GEORGE BERKELEY was born in Kilkenny, Ireland, in 1685. He was educated at Kilkenny School and at Trinity College, Dublin, where he was ordained priest and gained a reputation as a mathematician. He had become a Fellow of Trinity in 1707, and his first book, *An Essay Towards a New Theory of Vision,* appeared in 1709. His major work, *A Treatise Concerning the Principles of Human Knowledge,* followed in 1710, and *Three Dialogues between Hylas and Philonous* was published in 1713. In that year he went to London and soon entered the literary society of Swift, Addison, Steele and Pope. He then travelled widely in France and Italy, and returned to Dublin in 1721. In 1724 he was appointed Dean of Derry. He then spent much of his time trying to win support for the missionary project of founding a college in Bermuda. In 1728 he set sail for America and settled down at Newport, Rhode Island. But the money to found the college was not forthcoming and he returned to London in 1731. In 1734 he was appointed Bishop of Cloyne and he spent the rest of his life there, until in 1753 he died while on an extended visit to Oxford.

G. J. WARNOCK was born in 1923 and educated at Winchester College and New College, Oxford. He is the author of *English Philosophy since 1900* (1958) and *Contemporary Moral Philosophy* (1967).

The Principles of
Human Knowledge
Three Dialogues between
Hylas and Philonous

GEORGE BERKELEY

Edited with an introduction by G. J. Warnock, M.A.
Fellow of Magdalen College Oxford

COLLINS / FONTANA

The Principles of Human Knowledge
was first published in 1710
Three Dialogues between Hylas and Philonous
was first published in 1713
First issued in Fontana 1962
Ninth Impression July 1979

© in the Editor's Introduction and Notes
William Collins Sons & Co. Ltd.

Made and printed in Great Britain by
William Collins Sons & Co. Ltd. Glasgow

CONTENTS

INTRODUCTION BY G. J. WARNOCK $page$ 7

THE PRINCIPLES OF HUMAN
   KNOWLEDGE 41

THREE DIALOGUES BETWEEN
   HYLAS AND PHILONOUS 147

APPENDIX 263

BIBLIOGRAPHY 279

CHRONOLOGICAL TABLE 282

INDEX 284

INTRODUCTION

by G. J. Warnock

I

George Berkeley was born in Ireland, in the neighbourhood of Kilkenny, in 1685. Very little is known about his childhood : but it is clear that his family was in comfortable circumstances, and his education was well provided for. He was sent first to Kilkenny College, and then, at the early age of fifteen, to Trinity College, Dublin. This was in 1700. The vicissitudes of the English monarchy in the preceding century had involved Ireland in many years of warfare and civil disturbance; but all this had recently ended, and by the turn of the century education in Ireland was in a flourishing condition—Trinity College at that date was markedly more progressive than either Oxford or Cambridge. Berkeley read widely in the classics and acquired some Hebrew; he was well versed in mathematics and in the physical science of his day, particularly in the work of "the incomparable Mr. Newton." Also, and most importantly for his subsequent career, he became acquainted with John Locke's *Essay concerning Human Understanding*, published in 1690 and already recognized —except in Locke's own university of Oxford—as a work of major importance.

Berkeley took the degree of B.A. in 1704, and in June 1707, having remained in residence as a graduate, he was admitted as a Fellow of his College. The statutes required that Fellows should be in clerical orders, and Berkeley was ordained very shortly after his admission. He is among the most strikingly precocious of the great philosophers, and it is clear from two surviving notebooks which he filled at

7

this time that he had already progressed far towards his final philosophical position. Publications soon followed. His doctrines were partly revealed, but also, apparently by design, partly kept out of sight, in his *Essay towards a New Theory of Vision* (1709); and his major work, *The Principles of Human Knowledge,* was published in Dublin in May, 1710. The very pleasingly written *Three Dialogues between Hylas and Philonous* was published in London exactly three years later.

Berkeley never seriously modified the views thus early arrived at. By the age of twenty or so, he believed he had found the key to a completely satisfactory solution to a vast range of philosophical problems, and he was never conscious of any necessity to qualify this conviction. His surviving correspondence, in fact, shows that in later life his interest in philosophy was by no means continuous; there is little evidence that he read the philosophical works of his contemporaries, nor did he seek the acquaintance of other philosophers.

He had, in point of fact, many other interests. He left Ireland for the first time early in 1713, soon entered the literary society of Swift, Addison, Steele, and Pope, and travelled widely in France and Italy. Returning to Dublin in 1721, he was appointed Dean of Derry in 1724. It cannot be said, however, that he was a conscientious Dean : for at about this time his energies became entirely absorbed in the missionary project of founding a college in Bermuda.

Berkeley, whose charm all those who knew him agree to have been irresistible, was a most successful advocate of this (in fact) impracticable scheme. He secured a royal charter, large sums of money by private subscription, and a promise of a substantial grant from the English Parliament. In the autumn of 1728 he set sail for America, and settled down at Newport, Rhode Island, to wait for his schemes to mature. He occupied himself usefully and happily in America, corresponding (see *Appendix*) with one of the earliest of his serious critics and disciples, Samuel

Johnson. But so far as his main project was concerned, he waited in vain. With the withdrawal from London of his own persuasive energies, opposition gathered force; and the Prime Minister, Walpole, grew steadily more sceptical and lukewarm. At last it became clear that the essential Parliamentary grant would not be forthcoming, and by the end of 1731 Berkeley was back, somewhat disconsolate, though in no way discredited, in London.

In 1734—having, it appears, never visited his Deanery at Derry at all—he was appointed Bishop of Cloyne, in the extreme south of Ireland. He had married in 1728, and now he and his family began a long period of quiet and conscientious episcopal life. Berkeley was always keenly and most intelligently concerned with the social and economic condition of Ireland; but perhaps the major interest of his later years was in the virtues of " tar-water," a resinous solution which, largely owing to Berkeley's advocacy, became immensely popular for its supposed medicinal properties.

In the summer of 1752, already in bad health, Berkeley planned to make an extended visit to Oxford, where George, his second son, had just been admitted to Christ Church. He took a house in Holywell with his wife and daughter and lived there for several months, intending however to return to Cloyne in due course : but on Sunday evening of 14th January, 1753, he suddenly died. A few days later he was buried in the cathedral at Christ Church.

II

The age in which Berkeley flourished could be said to have been one of the peaks of English, and indeed of European, intellectual achievement. In 1700 Isaac Newton was nearly sixty, his great work accomplished. Galileo, Harvey, and Boyle were only recently dead. In philosophy Bacon,

Hobbes, Descartes, and Spinoza had, in their different ways, powerfully re-animated the tradition of argument and speculation; and Locke, Leibnitz, and Malebranche were still alive. Berkeley was the beneficiary of all this activity, progress, and achievement; yet he was also, in a certain sense, its implacable enemy. The philosophers, he thought, had not only failed to lay, but had actually made thicker, the "learned dust" of the middle ages : they had given countenance to old errors and introduced new ones, and in general had made to seem complicated and deeply obscure questions to which Berkeley believed, in his youthful zeal, the true answers were at once quite simple and luminously clear. The scientists, even more harmfully, had troubled the minds of the public with the notion that the Universe was a vast machine, a gigantic piece of clockwork, in which God and the human soul kept a foothold only on sufferance. And both groups combined to dismiss with contempt the beliefs of Common Sense, thus insinuating a general uncertainty, or a positive scepticism, most dangerous to true religion and, therefore, also to good morals. But these errors were avoidable, these alarming complications were of the theorists' own making : and if once the great encumbrance of new and old blunders could be thrown off, the purified sciences could be expected to bring innumerable benefits to an unquestioningly devout and virtuous public. Berkeley believed that he could bring this about at a single blow.

In this enterprise he was fired by a mixture of motives which makes him a quite unique figure in the history of philosophy. Many philosophers have been largely concerned with the defence of religious doctrine or of moral convictions. Many have wished to elaborate and expound a more or less personal, more or less idiosyncratic, metaphysical view of the nature of reality as a whole. Some, though perhaps not many, have been chiefly concerned to expose the pretensions of philosophical ambition and to re-affirm the "common-sense" convictions of all sensible men. It is the unique achievement of Berkeley to have presented himself in all three of these—not easily compatible—roles at once. He was sincerely, and perhaps predominantly, concerned to defeat what he took to be the irreligious, even atheistic, tendencies of his age; he was genuinely shocked by what he regarded as the wanton defiance by theorists in general of plain common sense; and further, he had a personal view of the nature of reality which, for very personal and perhaps now not discoverable reasons, he was determined to oppose to the "scientific" world-view which he rightly believed to be gaining ground every day. It is not surprising that he has been very widely misunderstood: for it is extremely difficult, in fact, to interpret his position consistently. He cannot, because of his strange metaphysical convictions, be regarded as *merely* the friend and defender of "common sense"; and yet, since his attachment to "common sense" was, in its way, both genuine and justified, he cannot be seen either as *merely* a high-flying metaphysician. He really was both, and a religious apologist as well: and it is essential to the right understanding of his position to see by what insight and ingenuity he was able to make his three roles fit (at first sight at least) so naturally together.

III

It is not, I believe, excessively unjust to Berkeley to say that his views were parasitic on the doctrines of Locke. Certainly he might, in principle, have reached just the views he did, if Locke had never existed; but in fact he was stirred into action primarily by his study of Locke, and in theory his position is most easily understood as the outcome of a very simple, but very far-reaching, amendment to the Lockean view. It is essential, then, to have before us at least an outline of Locke's position.

A major motive in Locke's philosophy was the desire

to work out the philosophical implications of the achievements of seventeenth-century science. Locke took it to have been established beyond all question that the material world was fundamentally mechanical in its nature and operations, and that matter on the gross scale on which we were capable of perceiving it was " corpuscular," or atomic, in structure—really made up of agglomerations of innumerable " insensible particles," acting upon each other and upon our sense-organs mechanically, " by impulse," " the only way we can conceive bodies operate." So confident was Locke of the fundamental correctness of the current, somewhat primitive, atomic theory of matter that he incorporated it in his definition of the " real essence " of material things. If, that is, we ask what it is that, fundamentally, *makes* each kind of object an object of that kind, or in what *being* of that kind ultimately consists, we must answer, in Locke's view, that it is its atomic structure—the dispositions, motions, and inter-actions of its " insensible parts." Now all this has important implications both for perception and, consequently, for knowledge.

Locke's account of perception is in large part simply a transcription of the doctrine set forth in contemporary scientific text-books. The sense-organs, it was supposed, in perception were mechanically stimulated, either by actual contact with an " external object " or, as in vision, by " insensible particles " emitted or reflected from it : this mechanical stimulus was then transmitted, through the appropriate nerves, to the brain. But when the stimulus reaches the brain something quite different happens; the mechanical cause at this stage produces a non-mechanical effect, namely the occurrence " in the mind " of what Locke calls an " idea," or, more fully, an " idea of sensation." But—and this is a crucial point—in Locke's view to have an idea in one's mind is *not,* as perhaps one might expect, to be made aware of that object in the world from which the original stimulus emanated; to have an idea *is* to be aware *of the idea*; and it is an essential feature of Locke's doctrine that, strictly speaking, we are directly aware *only* of ideas in our own minds. These mental entities, the only objects of which we are directly aware, "represent" to us those external objects from whose operations they are supposed to originate : of external objects themselves we cannot be directly aware.

Now this raises a question : do the ideas that occur " in our minds " *faithfully, veridically* represent the external world which is taken to be their cause? Is that world really as our ideas represent it to be? Locke holds that in some respects it is, but in others not. At this point he makes his celebrated distinction between *primary* and *secondary* qualities : the former, he argues, really are " in " external objects, but the latter, though " by mistake " we naturally take them for " real qualities " of objects, strictly speaking are nothing more than modes in which objects happen to affect such sensitive organisms as we are. The actual contents of the physical world really are solid, extended, moving, of certain sizes and shapes and weights; by contrast, owing to the nature of our sensibility, they merely *appear to us as being* coloured, or odorous, or warm, as making sounds, or having tastes. The actual *cause* of these appearances to us (as indeed of everything else) is simply the " bulk, figure, texture, and motion " of the " solid parts " of matter.

Turning now to the problem of knowledge, Locke finds himself in some difficulty. It is, for a start, difficult to see how we could justifiably claim to know *anything* of the " external world " if, as Locke insists, we are never directly aware of anything except the ideas in our own minds. Berkeley, as we shall see, rightly makes much of this point; but Locke, though rather uneasily conscious of it, glosses over the difficulty with the hopeful remark that of the external world we have " as much certainty as our condition needs." He dwells himself, however, with a certain gloomy relish, on what he regards as the insuperable obstacles to our knowing very much : in his view, what is really essential in material things is the minute atomic structure of their "insensible parts," and on this he followed Newton in the dismal conviction that we not only do not know, but in principle never can know, anything at all. Our senses are adapted to the perception only of objects of a certain bulk, and thus, Locke thinks, the *arcana* of the natural world are permanently and in principle inaccessible to us. It is certain that our "ideas of sensation" in certain respects misrepresent to us the actual character of the physical world; and although, in Locke's view, we are entitled to believe in a general way that it really has the primary qualities, the fine details that would give us genuine scientific understanding will be for ever beyond our grasp.

Finally, we must at least glance at Locke's rather desperate grapplings with the concept of *substance*; for this brings in two points on which Berkeley fastened with alacrity. What is *substance*, Locke asks? It is that to which *qualities* belong. And there must be substance, since we cannot intelligibly suppose mere qualities to exist in their own right, on their own, *sine re substante*. But what is substance itself? It seems to Locke that we just cannot say; for to say anything about substance is unavoidably to ascribe some quality to it, and this gets us no nearer to saying what it *is*. Locke finds himself left, then, with the bare idea of substance as being "something, I know not what"—that unperceivable, indescribable something of which all we can say is that it is that to which qualities belong, or in which they inhere.

Now this conclusion leads Locke into a further difficulty. He wishes to hold, on general grounds, that there are two kinds or varieties of substance—"material" substance, that something to which all the qualities of material things ultimately belong, and "immaterial" substance, in which inhere such non-material properties as consciousness, sensation, and the ability to think. But Locke sees, rightly, that he can really have no ground for this opinion. If all we can say of substance is that it is "something, we know not what," we can have no ground for saying that there are two varieties of substance; to say this we would have to know that the two varieties differed in some way; and we cannot know this since about substance we cannot know anything at all. Locke thus finds that, though he does not accept, he cannot disprove the supposition that the *same* substance which "supports" the qualities of matter might also have consciousness, sensation, the power of thinking : there might, that is, be only *one* thing "we know not what," and not, as Locke supposes, two.

IV

This, then, in barest outline is the doctrine on which Berkeley pondered in his undergraduate studies. He very quickly came to the conclusion that it was at once dangerous, ridiculous, and detestable. Let us now see why.

He thought it dangerous chiefly for the reason that it seemed to offer pretexts for religious scepticism. Locke's views were firmly founded on, and fully incorporated, the Newtonian idea that the physical universe is a vast mechanical system of bodies in motion, acting and interacting in accordance with rigorously formulable mechanical laws. Where then does God come in? Do the Newtonians admit the need for "this hypothesis"? Locke himself, who was not an unbeliever, had taken it for granted that God was the creator of the vast machine, and had, so to speak, set it going. But surely this assumption, on his principles, could easily be challenged. For suppose it were suggested that the universe had *existed eternally*. Locke, of course, could not hope to disprove this; but if not, he would surely be left with no reason at all for supposing any God to exist. If the universe was not created, no Creator would be required; if it has been in mechanical motion for ever, then no divine push could be supposed to have set it in motion. From Locke's principles, then, it is all too easy to conclude that God's existence is simply a redundant, quite unnecessary assumption.

And what about the soul? Locke indeed had supposed that the universe contained, besides matter, " immaterial " substances, minds or souls. But he had been obliged to confess that his system gave no grounds for this supposition, and that, for all he could show, consciousness might be merely one of the properties of matter. But it is, if not absolutely necessary, all too easy to conclude from this that consciousness may terminate absolutely with bodily death, or at least that we can have no reason whatever for believing that anything survives the dissolution of the body.

Berkeley firmly believed (as people often do) that his own age surpassed most others in vice and depravity, in the reckless pursuit of pleasure, in the wanton neglect of private and public duty. He believed this to be due entirely to a general weakening of religious conviction; and he thought this weakening directly attributable to the spread of the " corpuscularian," mechanistic view of the universe invented by scientists and popularized by, among others, Locke. He did not, indeed, accuse Newton and Locke themselves of being unbelievers; but he was convinced that they had propagated doctrines whose tendency *must* be to promote unbelief in others. For others would be only too ready to draw from their doctrines those atheistical implications which they indeed had not drawn, but had been unable to counter.

This aptness to induce religious scepticism, then, seemed to Berkeley highly dangerous; but he believed also that Locke's position gave countenance to scepticism of another variety, not in this case dangerous, but demonstrably absurd. The crucial point here is the way in which Locke distinguished the ideas in our minds, of which we are actually aware, from the *objects* in the world which our ideas are taken to " represent " to us. He had then argued, first of all, that objects certainly are not exactly as our ideas would lead us to suppose; for though they do indeed have primary qualities, such secondary qualities as colour are not really " in " objects at all. Berkeley objects to this conclusion on two grounds. First, it appeared to him plainly ridiculous to suppose, as he put it, that " the visible beauty of creation " is no more than a " false imaginary glare," that for instance the flowers in our gardens are not really coloured and have really no scent : Locke had owned that his view would seem to many to be " very extravagant," but it is worse than that, Berkeley holds—it is an outrage to plain good sense. But second, Locke has actually no ground for making this distinction. He detaches, so to speak, the so-called secondary qualities from objects by pointing out that, in respect of them, objects may *appear differently* as the conditions of observation, or the state of the observer, are varied : the state of the light may cause apparent colours to change, water feels cooler to a warm hand than to a cold one, and so on. But Berkeley points out, quite correctly, that exactly the same is true of primary qualities also : a changed angle of observation may change apparent shape, apparent speeds are affected by our distance from the moving object, and so on. So Locke's distinction is baseless as well as, on the face of it, absurd.

But worse is to come. For suppose we raise again the question that Locke glossed over : how could he *know* that our ideas are in some respects faithful representatives, in others not? If I am to know whether a portrait is a faithful likeness of a sitter, I must look at the sitter and compare him with his portrait. But Locke's principles completely rule out the corresponding operation. It is *only* our own ideas that we are actually aware of; and thus, though we are well enough in a position to tell whether any idea is like another *idea*, we cannot possibly have any ground at all for holding that ideas are in *any* respects like or unlike " external objects." These latter are simply inaccessible to inspection; and thus, if the sceptical suggestion be raised that the " external world " is perhaps *wholly* unlike what our ideas represent it as being, Locke is helpless; his principles leave him without any reply. But is not any system itself to be condemned as ridiculous, which permits the ridiculous supposition to be made that perhaps we know nothing at all of the material world?

But worse still—on Locke's principles the very *existence* of the " external world " must be completely uncertain. All that I am aware of is the ideas that occur in my mind; and if so, what ground could I have for the belief that there exists something else that I am never aware of at all? Locke insists, and rightly insists, that we must suppose our ideas to have causes; they occur whether we like it or not, and are plainly not under our control. But this gives no ground for Locke's particular assumption that the causes of our ideas are " external objects "; we could have grounds for this supposition only if, besides being aware of our own ideas, we could observe the causal operation of external objects; and this, as Locke readily admits, we cannot do. Thus Locke is again left without any reply in the face of the very extreme sceptical suggestion that perhaps there are really no objects in the world at all; but to allow this suggestion to go unanswered is very nearly insane. In any case, is there not something perfectly ridiculous in the conclusion which Locke himself openly avows— that what is really in the world, what the qualities of material things really belong to, must be helplessly accepted as " something, we know not what " ? There seems little to choose between " something, we know not what," and " nothing."

Further, Berkeley held very strongly that Locke's theory was useless as an *explanation*. He had undertaken to *explain* the occurrence of ideas in our minds by reference to the mechanical action upon our sense-organs and brains of " external bodies," acting " by impulse." But Berkeley held that this failed both in detail and in principle. It failed in detail because, as Locke himself confessed, it was impossible to explain *why* a particular mechanical agitation of the brain should produce an effect of a completely different character—the occurrence, say, of an idea of colour. The supposed connection between ideas in the mind and motions in the brain was one, Locke admitted, that we could not really understand; but if so, he was surely not entitled to claim that brain-motions *explained* the occurrence of our ideas. But more generally, Berkeley also rejected as non-explanatory the whole conception of mechanical causation : he held, in fact, that the term "causation" was improperly used in this context. A true cause, he held, originates something, makes something happen; we have examples of this in the exercise of *the will*. But events in nature do not make other events happen; one event precedes another, and, if it does so with regularity, may serve as a *sign* of the occurrence of its usual concomitant; but it is not a cause, for it is not an agent, it exerts no volition. Thus, Berkeley held that so-called mechanical causation was not really causation at all; it mentioned no agents, no exercises of the will, but merely described the regular successions of events; this might be good description, but was no sort of *explanation*.

There is also, I think, a rather less tangible respect in which the attitudes of Locke and Berkeley to mechanical explanation were totally opposed. For Locke the idea of a mechanism was completely satisfactory, a paradigm of the intelligible; he delighted to think of objects as "curious machines," to compare them with clocks, to envisage, as it were, the springs, levers, and wheels of their inner structure. Though pessimistic about our prospects of achieving truly "scientific" knowledge, he had no doubt whatever what form such knowledge would take—it would consist in comprehension of the detailed mechanisms of nature. Berkeley, on the contrary, found the notions of mechanism repulsive. He violently rejected the idea that they could explain anything; but further, he was oppressed by, and hostile to, the whole conception of nature as an enormous machine. He thought it ugly, "stupid," false to the true character of our experience, mindless, antipathetic to the human spirit. Thus he not only criticized, but profoundly hated, Locke's philosophy; the whole cast of mind which could embrace it was to him disagreeable.

v

Such, then, were the varied grounds on which Berkeley so strongly objected to the views of his distinguished predecessor. His temperamental hostility was re-inforced by his belief that Locke's system ran grossly counter to plain good sense, and permitted "sceptical" views intolerable to all sensible men; and this defence of common sense was further fortified by the conviction that Locke's principles were most dangerous to religion, and so also to morality. What then was to be done? Berkeley thought that the solution to all these perplexities was obvious, luminously simple, and lay ready to hand; as he wrote in his notebook, "I wonder not at my sagacity in discovering the obvious though amazing truth, I rather wonder at my stupid inadvertency in not finding it out before." The solution was *to deny the existence of matter*.

It is not difficult to see how this move seemed to solve Berkeley's problems. First, to deny the existence of matter was to make unnecessary Locke's tortuous struggles with the notion of "material substance"; that idea would simply drop out. Moreover, if there is no material substance, there are, in Locke's sense of the phrase, no "external bodies"; and this is a pure gain. It was always hard to see what purpose these entities could serve, since, as Locke himself insisted, we could not be aware of them; on the other hand, they afforded the sole and sufficient pretext for scepticism. If they are rejected, then the houses and trees, tables and stars that we perceive in the world can be *identified* with the ideas that we actually have, not *contrasted* with our ideas as their remote and bafflingly inaccessible causes; and since it is beyond dispute that we do have ideas, it will be at once put beyond dispute, as surely it should be, that houses and trees, tables and stars, do really exist and are (familiar abnormalities apart) just as they appear to us to be. Locke's fundamental mistake lay in his duplicating the world—one world of ideas that we actually perceive, and, inaccessibly *behind* that, a supposed other world of " external bodies." If these latter items are simply deleted, the actual course of our experience remains exactly as it was, but the very possibility of sceptical doubts and questionings must vanish.

But, it will be objected, in thus rejecting " external bodies," do we not run counter to the admitted principle that our ideas have *causes*? What causes in me the idea of a house, if not, as Locke supposed, an " external " house really existing in the world? But here Berkeley insists that the cause of our ideas could not be known to be, nor could be in fact, an " external world " as understood by Locke. This could not be known just because that world was " external," inaccessible to observation; but further, material things as described by Locke could not (for reasons outlined above) really be *causes*. The true cause of the occurrence of ideas can only be " an incorporeal active substance or spirit," by whose *will* ideas are implanted in our finite minds in an orderly, systematic, and rational manner.

Again, it will be objected that ideas cannot exist " without the mind "; if we say, then, that objects *are* " collections of ideas," do we not have to hold that they exist when and *only* when they are perceived? Certainly, says Berkeley; but where is the difficulty in this? There are objects, no doubt, which no human being perceives; but all alike are perceived by, and exist in the mind of, God—that " infinite, omnipresent spirit," " who works all in all, and by whom all things consist." " That the discovery of this great truth which lies so near and obvious to the mind, should be attained to by the reason of so very few, is a sad instance of the stupidity and inattention of men, who, though they are surrounded with such clear manifestations of the Deity, are yet so little affected by them, that they seem as it were blinded with excess of light."

Thus, we see further that the rejection of " external bodies " removes all threats to religious belief. In Locke's " material " world, that supposedly self-sufficient machine, God's tenure was that of a precariously tolerated outsider; in Berkeley's world, from which matter is totally banished, every natural event, every object that we perceive, " the whole choir of Heaven and furniture of the earth," are immediate effects and evidences of the will of God. God does not dwell remotely outside, but incessantly and everywhere sustains in existence, the material world, whose existence in fact cannot be coherently conceived without Him. In this manner, Berkeley thinks, we score at once over " every wretched sect of atheists " the "most complete and easy triumph in the world."

Finally, we can wholly rid ourselves of the nightmare of mechanism. We can hold that it cannot in any sense be true that the physical world is really a piece of gigantic and intricate machinery, since the material bodies of which all this was supposed to be true simply do not exist. There are simply no such bodies : there are finite minds, and there is the mind of God; and God communicates directly with our finite minds by the mediation of ideas, the order, regularity, and " admirable connexion " of which form the " rational discourse " of the infinite Spirit with his finite creatures. All depends on God's will; there is no place for unintelligent, mindless, ugly, cosmic machinery.

VI

This last point, however, raises a substantial issue : what account can Berkeley give of the physical sciences? Locke, of course, had been aware of no particular problem here. He had taken it for granted, doubtless too readily, that such theories as that of the "corpuscular" structure of matter were straightforwardly and literally true of objects in the world—that matter was literally composed of "insensible particles" very much as a building is literally composed of bricks. He thought of the physical scientist as discovering straightforward truths about the world—refined truths no doubt, sometimes startling and unfamiliar, but still truths in the same straightforward sense as those we can arrive at by ordinary observation. But plainly this simple line is not available to Berkeley. For him, the corpuscular theory of matter cannot possibly be true, for in his system there is nothing whatever for it to be true *of*. What is he to make, then, of the work of Galileo, of Newton, of Boyle, and many others?

When writing the *Principles* and *Dialogues* Berkeley seems not to have felt the full weight of this difficulty, and the solution he offers is not wholly satisfactory. Briefly, he contends that the sciences, rightly understood, do not require the supposition that anything exists which we do not perceive, and hence can be construed as referring only to ideas. It is the function of the scientist, he insists, not to *explain* our experience, but to bring it under "general rules"—to formulate, that is, empirical generalizations about the actual course of our experience. But nothing in this aim requires that any reference be made to anything that we do *not* experience; and since nothing exists except what we *do* experience, namely ideas, any such reference must be misguided and illegitimate. Hence, the physical sciences are to be understood as very general descriptions of the observable world; and to that, of course, Berkeley has no objection—in this sense, from his principles "no reason can be drawn, why the history of Nature should not still be studied."

Berkeley soon came to feel, however, that this would not do. He was too intelligent a man to be long content with simply dismissing, as at first he was inclined to do, all talk of an underlying, "insensible" mechanism in Nature as a mere misunderstanding; he could not but be aware that the "corpuscular" theories of matter, and of light, were both too fertile to be easily rejected, and too centrally characteristic of the whole ideal of scientific understanding. But it was still not open to him to admit that such theories were, as they stood, straightforwardly true; and so, with very striking insight and ingenuity, he fell back on a distinction between the observed *facts* of science, and the *theories* devised by scientists to account for them. The aim of science, he still holds, is to reduce to "general rules" the observed phenomena; but the achievement of this aim, he now argues, is greatly facilitated by the making of appropriate *suppositions*. If we think of light, for example, *as if it were* propagated in the form of a stream of "insensible particles," then the diverse phenomena of light can be comprehended within a theory capable of expression in simple mechanical terms, and highly apt for the precise use of measurement and mathematical calculation. This is certainly useful; but, Berkeley insists, it is *useful*, not *true*. As he wrote in his tract *De Motu* in 1721, "to be of service to reckoning and mathematical demonstrations is one thing, to set forth the nature of things is another." Thus, Berkeley does not now object, as formerly he did, to references to "insensible particles" and other items of supposed, unperceivable "corpuscular" machinery. He sees that such references serve a theoretical purpose, particularly in facilitating the application to physical phenomena of precise mathematical concepts and methods. But the resulting theories have the status of *serviceable fictions*; they are useful inventions; it cannot be objected that he leaves such theories with nothing to be true of, for in fact there is no need to suppose that they are *true* at all. They are theories, not facts; and the virtue of a theory consists not in truth, but in utility.

Berkeley's motives, of course, for arriving at this view were unusual and even idiosyncratic. Nevertheless it embodies an insight the significance of which has only quite recently come to be fully appreciated. For so long as physical theory retained, fundamentally, the fairly simple mechanistic character familiar to Locke and his contemporaries, those uninfluenced by Berkeley's peculiar pre-occupations felt little difficulty in construing physical theory as straightforwardly factual in character. In this century, however, the sophistication of theoretical physics has increased so greatly that its technical concepts can no longer be interpreted in terms of any simple model; it is indeed a question of current controversy whether *any* consistent physical model can be made to fit the mathematical theory. Thus there has been forced upon the attention of theorists just that distinction between observation and theory-construction on which Berkeley insisted 250 years ago; and to-day some physicists, not without fierce opposition, are inclined to argue exactly as he did, that physical theory is not a matter of factual truth, but essentially of mathematical and predictive convenience. It has been strenuously argued that to accept this idea is to lower intolerably the aspirations of the physical scientist—to substitute an ideal of ingenuity for the more exacting ideal of the pursuit of truth. And it must be admitted that just this was a large part of Berkeley's intentions; there is no doubt that he deeply disliked the high prestige accorded in his day to the physical scientist, and wished to maintain that in reality he had no claim whatever to be an authority on "the nature of things." In his own time he failed entirely to win acceptance for his view; it is by no means, however, plainly untenable, and in fact in our own day it has won far more general support than ever before.

VII

Brief mention must be made of another, but not quite independent, issue on which Berkeley vehemently dissented
from Locke—the problem, namely, of "abstract ideas,"
which is the topic of the Introduction to Berkeley's *Principles*.

The controversy here is concerned with the problem of
meaning. What is it for a word to be a *general* term, and
what is it for a general term to have a *meaning*? Locke's
answer to these questions is modelled on the notion of a
pattern, and the use of a pattern. Consider, for instance,
the general term "pink." First, Locke thinks, from observation of a number of particular pink things we must
"abstract" that feature which we find is common to them
all : leaving out of account all those respects in which one
pink thing may differ from another—shape, size, texture,
and so on—we must "frame" in our minds the "abstract
idea" of Pink. Next, if we choose, we may give a name to
this idea—in this case, the name "pink." The word
"pink," by being thus made the name of an abstract,
general idea, becomes itself a general term, the idea of
Pink being its "immediate signification." Finally, we
actually use the general term "pink," employ it in the
characterization of other particulars, by using the abstract
idea as a "pattern"; when we observe that some particular
object matches, or "conforms with," the pattern-idea laid
up in our minds, we may forthwith apply to that object
the general term that we have "annexed," as its name, to
the pattern, the abstract idea.

Berkeley objects to this theory, with surprising vehe-
mence, that it is both unnecessary and impossible. Simpli-
fying a little, we may state his objections as follows. First,
the explanation of general terms by reference to "abstract
ideas" is unnecessary : for a term to be general, and to
have a meaning, it is not necessary that it be "annexed,"

like a name, to any special variety of specially "framed" idea: what is needed is just that it be used to "denote indifferently" *any* of a class of particular things—those, namely, which are like one another in the relevant respect. Similarly, my recognition of an object as pink does not require reference to an "abstract idea" laid up in my mind as a pattern or standard of Pinkness; if I have already learned that a number of objects are called "pink," all that is needed is that I should observe the new object to be like *them*; there is no need to go through, nor do we in fact do so, the elaborate process of "framing" a pattern and comparing objects with *that*.

But second, and more seriously, Locke's theory is actually impossible; there just could not be pattern-ideas of the kind he requires. According to Locke's theory the pattern-idea of Pink instantiates Pink and nothing else whatever; but could a pattern of Pink be conceivably not also extended? Could it be of no shape, and have no dimensions at all? But consider particularly—Berkeley calls this in his notebook "the killing blow"—what Locke himself says of the abstract idea of a Triangle. If this is to serve as a pattern of triangles *in general*, it cannot be permitted to be isosceles in particular; but equally it cannot be equilateral, right-angled, or scalene. It appears that it must, if it is to play the general role as a pattern which Locke requires, be *all* of these, but also none in particular—it must, as Locke actually says, be "all and none" at once. But it is plain that this is a logical impossibility: it is logically impossible that a triangular figure should be of *none* of the possible varieties of triangles, and it is no less impossible that it should belong to *all* of the mutually incompatible species. It thus becomes clear that, in general, there could not be *patterns* of the kind which Locke wrongly supposes to be needed, if we are to use and understand general terms in our language. In fact, so Berkeley concludes, nothing else is required but the words that we use, and the particular experienced items that we use them to speak about; the generality of a general term lies in its *use,* and not in the peculiar nature of any special item of which it may, misguidedly, be thought of as the name.

Unfortunately, Berkeley does not make it absolutely clear why he attaches so much importance to this particular issue—so much that he sets it in the forefront of his major work. However, I think it is possible to attribute to him two motives, one very general, one more specific. In general he seems to have thought, undoubtedly with justice, that Locke's theory of abstract ideas was a standing invitation to confusion and needless perplexity. We understand the words that we use, for the most part, well enough so long as we think of the concrete contexts in which, and the everyday purposes for which, we actually use them; we are in no difficulties, for instance, with the word " time," so long as we think of the situations in which we enquire what time it is, promise to be back in a short time, or point out that a round of golf needs more time than a game of tennis. However, if we take seriously Locke's theory on this matter, we shall come to think that the true " signification " of the word " time " ought to be taken as the *abstract idea* of Time, an idea supposedly somewhere stored up " in our minds." We thus begin, as it were, to grope about in our minds, attempting to lay hands on, to bring before " the mind's eye," the abstract, general idea of Time. Not surprisingly, we fail; our minds on this subject appear to be entirely blank; and thus we may gloomily conclude that we do not understand the meaning of a word whose meaning, if only we had not looked for it in this way, would have been entirely familiar to us. In a less awkward case we may not draw blank altogether; but even so, the process of groping around in our own minds, the process to which Locke's theory naturally invites us, is inherently liable to issue in *mis*understanding, as reflection on the actual, concrete *uses* of terms is not.

But there is perhaps a more specific reason than this why Berkeley should wish to reject first of all Locke's

" abstract ideas." It was, after all, an essential feature of Locke's view of the world that very much in the world was supposed to be *unperceivable*; the whole notion that *behind* the ideas that we actually perceive lay a complicated, largely conjectural world of " external bodies " essentially required that it should at least *make sense* to speak of things that we never in fact perceive. Locke accepts this without difficulty; to understand what we say, in his view, we must have " abstract ideas," but since these are " framed " by us, and stored away in our minds, in *addition* to the particular ideas that we are furnished with in our sensory experience, there is no reason why their signification should be strictly confined to what we actually perceive. Conversely, if Berkeley can establish the impossibility of abstract ideas in the sense understood by Locke, then he can argue that all talk of unperceivable entities *must* be meaningless; if a general term has meaning in virtue of its use in discourse about any of a class of particular ideas, then it must be impossible to speak significantly of what is *not* a particular idea—that is, of anything supposed to be unperceivable. If so, Berkeley's other objections to Locke's view of the world would be reinforced by the far-reaching contention that it is not possible to speak significantly of anything except the entities we actually perceive.

Berkeley cannot and does not, however, apply this principle quite consistently. From the first he had recognized that he could not square with it his own talk of " spirits," of our own minds and of God; for these are perceivers, not among the objects of perception. Thus he says, rather weakly and without elucidation, that in addition to our ideas we also have " notions "—we know what it means to speak of " spirits " and their operations. Moreover, as we have seen, he soon came to admit that we can after all, as for instance in physics, speak in some sense intelligibly of the unperceivable; our terms can be given a quite clear theoretical use, even if they refer to no items in our sensory experience. His sharp criticism of the theory of abstract ideas may thus be said to reduce to a (still very valuable) insistence upon attention to the concrete uses and contexts of our words, and a highly salutary objection to the not uncommon notion that their "real meanings" are to be sought *elsewhere,* dredged up from the recesses of our minds. This was a lesson which, in the present century, philosophers have found it necessary painfully to re-learn.

VIII

Did Berkeley succed, then, in what he undertook to do? Did he really succeed, as he so confidently believed, in completely eliminating religious and philosophical scepticism, while at the same time re-instating the convictions of common sense?

It must, I believe, be clear that he did not succeed completely. It cannot be argued here—it may even be impossible to show conclusively—that his own vision of "the nature of things" is incorrect; but at least it must be said that, as most of his readers have felt, he is not really entitled to claim the support of "common sense." In denying the existence of matter he meant just what he said; he really meant to insist that nothing whatever exists except minds and their contents, "spirits" and their "ideas." Admittedly, given the initial supposition that ideas and only ideas are actually perceived, he could argue that a world in which only ideas and their perceivers exist would *look* just the same as—would in no way diverge in *appearance* from—a world supposed to consist of common-sensical "material things"; but he can scarcely maintain that the two are exactly the same. To put it bluntly, his axiom that *esse* is *percipi* or *percipere,* that to exist is to be perceived or to perceive, is certainly true of his world, but false of ours. His rejection of matter and retention only of ideas obliges him to hold that it is *self-*

contradictory to suppose that any object exists that is not actually perceived; it can only be answered that the "common sense" view finds no difficulty in that supposition. Berkeley's world, in a clear sense, is genuinely *insubstantial*, and thus *is* not the same (however it may appear) as the intractably substantial world in which we all ordinarily suppose ourselves to be living. It would perhaps need more argument than we here have space for to make good this contention—Berkeley would certainly not have surrendered to it easily—but it is, I think, both a natural comment at first sight, and ultimately a sound one.

But how, it may be asked, can Berkeley's conclusion be avoided, without falling back into that position of Locke's against which Berkeley justly urged so many highly cogent objections? If we cannot do without Locke's world of "external objects," are we any the less uncomfortable in trying to put up with it?

Well, here we must raise a fundamental question which neither Berkeley, nor many of his critics, ever considered. It was, we remember, one of Berkeley's main criticisms of Locke that he, absurdly, *duplicated* the world : he supposed that all we could ever actually be aware of was the ideas in our own minds, and then postulated *behind* these ideas a necessarily inaccessible "external world." Berkeley's solution consisted in deleting half this duplication; the perplexities of Locke's position, he argued, must vanish, if we simply deny that his "external world" exists. However, if we do this, we are left with Berkeley's "immaterial" world of spirits and their ideas; and this, we have suggested, is distressingly insubstantial. Should we not ask, then, whether we might not be better advised to delete the *other* half of Locke's duplication—to reject, that is, not his world of external objects, but the supposedly impenetrable screen of "our own ideas"? Should we not argue that there are indeed external objects, but that these are not, as Locke supposed, inaccessible to us—that it is *objects*, not our own ideas, that we are aware of in perception, and that we know to exist because we actually observe that they do?

It is true, though astonishing, that Berkeley never even considered this possibility. Indeed, the proposition that we perceive only ideas is dogmatically laid down in the very first sentence of the *Principles,* and never seriously argued for. And yet, when one comes to think of it, what a strange notion it is! There is a lengthy tradition of philosophical argument on this matter, and it will not do to suggest that it is a purely gratuitous *mistake* to hold that "ideas or sensations" are all that we ever perceive. But at least we are entitled to insist that this opinion runs quite counter to what we all ordinarily believe; we are entitled to demand that very strong arguments be carefully deployed, if we are to be brought to accept it or even to take it very seriously. It surely will not do to assume at the very beginning, as Berkeley does, that this extraordinary doctrine can simply be stated as "evident"—particularly since, as we are now in a position to see, its acceptance leads us straight into philosophical perplexities. No doubt Berkeley felt that the principle that we perceive only "ideas" stood in need of no argument partly for the reason that, on this point at least, he and Locke were in agreement; but may it not be just *because* they were in agreement on this that they appear to force upon us a choice between alternative doctrines, with *neither* of which we are really inclined to agree? In philosophy it is always good policy, when two theorists appear to offer a choice between two positions neither of which is acceptable, to consider whether, underlying the divergences between them, there may not be some dubious principle which they have in common. In this case, we do not have to agree with either Locke or Berkeley *unless* we accept, as they both did, the initial supposition that in perception we are aware *only* of "our own ideas." But neither—I must here state dogmatically—actually produces any arguments sufficient to establish so strange a view.

IX

Berkeley's first published work, the *Essay towards a New Theory of Vision,* stands somewhat apart from his central philosophical writings. In it he is not concerned to lay before the public his general metaphysical views; his great thesis of " immaterialism " is kept firmly out of sight, though his notebooks make clear that at this time—1709— he was already perfectly convinced of its truth. His particular concern in the *Essay* is with the nature of vision, and with the correct understanding of the relation between optical theory and the making of visual judgments. Berkeley rightly maintains, in a number of specific instances, that physical and geometrical optics contribute little to the explanation of, or to the making of, visual judgments, and offers many shrewd explanatory suggestions of his own. His general thesis about vision—that the " proper objects " of sight are not, as we might ordinarily suppose, material objects, but " light and colours "—may seem to be preparing the way for the doctrine of the *Principles*; but in the *Essay* this thesis is explicitly contrasted with the supposition that, by at least the sense of touch, we are made directly acquainted with material things " in circumambient space." This concession to common sense—even if, as seems likely, it was meant only to be temporary and provisional—had the effect of gaining for the *Essay* far more serious and more prolonged attention than Berkeley's early readers ever felt that the *Principles* deserved.

The reception of the *Principles* distressed and astonished Berkeley. He knew himself to be a warm friend of religious orthodoxy; he felt himself seriously outraged by what he regarded as the absurd " sceptical " implications of Locke's doctrine, and he supposed that he had, with robust common sense, rejected them. He hoped, then, that all good men, and all sensible men, would at once recognize the force and the merits of his case. Quite the opposite occurred. Some thought he was insane, and some that he could not be wholly serious; some thought he was corrupted by an Irish propensity to paradox and novelty; almost no one took him seriously. Nor is it, in fact, very difficult for us to see why. Berkeley's *negative* case—his particular criticism of Locke—is for the most part well-taken and genuinely on the side of common sense; but his positive thesis, his strange immaterialist ontology, is, and was rightly felt to be, exceedingly eccentric. Berkeley could not see, and doubtless had no wish to see, how the two could be separated : he firmly believed that his idiosyncratic ontology was just the reverse side of his objections to Locke, and so *must* be accepted if those were acceptable. But his readers, while doubtless not many, if any, saw clearly just how and why this was not so, felt almost unanimously that it *could* not be so. Berkeley, supposing with some justice that he had not been properly understood, appealed to the public with as much patient clarity as he could muster in the *Three Dialogues between Hylas and Philonous*. But the merits of his case, and even its prodigious ingenuity and considerable insight, still went largely unrecognized.

Berkeley's later writings do not compare in importance with the *Essay*, *Principles*, and *Dialogues*, all of which were completed when he was still in his twenties. Nor are they voluminous. His short Latin tract *De Motu* (1721), an essay submitted—unsuccessfully—for a prize offered by the French Royal Academy of Sciences, is chiefly of interest in that it modifies, as noted above, his account of the legitimate pursuits of the physical scientist. His next large-scale work, the long dialogue *Alciphron* (1732), is an elegant, able, once popular, but inevitably somewhat faded and dated defence of the Anglican form of Christianity against the attacks of various types of Deist and " freethinker." The *Theory of Vision Vindicated* (1733) takes up the defence of his first published work, but again makes some interesting modifications in his account of the nature of the sciences and of mathematics. The *Anaylst* (1734) is again concerned with mathematical theory, and here Berkeley stirred up a hornets' nest of controversy by his polemical conclusion that mathematics itself contains confusions and "mysteries" no less baffling than those imputed by infidels to religion.

Berkeley's last philosophical work, and a very strange one, was *Siris: A Chain of Philosophical Reflexions and Inquiries* (1744). This "chain," the links of which hold together very tenuously, owed its genesis to Berkeley's preoccupation in later life with the virtues of tar-water. It consists largely of a sadly rambling, often distressingly speculative, dissertation on a variety of medical, chemical, and physical topics. The display of varied learning is certainly impressive, and of course it must also be remembered that much which may strike us to-day as absurd or superstitious would have seemed quite otherwise two hundred years ago. The work contains occasional echoes of the "anti-corpuscularian" arguments of Berkeley's youth, and strongly emphasizes his temperamental preference for Mind over Mattèr; doctrinally, it is not inconsistent with his earlier views. In points of style, however, in order and clarity, and in vigour of argument, it is so far different that one would not easily believe it to be the work of the same hand.

x

Though Berkeley's major works, as has been said, fared ill with the public, they have never been far from the attention of philosophers. It is notable that Berkeley's great successor, David Hume, appears to have learned nothing from Berkeley and to have taken small account of him, with the single exception of his powerful *critique* of Locke's doctrine of abstract ideas.[1] Kant also, though he mentions "the good Berkeley" occasionally in his writings, evidently did not regard him as a major figure and perhaps was not very well acquainted with his actual writings. However, if Locke gave the classic exposition of one of the traditional accounts of perception and the material world, Berkeley set out no less ably the classic rejoinder; and between them they established a pattern of argument on this subject which has remained central in philosophy right down to the present day.

Berkeley's descendant in the philosophy of the present century is the theory commonly known as Phenomenalism. As Berkeley's doctrine was prompted by criticism of Locke, so Phenomenalism arises by a natural reaction to Locke's own descendant, the so-called Causal Theory of perception. The Causal Theory holds that the objects of "direct awareness" are "sense-data," these being usually regarded, as "ideas" were in the eighteenth century, as mental entities, or at least as being mind-dependent : material things or physical objects are then distinguished as being the causes (at least in part) of the occurrence of sense-data. To this position it has been objected, in the manner of Berkeley, that if we are directly aware only of sense-data, and if material things are distinguished from these as their causes, then it cannot be satisfactorily explained how we could ever come to have knowledge of material things; for we cannot perceive them, if perception is always of sense-data. It has then seemed a natural enough next move to maintain that, again precisely in the manner of Berkeley, material things must be *identified* with sense-data, for only so can our discourse and knowledge of material things be made intelligible. This thesis, the "reduction" of physical objects to "phenomena," is usually known in its diverse forms by the name of Phenomenalism.

[1] See Hume's *Treatise,* Book I, Part I, section VII.

It must be emphasized, however, that in certain respects this contemporary thesis differs most crucially from Berkeley's. Berkeley wrote openly, insistently, and defiantly, as an ontologist : he held that matter, and therefore also Locke's " external bodies," *did not exist*; he held further that the only entities which *did* exist were, in reality, *spirits* and their *ideas*. Moreover, he felt it both necessary and highly desirable to maintain that, if " the choir of Heaven and furniture of the earth " were to be held to exist continuously, they must be held to exist as ideas " in the mind of God." But the modern theory is thought to have no such theistic implications; nor has it, at least in the hands of its most sophisticated exponents, any avowed ontological commitments. The phenomenalist, that is, does not represent himself as *denying* that material objects exist, or as asserting that nothing whatever exists but sense-data. In the words of Professor A. J. Ayer, " it must be made clear that what the statement that material things consist of sense-data must be understood to designate is not a factual but a linguistic relationship. What is being claimed is simply that the propositions which are ordinarily expressed by sentences which refer to material things could also be expressed by sentences which referred exclusively to sense-data." Moreover, if we wish to maintain that material things still exist when nobody perceives them, we bring in not the mind of God, but " possible sense-data "; and " the inclusion of possible as well as actual sense-data among the elements of the material things must be taken only to imply a recognition that some of these statements about sense-data will have to be hypothetical."[2] The phenomenalist thesis, that is, is supposed to be concerned only with the meaning, or analysis, of " sentences which refer to material things." It is not intended, officially at least, to be a factual thesis, or either to deny or assert any

[2] Ayer, *The Foundations of Empirical Knowledge,* London, 1940, p. 232.

doctrine as to what exists in the world. It may be doubted,
and has been questioned, to what extent this official ontological neutrality is observed in practice;[3] but even its
official avowal serves to mark an important difference of
intention from Berkeley's.

I said earlier that " in the present century, philosophers
have found it necessary painfully to re-learn " some of the
lessons contained in Berkeley's criticism of abstract ideas.
Early in this century G. E. Moore was conspicuous for his
tendency to seek for the meanings of words by a kind of
inward gazing, or groping among the contents of his mind,
very much in the manner of one searching for a Lockean
abstract idea; and it was in part a keen sense of the
dangers inherent in this tendency which led Wittgenstein
to insist upon attenion to the actual *uses* of words. There
is an analogy here with Berkeley's criticism of Locke; but
it is not, I believe, a case of historical influence. There is
no evidence that either Wittgenstein himself, or many of
his admirers, ever realized how closely many of his ideas
had been foreshadowed by Berkeley more than two cen-
turies before.

Perhaps we may conclude with the observation that a
form of the objection urged above against Berkeley is still
highly pertinent to-day to the case of Phenomenalism. We
saw that Berkeley's doctrine gained much of its persuasive
force from the fact that it appeared to be the only alternative to Locke's : if so-called material things are not
" collections of ideas," are we not condemned to the most
unwelcome conclusion that they are inaccessible to observation, cut off from us, as it were, by the iron curtain of
our own ideas? Rather similarly Phenomenalism, which
is scarcely plausible in itself, may come to seem plausible
and indeed inescapable, if it appears as the only possible
alternative to the Causal Theory : is it not at least better to
hold that (in the sense explained) material things consist of

[3] Notably by J. L. Austin, in his *Sense and Sensibilia,* Oxford,
1962.

sense-data, than that they are the remotely-inferred, unobservable causes of the sense-data with which alone we are "directly" acquainted? We saw, however, that Berkeley's theory must result from the rejection of Locke's *only if* one accepts, as Berkeley did without question, the principle that in perception we are aware of nothing but "our own ideas or sensations"; if this principle is denied, it seems that Locke's difficulties can be avoided at a lesser price than acceptance of Berkeley's immaterialism. Analogously, Phenomenalism appears to be naturally engendered by the difficulties of the Causal Theory only if the supposition, common to both, is accepted that in perception we are "directly" aware only of sense-data. It is at this early stage that most careful attention is needed; it is necessary to ask insistently, and even obstinately, whether any clear meaning has really been attached to this principle, and if so, whether any sufficient grounds have been adduced for supposing it, with all its perplexing implications, to be true. It is at this point that there lies the best hope of escaping from the narrow circle in which, for so many years, with such industry and ingenuity, the philosophy of perception has laboured. It has laboured along tracks laid down by Locke and by Berkeley; and it is far from implying disrespect for the force and merits of their exertions, to hope that we need not be thus attached to their coat-tails for ever.

A TREATISE

CONCERNING

THE PRINCIPLES OF
HUMAN KNOWLEDGE

PREFACE

What I here make public has, after a long and scrupulous inquiry, seemed to me evidently true, and not unuseful to be known—particularly to those who are tainted with Scepticism, or want a demonstration of the Existence and Immateriality of God, or the Natural Immortality of the Soul. Whether it be so or no I am content the reader should impartially examine; since I do not think myself any farther concerned for the success of what I have written than as it is agreeable to truth. But, to the end this may not suffer, I make it my request that the reader suspend his judgment till he has once at least read the whole through with that degree of attention and thought which the subject-matter shall seem to deserve. For, as there are some passages that, taken by themselves, are very liable (nor could it be remedied) to gross misinterpretation, and to be charged with most absurd consequences, which, nevertheless, upon an entire perusal will appear not to follow from them; so likewise, though the whole should be read over, yet, if this be done transiently, it is very probable my sense may be mistaken; but to a thinking reader I flatter myself it will be throughout clear and obvious.—As for the characters of novelty and singularity which some of the following notions may seem to bear, it is, I hope, needless to make any apology on that account. He must surely be either very weak, or very little acquainted with the sciences, who shall reject a truth that is capable of demonstration, for no other reason but because it is newly known, and contrary to the prejudices of mankind. Thus much I thought fit to premise, in order to prevent, if possible, the hasty censures of a sort of men who are too apt to condemn an opinion before they rightly comprehend it.

INTRODUCTION

1. Philosophy, being nothing else but the study of wisdom and truth, it may with reason be expected that those who have spent most time and pains in it should enjoy a greater calm and serenity of mind, a greater clearness and evidence of knowledge, and be less disturbed with doubts and difficulties than other men. Yet so it is, we see the illiterate bulk of mankind, that walk the high-road of plain common sense, and are governed by the dictates of nature, for the most part easy and undisturbed. To them nothing that is familiar appears unaccountable or difficult to comprehend. They complain not of any want of evidence in their senses, and are out of all danger of becoming Sceptics. But no sooner do we depart from Sense and Instinct to follow the light of a superior Principle—to reason, meditate, and reflect on the nature of things, but a thousand scruples spring up in our minds concerning those things which before we seemed fully to comprehend. Prejudices and errors of sense do from all parts discover themselves to our view; and, endeavouring to correct these by reason, we are insensibly drawn into uncouth paradoxes, difficulties, and inconsistencies, which multiply and grow upon us as we advance in speculation, till at length, having wandered through many intricate mazes, we find ourselves just where we were, or, which is worse, sit down in a forlorn Scepticism.

2. The cause of this is thought to be the obscurity of things, or the natural weakness and imperfection of our understandings. It is said, " the faculties we have are few, and those designed by nature for the support and pleasure of life, and not to penetrate into the inward essence and constitution of things. Besides, the mind of man being

finite, when it treats of things which partake of infinity, it is not to be wondered at if it run into absurdities and contradictions, out of which it is impossible it should ever extricate itself, it being of the nature of infinite not to be comprehended by that which is finite."

3. But, perhaps, we may be too partial to ourselves in placing the fault originally in our faculties, and not rather in the wrong use we make of them. It is a hard thing to suppose that right deductions from true principles should ever end in consequences which cannot be maintained or made consistent. We should believe that God has dealt more bountifully with the sons of men than to give them a strong desire for that knowledge which he had placed quite out of their reach. This were not agreeable to the wonted indulgent methods of Providence, which, whatever appetites it may have implanted in the creatures, doth usually furnish them with such means as, if rightly made use of, will not fail to satisfy them. Upon the whole, I am inclined to think that the far greater part, if not all, of those difficulties which have hitherto amused philosophers, and blocked up the way to knowledge, are entirely owing to ourselves—that we have first raised a dust and then complain we cannot see.

4. My purpose therefore is, to try if I can discover what those Principles are which have introduced all that doubtfulness and uncertainty, those absurdities and contradictions, into the several Sects of Philosophy; insomuch that the wisest men have thought our ignorance incurable, conceiving it to arise from the natural dullness and limitation of our faculties. And surely it is a work well deserving our pains to make a strict inquiry concerning the First Principles of Human Knowledge, to sift and examine them on all sides; especially since there may be some grounds to suspect that those lets and difficulties, which stay and embarrass the mind in its search after truth, do not spring from any darkness and intricacy in the objects, or natural defect in the understanding, so much as from False Prin-

ciples which have been insisted on, and might have been avoided.

5. How difficult and discouraging soever this attempt may seem, when I consider what a number of very great and extraordinary men have gone before me in the like designs, yet I am not without some hopes—upon the consideration that the largest views are not always the clearest, and that he who is short-sighted will be obliged to draw the object nearer, and may, perhaps, by a close and narrow survey, discern that which had escaped far better eyes.

6. In order to prepare the mind of the reader for the easier conceiving what follows, it is proper to premise somewhat, by way of Introduction, concerning the Nature and Abuse of Language. But the unravelling this matter leads me in some measure to anticipate my design, by taking notice of what seems to have had a chief part in rendering speculation intricate and perplexed, and to have occasioned innumerable errors and difficulties in almost all parts of knowledge. *And this is the opinion that the mind hath a power of framing abstract ideas or notions of things.* He who is not a perfect stranger to the writings and disputes of philosophers must needs acknowledge that no small part of them are spent about *abstract ideas*. These are in a more especial manner thought to be the object of those sciences which go by the name of Logic and Metaphysics, and of all that which passes under the notion of the most abstracted and sublime learning, in all which one shall scarce find any question handled in such a manner as does not suppose their existence in the mind, and that it is well acquainted with them.

7. It is agreed on all hands that the qualities or modes of things do never *really exist* each of them apart by itself, and separated from all others, but are mixed, as it were, and blended together, several in the same object. But, we are told, the mind being able to *consider* each quality singly, or abstracted from those other qualities with which it is united, does by that means frame to itself abstract

ideas. For example, there is perceived by sight an object extended, coloured, and moved: this mixed or compound idea the mind resolving into its simple, constituent parts, and viewing each by itself, exclusive of the rest, does frame the abstract ideas of extension, colour, and motion. Not that it is possible for colour or motion to exist without extension; but only that the mind can frame to itself by *abstraction* the *idea* of colour exclusive of extension, and of motion exclusive of both colour and extension.

8. Again, the mind having observed that in the particular extensions perceived by sense there is something common and alike in all, and some other things peculiar, as this or that figure or magnitude, which distinguish them one from another; it considers apart or singles out by itself that which is common, making thereof a most abstract idea of extension, which is neither line, surface, nor solid, nor has any figure or magnitude, but is an idea entirely prescinded from all these. So likewise the mind, by leaving out of the particular colours perceived by sense that which distinguishes them one from another, and retaining that only which is common to all, makes an idea of colour in abstract which is neither red, nor blue, nor white, nor any other determinate colour. And, in like manner, by considering motion abstractedly not only from the body moved, but likewise from the figure it describes, and all particular directions and velocities, the abstract idea of motion is framed; which equally corresponds to all particular motions whatsoever that may be perceived by sense.

9. And as the mind frames to itself abstract ideas of qualities or modes, so does it, by the same *precision* or mental separation, attain abstract ideas of the more compounded beings which include several co-existent qualities. For example, the mind, having observed that Peter, James, and John resemble each other in certain common agreements of shape and other qualities, leaves out of the complex and compounded idea it has of Peter, James and any other particular man, that which is peculiar to each,

retaining only what is common to all, and so makes an abstract idea wherein all the particulars equally partake—abstracting entirely from and cutting off all those circumstances and differences which might determine it to any particular existence. And after this manner it is said we come by the abstract idea of *man,* or, if you please, *humanity* or *human nature*; wherein it is true there is included colour, because there is no man but has some colour, but then it can be neither white, nor black, nor any particular colour, because there is no one particular colour wherein all men partake. So likewise there is included stature, but then it is neither tall stature, nor low stature, nor yet middle stature, but something abstracted from all these. And so of the rest. Moreover, there being a great variety of other creatures that partake in some parts, but not all, of the complex idea of man, the mind, leaving out those parts which are peculiar to men, and retaining those only which are common to all the living creatures, frames the idea of *animal,* which abstracts not only from all particular men, but also all birds, beasts, fishes, and insects. The constituent parts of the abstract idea of animal are body, life, sense, and spontaneous motion. By *body* is meant body without any particular shape or figure, there being no one shape or figure common to all animals, without covering, either of hair, or feathers, or scales, &c., nor yet naked : hair, feather, scales and nakedness being the distinguishing properties of particular animals, and for that reason left out of the *abstract idea.* Upon the same account the spontaneous motion must be neither walking, nor flying, nor creeping; it is nevertheless a motion, but what that motion is it is not easy to conceive.

10. Whether others have this wonderful faculty of abstracting their ideas, they best can tell. For myself, I find indeed I have a faculty of imagining, or representing to myself, the idea of those *particular* things I have perceived, and of variously compounding and dividing them. I can

imagine a man with two heads, or the upper parts of a man joined to the body of a horse. I can consider the hand, the eye, the nose, each by itself abstracted or separated from the rest of the body.—But then whatever hand or eye I imagine, it must have some particular shape and colour. Likewise the idea of man that I frame to myself must be either of a white, or a black, or a tawny, a straight, or a crooked, a tall, or a low, or a middle-sized man. I cannot by any effort of thought conceive the *abstract* idea above described.—And it is equally impossible for me to form the abstract idea of motion distinct from the body moving, and which is neither swift nor slow, curvilinear nor rectilinear; and the like may be said of all other abstract general ideas whatsoever. To be plain, I own myself able to abstract *in one sense,* as when I consider some particular parts or qualities separated from others, with which, though they are united in some object, yet it is possible they may really exist without them. But I deny that I can abstract from one another, or conceive separately, those qualities which it is impossible should exist so separated; or that I can frame a general notion, by abstracting from particulars in the manner aforesaid—which last are the two proper acceptations of *abstraction.* And there is ground to think most men will acknowledge themselves to be in my case. The generality of men which are simple and illiterate never pretend to *abstract* notions. It it said they are difficult and not to be attained without pains and study; we may therefore reasonably conclude that, if such there be, they are confined only to the learned.

11. I proceed to examine what can be alleged in defence of the doctrine of abstraction, and try if I can discover what it is that inclines the men of speculation to embrace an opinion so remote from Common Sense as that seems to be. There has been a late deservedly esteemed philosopher[1] who, no doubt, has given it very much counten-

[1] Locke.

ance, by seeming to think the having abstract general ideas is what puts the widest difference in point of understanding betwixt man and beast. "The having of general ideas," saith he, "is that which puts a perfect distinction betwixt man and brutes, and is an excellency which the faculties of brutes do by no means attain unto. For, it is evident we observe no footsteps in them of making use of general signs for universal ideas; from which we have reason to imagine that they have not the faculty of abstracting, or making general ideas, since they have no use of words or any other general signs." And a little after: "Therefore, I think, we may suppose that it is in this that the species of brutes are discriminated from men, and it is that proper difference wherein they are wholly separated, and which at last widens to so wide a distance. For, if they have any ideas at all, and are not bare machines (as some would have them), we cannot deny them to have some reason. It seems as evident to me that they do, some of them, in certain instances reason as that they have sense; but it is only in particular ideas, just as they receive them from their senses. They are the best of them tied up within those narrow bounds, and have not (as I think) the faculty to enlarge them by any kind of abstraction."—*Essay on Human Understanding*, b. II, ch. 11. §§ 10 and 11. I readily agree with this learned author, that the faculties of brutes can by no means attain to abstraction. But then if this be made the distinguishing property of that sort of animals, I fear a great many of those that pass for men must be reckoned into their number. The reason that is here assigned why we have no grounds to think brutes have abstract general ideas is, that we observe in them no use of words or any other general signs; which is built on this supposition—that the making use of words implies the having general ideas. From which it follows that men who use language are able to abstract or generalise their ideas. That this is the sense and arguing of the author will further appear by his answering the question he in another place puts:

" Since all things that exist are only particulars, how come
we by general terms?" His answer is: " Words become
general by being made the signs of general ideas."—*Essay
on Human Understanding,* b. III, ch. 3, § 6.—But it
seems that a word becomes general by being made the
sign, not of an abstract general idea, but of several particular ideas, any one of which it indifferently suggests to the
mind. For example, when it is said " the change of
motion is proportional to the impressed force," or that
" whatever has extension is divisible," these propositions
are to be understood of motion and extension in general,
and nevertheless it will not follow that they suggest to my
thoughts an idea of motion without a body moved, or any
determinate direction and velocity, or that I must conceive an abstract general idea of extension, which is neither
line, surface, nor solid, neither great nor small, black,
white, nor red, nor of any other determinate colour. It is
only implied that whatever *particular* motion I consider,
whether it be swift or slow, perpendicular, horizontal,
or oblique, or in whatever object, the axiom concerning it
holds equally true. As does the other of every *particular*
extension, it matters not whether line, surface, or solid,
whether of this or that magnitude or figure.

12. By observing how ideas become general, we may the
better judge how words are made so. And here it is to be
noted that I do not deny absolutely there are general
ideas, but only that there are any *abstract* general ideas;
for, in the passages we have quoted wherein there is mention of general ideas, it is always supposed that they are
formed by abstraction, after the manner set forth in sections 8 and 9. Now, if we will annex a meaning to our
words, and speak only of what we can conceive, I believe
we shall acknowledge that an idea which, considered in
itself, is particular, becomes general by being made to
represent or stand for all other particular ideas of the same
sort.—To make this plain by an example, suppose a geo-
metrician is demonstrating the method of cutting a line in

two equal parts. He draws, for instance, a black line of an inch in length : this, which in itself is a particular line, is nevertheless with regard to its signification general, since, as it is there used, it represents all particular lines whatsoever; so that what is demonstrated of it is demonstrated of all lines, or, in other words, of a line in general. And, as *that particular line* becomes general by being made a sign, so the *name* " line," which taken absolutely is particular, by being a sign is made general. And as the former owes its generality not to its being the sign of an abstract or general line, but of all particular right lines that may possibly exist, so the latter must be thought to derive its generality from the same cause, namely, the various particular lines which it indifferently denotes.

13. To give the reader a yet clearer view of the nature of abstract ideas, and the uses they are thought necessary to, I shall add one more passage out of the *Essay on Human Understanding,* which is as follows :—" Abstract ideas are not so obvious or easy to children or the yet unexercised mind as particular ones. If they seem so to grown men it is only because by constant and familiar use they are made so. For, when we nicely reflect upon them, we shall find that general ideas are fictions and contrivances of the mind, that carry difficulty with them, and do not so easily offer themselves as we are apt to imagine. For example, does it not require some pains and skill to form the general idea of a triangle (which is yet none of the most abstract, comprehensive, and difficult); for it must be neither oblique nor rectangle, neither equilateral, equicrural, nor scalenon, but all and none of these at once? In effect, it is something imperfect that cannot exist, an idea wherein some parts of several different and inconsistent ideas are put together. It is true the mind in this imperfect state has need of such ideas, and makes all the haste to them it can, for the conveniency of communication and enlargement of knowledge, to both which it is naturally very much inclined. But yet one has reason to

suspect such ideas are marks of our imperfection. At least this is enough to shew that the most abstract and general ideas are not those that the mind is first and most easily acquainted with, nor such as its earliest knowledge is conversant about."—B. IV, ch. 7, § 9. If any man has the faculty of framing in his mind such an idea of a triangle as is here described, it is in vain to pretend to dispute him out of it, nor would I go about it. All I desire is that the reader would fully and certainly inform himself whether he has such an idea or no. And this, methinks, can be no hard task for anyone to perform. What more easy than for anyone to look a little into his own thoughts, and there try whether he has, or can attain to have, an idea that shall correspond with the description that is here given of the general idea of a triangle—which is neither oblique nor rectangle, equilateral, equicrural nor scalenon, but all and none of these at once?

14. Much is here said of the difficulty that abstract ideas carry with them, and the pains and skill requisite to the forming them. And it is on all hands agreed that there is need of great toil and labour of the mind, to emancipate our thoughts from particular objects, and raise them to those sublime speculations that are conversant about abstract ideas. From all which the natural consequence should seem to be, that so difficult a thing as the forming abstract ideas was not necessary for *communication*, which is so easy and familiar to all sorts of men. But, we are told, if they seem obvious and easy to grown men, it is only because by constant and familiar use they are made so. Now, I would fain know at what time it is men are employed in surmounting that difficulty, and furnishing themselves with those necessary helps for discourse. It cannot be when they are grown up, for then it seems they are not conscious of any such painstaking; it remains therefore to be the business of their childhood. And surely the great and multiplied labour of framing abstract notions will be found a hard task for that tender age. Is it not a hard

thing to imagine that a couple of children cannot prate together of their sugar-plums and rattles and the rest of their little trinkets, till they have first tacked together numberless inconsistencies, and so framed in their minds abstract general ideas, and annexed them to every common name they make use of?

15. Nor do I think them a whit more needful for the *enlargement of knowledge* than for communication. It is, I know, a point much insisted on, that all knowledge and demonstration are about universal notions, to which I fully agree : but then it does not appear to me that those notions are formed by abstraction in the manner premised—*universality,* so far as I can comprehend, not consisting in the absolute, positive nature or conception of anything, but in the *relation* it bears to the particulars signified or represented by it; by virtue whereof it is that things, names, or notions, being in their own nature *particular,* are rendered *universal.* Thus, when I demonstrate any proposition concerning triangles, it is to be supposed that I have in view the universal idea of a triangle; which ought not to be understood as if I could frame an idea of a triangle which was neither equilateral, nor scalenon, nor equicrural; but only that the particular triangle I consider, whether of this or that sort it matters not, doth equally stand for and represent all rectilinear triangles whatsoever, and is *in that sense universal.* All which seems very plain and not to include any difficulty in it.

16. But here it will be demanded, how we can know any proposition to be true of all particular triangles, except we have first seen it demonstrated of the abstract idea of a triangle which equally agrees to all? For, because a property may be demonstrated to agree to some one particular triangle, it will not thence follow that it equally belongs to any other triangle, which in all respects is not the same with it. For example, having demonstrated that the three angles of an isosceles rectangular triangle are equal to two right ones, I cannot therefore conclude this affection agrees

to all other triangles which have neither a right angle nor two equal sides. It seems therefore that, to be certain this proposition is universally true, we must either make a particular demonstration for every particular triangle, which is impossible, or once for all demonstrate it of the abstract idea of a triangle, in which all the particulars do indifferently partake and by which they are all equally represented.—To which I answer, that, though the idea I have in view whilst I make the demonstration be, for instance, that of an isosceles rectangular triangle whose sides are of a determinate length, I may nevertheless be certain it extends to all other rectilinear triangles, of what sort or bigness soever. And that because neither the right angle, nor the equality, nor determinate length of the sides are at all concerned in the demonstration. It is true the diagram I have in view includes all these particulars, but then there is not the least mention made of them in the proof of the proposition. It is not said the three angles are equal to two right ones, because one of them is a right angle, or because the sides comprehending it are of the same length. Which sufficiently shews that the right angle might have been oblique, and the sides unequal, and for all that the demonstration have held good. And for this reason it is that I conclude that to be true of any obliquangular or scalenon which I had demonstrated of a particular right-angled equicrural triangle, and not because I demonstrated the proposition of the abstract idea of a triangle. [And here it must be acknowledged that a man may consider a figure merely as triangular, without attending to the particular qualities of the angles, or relations of the sides. So far he may abstract; but this will never prove that he can frame an abstract, general, inconsistent idea of a triangle. In like manner we may consider Peter so far forth as man, or so far forth as animal, without framing the forementioned abstract idea, either of man or of animal, inasmuch as all that is perceived is not considered.][2]

[2] Added in Berkeley's third edition (1734).

17. It were an endless as well as an useless thing to trace the Schoolmen, those great masters of abstraction, through all the manifold inextricable labyrinths of error and dispute which their doctrine of abstract natures and notions seems to have led them into. What bickerings and controversies, and what a learned dust have been raised about those matters, and what mighty advantage has been from thence derived to mankind, are things at this day too clearly known to need being insisted on. And it had been well if the ill effects of that doctrine were confined to those only who make the most avowed profession of it. When men consider the great pains, industry, and parts that have for so many ages been laid out on the cultivation and advancement of the sciences, and that notwithstanding all this the far greater part of them remain full of darkness and uncertainty and disputes that are like never to have an end, and even those that are thought to be supported by the most clear and cogent demonstrations contain in them paradoxes which are perfectly irreconcilable to the understandings of men, and that, taking all together, a very small portion of them does supply any real benefit to mankind, otherwise than by being an innocent diversion and amusement—I say, the consideration of all this is apt to throw them into a despondency and perfect contempt of all study. But this may perhaps cease upon a view of the False Principles that have obtained in the world, amongst all which there is none, methinks, hath a more wide and extended sway over the thoughts of speculative men than this of *abstract* general ideas.

18. I come now to consider the *source* of this prevailing notion, and that seems to me to be Language. And surely nothing of less extent than reason itself could have been the source of an opinion so universally received. The truth of this appears as from other reasons so also from the plain confession of the ablest patrons of abstract ideas, who acknowledge that they are made in order to naming; from

which it is a clear consequence that if there had been no such thing as speech or *universal* signs there never had been any thought of abstraction. See b. III. ch. 6. § 39, and elsewhere of the *Essay on Human Understanding.* Let us examine the manner wherein Words have contributed to the origin of that mistake.—First then, it is thought that every name has, or ought to have, one only precise and settled signification; which inclines men to think there are certain abstract, determinate ideas that constitute the true and only immediate signification of each general name, and that it is by the mediation of these abstract ideas that a general name comes to signify any particular thing. Whereas, in truth, there is no such thing as one precise and definite signification annexed to any general name, they all signifying indifferently a great number of particular ideas. All which does evidently follow from what has been already said, and will clearly appear to anyone by a little reflection. To this it will be objected that every name that has a definition is thereby restrained to one certain signification. For example, a triangle is defined to be " a plain surface comprehended by three right lines," by which that name is limited to denote one certain idea and no other. To which I answer, that in the definition it is not said whether the surface be great or small, black or white, nor whether the sides are long or short, equal or unequal, nor with what angles they are inclined to each other; in all which there may be great variety, and consequently there is no one settled idea which limits the signification of the word triangle. It is one thing for to keep a name constantly to the same definition, and another to make it stand everywhere for the same idea; the one is necessary, the other useless and impracticable.

19. But, to give a further account how words came to produce the doctrine of abstract ideas, it must be observed that it is a received opinion that language has no other end but the communicating our ideas, and that every significant name stands for an idea. This being so, and it being

withal certain that names which yet are not thought altogether insignificant do not always mark out particular conceivable ideas, it is straightway concluded that they stand for abstract notions. That there are many names in use amongst speculative men which do not always suggest to others determinate particular ideas, or in truth anything at all, is what nobody will deny. And a little attention will discover that it is not necessary (even in the strictest reasonings) significant names which stand for ideas should, every time they are used, excite in the understanding the ideas they are made to stand for—in reading and discoursing, names being for the most part used as letters are in Algebra, in which, though a particular quantity be marked by each letter, yet to proceed right it is not requisite that in every step each letter suggest to your thoughts that particular quantity it was appointed to stand for.

20. Besides, the communicating of ideas marked by words is not the chief and only end of language, as is commonly supposed. There are other ends, as the raising of some passion, the exciting to or deterring from an action, the putting the mind in some particular disposition—to which the former is in many cases barely subservient, and sometimes entirely omitted, when these can be obtained without it, as I think does not unfrequently happen in the familiar use of language. I entreat the reader to reflect with himself, and see if it does not often happen, either in hearing or reading a discourse, that the passions of fear, love, hatred, admiration, and disdain, and the like, arise immediately in his mind upon the perception of certain words, without any ideas coming between. At first, indeed, the words might have occasioned ideas that were fitting to produce those emotions; but, if I mistake not, it will be found that, when language is once grown familiar, the hearing of the sounds, or sight of the characters, is oft immediately attended with those passions which at first were wont to be produced by the intervention of ideas that

are now quite omitted. May we not, for example, be affected with the promise of a *good thing,* though we have not an idea of what it is? Or is not the being threatened with *danger* sufficient to excite a dread, though we think not of any particular evil likely to befall us, nor yet frame to ourselves an idea of danger in abstract? If anyone shall join ever so little reflexion of his own to what has been said, I believe that it will evidently appear to him that general names are often used in the propriety of language without the speaker's designing them for marks of ideas in his own, which he would have them raise in the mind of the hearer. Even proper names themselves do not seem always spoken with a design to bring into our view the ideas of those individuals that are supposed to be marked by them. For example, when a schoolman tells me " Aristotle hath said it," all I conceive he means by it is to dispose me to embrace his opinion with the deference and submission which custom has annexed to that name. And this effect is often so instantly produced in the mind of those who are accustomed to resign their judgment to the authority of that philosopher, as it is impossible any idea either of his person, writings, or reputation should go before. So close and immediate a connexion may custom establish betwixt the very *word* Aristotle and the motions of assent and reverence in the minds of some men. Innumerable examples of this kind may be given, but why should I insist on those things which everyone's experience will, I doubt not, plentifully suggest unto him?

21. We have, I think, shewn the impossibility of Abstract Ideas. We have considered what has been said for them by their ablest patrons; and endeavoured to shew they are of no use for those ends to which they are thought necessary. And lastly, we have traced them to the source from whence they flow, which appears evidently to be language. —It cannot be denied that words are of excellent use, in that by their means all that stock of knowledge which has been purchased by the joint labours of inquisitive men in

all ages and nations may be drawn into the view and made the possession of one single person. But most parts of knowledge have been strangely perplexed and darkened by the *abuse* of words and general ways of speech wherein they are delivered. Since therefore words are so apt to impose on the understanding, whatever *ideas* I consider, I shall endeavour to take *them* bare and naked into my view, keeping out of my thoughts, so far as I am able, those *names* which long and constant use hath so strictly united with them; from which I may expect to derive the following advantages :—

22. *First,* I shall be sure to get clear of all controversies purely verbal—the springing up of which weeds in almost all the sciences has been a main hindrance to the growth of true and sound knowledge. *Secondly,* this seems to be a sure way to extricate myself out of that fine and subtle net of *abstract ideas* which has so miserably perplexed and entangled the minds of men; and that with this peculiar circumstance, that by how much the finer and more curious was the wit of any man, by so much the deeper was he likely to be ensnared and faster held therein. *Thirdly,* so long as I confine my thoughts to my own ideas divested of words, I do not see how I can easily be mistaken. The objects I consider, I clearly and adequately know. I cannot be deceived in thinking I have an idea which I have not. It is not possible for me to imagine that any of my own ideas are alike or unlike that are not truly so. To discern the agreements or disagreements there are between my ideas, to see what ideas are included in any compound idea and what not, there is nothing more requisite than an attentive perception of what passes in my own understanding.

23. But the attainment of all these advantages does presuppose an entire deliverance from the deception of words which I dare hardly promise myself; so difficult a thing it is to dissolve an union so early begun, and confirmed by so long a habit as that betwixt words and ideas.

Which difficulty seems to have been very much increased by the doctrine of *abstraction*. For, so long as men thought abstract ideas were annexed to their words, it does not seem strange that they should use words for ideas—it being found an impracticable thing to lay aside the word, and retain the *abstract* idea in the mind, which in itself was perfectly inconceivable.

This seems to me the principal cause why those who have so emphatically recommended to others the laying aside all use of words in their meditations, and contemplating their bare ideas, have yet failed to perform it themselves. Of late many have been very sensible of the absurd opinions and insignificant disputes which grow out of the abuse of words. And, in order to remedy these evils, they advise well, that we attend to the ideas signified, and draw off our attention from the words which signify them. But, how good soever this advice may be they have given others, it is plain they could not have a due regard to it themselves, so long as they thought the only immediate use of words was to signify ideas, and that the immediate signification of every general name was a determinate abstract idea.

24. But, these being known to be mistakes, a man may with greater ease prevent his being imposed on by words. He that knows he has no other than *particular* ideas, will not puzzle himself in vain to find out and conceive the *abstract* idea annexed to any name. And he that knows names do not always stand for ideas will spare himself the labour of looking for ideas where there are none to be had. It were, therefore, to be wished that every one would use his utmost endeavours to obtain a clear view of the ideas he would consider, separating from them all that dress and incumbrance of words which so much contribute to blind the judgment and divide the attention. In vain do we extend our view into the heavens and pry into the entrails of the earth, in vain do we consult the writings of learned men and trace the dark footsteps of antiquity—we need

only draw the curtain of words, to behold the fairest tree of knowledge, whose fruit is excellent, and within the reach of our hand.

25. Unless we take care to clear the First Principles of Knowledge from the embarras and delusion of words, we may make infinite reasonings upon them to no purpose; we may draw consequences from consequences, and be never the wiser. The farther we go, we shall only lose ourselves the more irrecoverably, and be the deeper entangled in difficulties and mistakes. Whoever therefore designs to read the following sheets, I entreat him that he would make my words the occasion of his own thinking, and endeavour to attain the same train of thoughts in reading that I had in writing them. By this means it will be easy for him to discover the truth or falsity of what I say. He will be out of all danger of being deceived by my words, and I do not see how he can be led into an error by considering his own naked, undisguised ideas.

PART I[1]

1. It is evident to anyone who takes a survey of the objects of human knowledge, that they are either *ideas* actually imprinted on the senses; or else such as are perceived by attending to the passions and operations of the mind; or lastly, *ideas* formed by help of memory and imagination—either compounding, dividing, or barely representing those originally perceived in the aforesaid ways.— By sight I have the ideas of light and colours, with their several degrees and variations. By touch I perceive hard and soft, heat and cold, motion and resistance, and of all these more and less either as to quantity or degree. Smelling furnishes me with odours; the palate with tastes; and hearing conveys sounds to the mind in all their variety of tone and composition.—And as several of these are observed to accompany each other, they come to be marked by one name, and so to be reputed as one THING. Thus, for example, a certain colour, taste, smell, figure and consistence having been observed to go together, are accounted one distinct thing, signified by the name *apple*; other collections of ideas constitute a stone, a tree, a book, and the like sensible things—which as they are pleasing or disagreeable excite the passions of love, hatred, joy, grief, and so forth.

2. But, besides all that endless variety of ideas or objects of knowledge, there is likewise something which knows or perceives them; and exercises divers operations, as willing, imagining, remembering, about them. This perceiving, active being is what I call MIND, SPIRIT, SOUL, or MYSELF.

[1] Though the *Principles* was thus issued as " Part I," no further parts were ever published. Berkeley said, some years later, that he had made some progress with the projected later parts, but had lost the manuscript while travelling in Italy.

By which words I do not denote any one of my ideas, but a thing entirely distinct from them, wherein they exist, or, which is the same thing, whereby they are perceived—for the existence of an idea consists in being perceived.

3. That neither our thoughts, nor passions, nor ideas formed by the imagination, exist without the mind, is what everybody will allow.—And to me it is no less evident that the various SENSATIONS, or *ideas imprinted on the sense,* however blended or combined together (that is, whatever *objects* they compose), cannot exist otherwise than in a mind perceiving them—I think an intuitive knowledge may be obtained of this by anyone that shall attend to *what is meant by the term exist when applied to sensible things.* The table I write on I say exists, that is, I see and feel it; and if I were out of my study I should say it existed—meaning thereby that if I was in my study I might perceive it, or that some other spirit actually does perceive it. There was an odour, that is, it was smelt; there was a sound, that is, it was heard; a colour or figure, and it was perceived by sight or touch. This is all that I can understand by these and the like expressions.—For as to what is said of the absolute existence of unthinking things without any relation to their being perceived, that is to me perfectly unintelligible. Their *esse* is *percipi,* nor is it possible they should have any existence out of the minds or thinking things which perceive them.

4. It is indeed an opinion strangely prevailing amongst men, that houses, mountains, rivers, and in a word all sensible objects, have an existence, natural or real, distinct from their being perceived by the understanding. But, with how great an assurance and acquiescence soever this principle may be entertained in the world, yet whoever shall find in his heart to call it in question may, if I mistake not, perceive it to involve a manifest contradiction. For, what are the forementioned objects but the things we perceive by sense? and what do we perceive besides our own ideas or sensations? and is it not plainly repugnant that any one

of *these,* or any combination of them, should exist unperceived?

5. If we thoroughly examine this tenet it will, perhaps, be found at bottom to depend on the doctrine of *abstract ideas.* For can there be a nicer strain of abstraction than to distinguish the *existence* of sensible objects from their *being perceived,* so as to conceive them existing unperceived? Light and colours, heat and cold, extension and figures—in a word the things we see and feel—what are they but so many sensations, notions, ideas, or impressions on the sense? and is it possible to separate, even in thought, any of these from perception? For my part, I might as easily divide a thing from itself. I may, indeed, divide in my thoughts, or conceive apart from each other, those things which, perhaps, I never perceived by sense so divided. Thus, I imagine the trunk of a human body without the limbs, or conceive the smell of a rose without thinking on the rose itself. So far, I will not deny, I can abstract—if that may properly be called *abstraction* which extends only to the conceiving separately such objects as it is possible may really exist or be actually perceived asunder. But my conceiving or imagining power does not extend beyond the possibility of real existence or perception. Hence, as it is impossible for me to see or feel anything without an actual sensation of that thing, so is it impossible for me to conceive in my thoughts any sensible thing or object distinct from the sensation or perception of it.

6. Some truths there are so near and obvious to the mind that a man need only open his eyes to see them. Such I take this important one to be, viz. that all the choir of heaven and furniture of the earth, in a word all those bodies which compose the mighty frame of the world, have not any subsistence without a mind—that their *being* is *to be perceived or known*; that consequently so long as they are not actually perceived by me, or do not exist in my mind or that of any other created spirit, they must either have no existence at all, or else subsist in the mind of some

Eternal Spirit—it being perfectly unintelligible, and involving all the absurdity of abstraction, to attribute to any single part of them an existence independent of a spirit. To be convinced of which, the reader need only reflect, and try to separate in his own thoughts the *being* of a sensible thing from its *being perceived*.

7. From what has been said it is evident there is not any other Substance than SPIRIT, or *that which perceives*. But, for the fuller demonstration of this point, let it be considered the sensible qualities are colour, figure, motion, smell, taste, &c., *i.e.* the ideas perceived by sense. Now, for an idea to exist in an unperceiving thing is a manifest contradiction; for to have an idea is all one as to perceive; that therefore wherein colour, figure, &c. exist must perceive them; hence it is clear there can be no unthinking substance or *substratum* of those ideas.

8. But, say you, though the ideas themselves do not exist without the mind, yet there may be things like them, whereof they are copies or resemblances, which things exist without the mind in an unthinking substance. I answer, an idea can be like nothing but an idea; a colour or figure can be like nothing but another colour or figure. If we look but never so little into our own thoughts, we shall find it impossible for us to conceive a likeness except only between our ideas. Again, I ask whether those supposed originals or external things, of which our ideas are the pictures or representations, be themselves perceivable or no? If they are, then they are ideas and we have gained our point; but if you say they are not, I appeal to anyone whether it be sense to assert a colour is like something which is invisible; hard or soft, like something which is intangible; and so of the rest.

9. Some there are who make a distinction betwixt *primary* and *secondary* qualities.[2] By the former they mean extension, figure, motion, rest, solidity, impenetrability,

[2] Locke: See *Essay*, b. II, ch. 8.

and number; by the latter they denote all other sensible qualities, as colours, sounds, tastes, and so forth. The ideas we have of these last they acknowledge not to be the resemblances of anything existing without the mind, or unperceived, but they will have our ideas of the primary qualities to be patterns or images of things which exist without the mind, in an unthinking substance which they call Matter.—By Matter, therefore, we are to understand *an inert, senseless substance, in which extension, figure and motion do actually subsist.* But it is evident, from what we have already shewn, that extension, figure, and motion are only ideas existing in the mind, and that an idea can be like nothing but another idea, and that consequently neither they nor their archetypes can exist in an unperceiving substance. Hence, it is plain that the very notion of what is called *Matter* or *corporeal substance* involves a contradiction in it.

10. They who assert that figure, motion, and the rest of the primary or original qualities do exist without the mind, in unthinking substances, do at the same time acknowledge that colours, sounds, heat, cold, and suchlike secondary qualities, do not—which they tell us are sensations existing in the mind alone, that depend on and are occasioned by the different size, texture, and motion of the minute particles of matter. This they take for an undoubted truth, which they can demonstrate beyond all exception. Now, if it be certain that those original qualities are inseparably united with the other sensible qualities, and not, even in thought, capable of being abstracted from them, it plainly follows that they exist only in the mind. But I desire any one to reflect and try whether he can, by any abstraction of thought, conceive the extension and motion of a body without all other sensible qualities. For my own part, I see evidently that it is not in my power to frame an idea of a body extended and moving, but I must withal give it some colour or other sensible quality which is acknowledged to exist only in the mind. In short, extension, figure, and

motion, abstracted from all other qualities, are inconceivable. Where therefore the other sensible qualities are, there must these be also, to wit, in the mind and no where else.

11. Again, *great* and *small, swift* and *slow,* are allowed to exist nowhere without the mind, being entirely relative, and changing as the frame or position of the organs of sense varies. The extension therefore which exists without the mind is neither great nor small, the motion neither swift nor slow, that is, they are nothing at all. But, say you, they are extension in general, and motion in general : thus we see how much the tenet of extended moveable substances existing without the mind depends on that strange doctrine of *abstract* ideas. And here I cannot but remark how nearly the vague and indeterminate description of Matter or corporeal substance, which the modern philosophers are run into by their own principles, resembles that antiquated and so much ridiculed notion of *materia prima,* to be met with in Aristotle and his followers. Without extension solidity cannot be conceived; since therefore it has been shewn that extension exists not in an unthinking substance, the same must also be true of solidity.

12. That number is entirely the creature of the mind, even though the other qualities be allowed to exist without, will be evident to whoever considers that the same thing bears a different denomination of number as the mind views it with different respects. Thus, the same extension is one, or three, or thirty-six, according as the mind considers it with reference to a yard, a foot, or an inch. Number is so visibly relative, and dependent on men's understanding, that it is strange to think how anyone should give it an absolute existence without the mind. We say one book, one page, one line, &c.; all these are equally units, though some contain several of the others, And in each instance, it is plain, the unit relates to some particular combination of ideas arbitrarily put together by the mind.

13. Unity I know some will have to be a simple or uncompounded idea, accompanying all other ideas into the

mind. That I have any such idea answering the word *unity* I do not find; and if I had, methinks I could not miss finding it : on the contrary, it should be the most familiar to my understanding, since it is said to accompany all other ideas, and to be perceived by all the ways of sensation and reflexion. To say no more, it is an *abstract* idea.

14. I shall further add, that, after the same manner as modern philosophers prove certain sensible qualities to have no existence in Matter, or without the mind, the same thing may be likewise proved of all other sensible qualities whatsoever. Thus, for instance, it is said that heat and cold are affections only of the mind, and not at all patterns of real beings existing in the corporeal substances which excite them, for that the same body which appears cold to one hand seems warm to another. Now, why may we not as well argue that figure and extension are not patterns or resemblances of qualities existing in Matter, because to the same eye at different stations, or eyes of a different texture at the same station, they appear various, and cannot therefore be the images of anything settled and determinate without the mind? Again, it is proved that sweetness is not really in the sapid thing, because the thing remaining unaltered the sweetness is changed into bitter, as in the case of a fever or otherwise vitiated palate. Is it not as reasonable to say that motion is not without the mind, since if the succession of ideas in the mind become swifter the motion, it is acknowledged, shall appear slower without any alteration in any external object.

15. In short, let anyone consider those arguments which are thought manifestly to prove that colours and tastes exist *only* in the mind, and he shall find they may with equal force be brought to prove the same thing of extension, figure, and motion.—Though it must be confessed this method or arguing does not so much prove that there is no extension of colour in an outward object, as that *we* do not know by *sense* which is the *true* extension or colour

of the object. But the arguments foregoing plainly shew it to be impossible that any colour or extension at all, or other sensible quality whatsoever, should exist in an unthinking subject without the mind, or in truth, that there should be any such thing as an outward object.

16. But let us examine a little the received opinion.—It is said extension is a mode or accident of Matter, and that Matter is the *substratum* that supports it. Now I desire that you would explain to me what is meant by Matter's *supporting* extension. Say you, I have no idea of Matter and therefore cannot explain it. I answer, though you have no positive, yet, if you have any meaning at all, you must at least have a relative idea of Matter; though you know not what it is, yet you must be supposed to know what relation it bears to accidents, and what is meant by its supporting them. It is evident " support " cannot here be taken in its usual or literal sense—as when we say that pillars support a building; in what sense therefore must it be taken?

17. If we inquire into what the most accurate philosophers declare themselves to mean by *material substance*, we shall find them acknowledge they have no other meaning annexed to those sounds but the idea of *being in general*, together with the relative notion of its *supporting accidents*. The general idea of Being appeareth to me the most abstract and incomprehensible of all other; and as for its supporting accidents, this, as we have just now observed, cannot be understood in the common sense of those words; it must therefore be taken in some other sense, but what that is they do not explain. So that when I consider the two parts or branches which make the signification of the words *material substance,* I am convinced there is no distinct meaning annexed to them. But why should we trouble ourselves any farther, in discussing this material *substratum* or " support " of figure, and motion, and other sensible qualities? Does it not suppose *they* have an

existence without the mind? And is not this a direct repugnancy, and altogether inconceivable?

18. But, though it were possible that solid, figured, moveable *substances* may exist without the mind, corresponding to the ideas we have of bodies, yet how is it possible for us to know this? Either we must know it by Sense or by Reason.—As for our senses, by them we have the knowledge only of our sensations, ideas, or those things that are immediately perceived by sense, call them what you will : but they do not inform us that things exist without the mind, or unperceived, like to those which are perceived. This the Materialists themselves acknowledge.— It remains therefore that if we have any knowledge at all of external things, it must be by Reason inferring their existence from what is immediately perceived by sense. But what reason can induce us to believe the existence of bodies without the mind, from what we perceive, since the very patrons of Matter themselves do not pretend there is any *necessary* connexion betwixt them and our ideas? I say it is granted on all hands—and what happens in dreams, frenzies, and the like, puts it beyond dispute—that it is possible we might be affected with all the ideas we have now, though there were no bodies existing without resembling them. Hence, it is evident the supposition of external bodies is not necessary for the producing our ideas; since it is granted they are produced sometimes, and might possibly be produced always in the same order we see them in at present, without their concurrence.

19. But, though we might possibly have all our sensations without them, yet perhaps it may be thought easier to conceive and explain the manner of their production, by supposing external bodies in their likeness rather than otherwise; and so it might be at least probable there are such things as bodies that excite their ideas in our minds. But neither can this be said; for, though we give the materialists their external bodies, they by their own confession are never the nearer knowing *how* our ideas are

produced; since they own themselves unable to comprehend in what manner body can act upon spirit, or how it is possible it should imprint any idea in the mind. Hence it is evident the production of ideas or sensations in our minds can be no reason why we should suppose Matter or corporeal substances, since *that* is acknowledged to remain equally inexplicable with or without this supposition. If therefore it were possible for bodies to exist without the mind, yet to hold they do so must needs be a very precarious opinion; since it is to suppose, without any reason at all, that God has created innumerable beings that are entirely useless, and serve to no manner of purpose.

20. In short, if there were external bodies, it is impossible we should ever come to know it; and if there were not, we might have the very same reasons to think there were that we have now. Suppose—what no one can deny possible—an intelligence *without the help of external bodies,* to be affected with the same train of sensations or ideas that you are, imprinted in the same order and with like vividness in his mind. I ask whether that intelligence hath not all the reason to believe the existence of corporeal substances, represented by his ideas, and exciting them in his mind, that you can possibly have for believing the same thing? Of this there can be no question—which one consideration were enough to make any reasonable person suspect the strength of whatever arguments he may think himself to have, for the existence of bodies without the mind.

21. Were it necessary to add any farther proof against the Existence of Matter, after what has been said, I could instance several of those errors and difficulties (not to mention impieties) which have sprung from that tenet. It has occasioned numberless controversies and disputes in philosophy, and not a few of far greater moment in religion. But I shall not enter into the detail of them in this place, as well because I think arguments *a posteriori* are unnecessary for confirming what has been, if I mistake not, suf-

ficiently demonstrated *a priori,* as because I shall hereafter find occasion to speak somewhat of them.

22. I am afraid I have given cause to think me needlessly prolix in handling this subject. For, to what purpose is it to dilate on that which may be demonstrated with the utmost evidence in a line or two, to anyone that is capable of the least reflection? It is but looking into your own thoughts, and so trying whether you can conceive it possible for a sound, or figure, or motion, or colour to exist without the mind or unperceived. This easy trial may perhaps make you see that what you contend for is a downright contradiction. Insomuch that I am content to put the whole upon this issue :—If you can but conceive it possible for one extended moveable substance, or, in general, for any one idea, or anything like an idea, to exist otherwise than in a mind perceiving it, I shall readily give up the cause. And, as for all that compages of external bodies you contend for, I shall grant you its existence, though you cannot either give me any reason why you believe it exists, or assign any use to it when it is supposed to exist. I say, the bare possibility of your opinion's being true shall pass for an argument that it is so.

23. But, say you, surely there is nothing easier than for me to imagine trees, for instance, in a park, or books existing in a closet, and nobody by to perceive them. I answer, you may so, there is no difficulty in it; but what is all this, I beseech you, more than framing in *your* mind certain ideas which you call books and trees, and at the same time omitting to frame the idea of any one that may perceive them? But do not you yourself perceive or think of them all the while? This therefore is nothing to the purpose : it only shews you have the power of imagining or forming ideas in your mind; but it does not shew that you can conceive it possible the objects of your thought may exist without the mind. To make out this, it is necessary that *you* conceive them existing unconceived or unthought

of, which is a manifest repugnancy. When we do our utmost to conceive the existence of external bodies, we are all the while only contemplating our own ideas. But the mind, *taking no notice of itself,* is deluded to think it can and does conceive bodies existing unthought of or without the mind, though at the same time they are apprehended by or exist in itself. A little attention will discover to any one the truth and evidence of what is here said, and make it unnecessary to insist on any other proofs against the existence of *material substance.*

24. It is very obvious, upon the least inquiry into our own thoughts, to know whether it be possible for us to *understand* what is meant by the *absolute* existence of sensible objects *in themselves,* or *without the mind.* To me it is evident those words mark out either a direct contradiction, or else nothing at all. And to convince others of this, I know no readier or fairer way than to entreat they would calmly attend to their own thoughts; and if by this attention the emptiness or repugnancy of those expressions does appear, surely nothing more is requisite for their conviction. It is on this therefore that I insist, to wit, that the absolute existence of unthinking things are words without a meaning, or which include a contradiction. This is what I repeat and inculcate, and earnestly recommend to the attentive thoughts of the reader.

25. All our ideas, sensations, notions, or the things which we perceive, by whatsoever names they may be distinguished, are visibly inactive—there is nothing of Power or Agency included in them. So that one idea or object of thought cannot produce or make any alteration in another.—To be satisfied of the truth of this, there is nothing else requisite but a bare observation of our ideas. For, since they and every part of them exist only in the mind, it follows that there is nothing in them but what is perceived : but whoever shall attend to his ideas, whether of sense or reflection, will not perceive in them any power

or activity; there is, therefore, no such thing contained in them. A little attention will discover to us that the very being of an idea implies passiveness and inertness in it, insomuch that it is impossible for an idea to do anything, or, strictly speaking, to be the cause of anything: neither can it be the resemblance or pattern of any active being, as is evident from sect. 8. Whence it plainly follows that extension, figure, and motion cannot be the cause of our sensations. To say, therefore, that these are the effects of powers resulting from the configuration, number, motion, and size of corpuscles, must certainly be false.

26. We perceive a continual *succession* of ideas; some are anew excited, others are changed or totally disappear. There is therefore some Cause of these ideas, whereon they depend, and which produces and changes them. That this cause cannot be any quality, or idea, or combination of ideas is clear from the preceding section. It must therefore be a substance; but it has been shewn that there is no corporeal or material substance : it remains therefore that the cause of ideas is an incorporeal active substance or Spirit.

27. A Spirit is one simple, undivided, active being—as it *perceives* ideas it is called the *Understanding*, and as it *produces* or otherwise *operates* about them it is called the *Will*. Hence there can be no *idea* formed of a soul or spirit; for, all ideas whatever, being passive and inert, (vid. sect. 25,) cannot represent unto us, by way of image or likeness, that which acts. A little attention will make it plain to any one that to have an idea which shall be *like* that active principle of motion and change of ideas is absolutely impossible. Such is the nature of Spirit, or that which acts, that it cannot be of itself perceived, but only by the effects which it produceth.—If any man shall doubt of the truth of what is here delivered, let him but reflect and try if he can frame the idea of any Power or Active Being; and whether he has ideas of two principal powers, marked by the names *Will* and *Understanding*, distinct from each

other, as well as from a third idea of Substance or Being in general, with a relative notion of its supporting or being the subject of the aforesaid powers—which is signified by the name Soul or Spirit. This is what some hold; but, so far as I can see, the words *will, soul, spirit,* do not stand for different ideas, or, in truth, for any idea at all, but for something which is very different from ideas, and which, being an Agent, cannot be like unto, or represented by, any idea whatsoever. Though it must be owned at the same time that we have some *notion* of soul, spirit, and the operations of the mind; such as willing, loving, hating —inasmuch as we know or understand the meaning of these words.

28. I find I can excite ideas in my mind at pleasure, and vary and shift the scene as oft as I think fit. It is no more than willing, and straightway this or that idea arises in my fancy; and by the same power it is obliterated and makes way for another. This making and unmaking of ideas doth very properly denominate the mind active. Thus much is certain and grounded on experience : but when we talk of unthinking agents, or of exciting ideas exclusive of Volition, we only amuse ourselves with words.

29. But, whatever power I may have over my own thoughts, I find the ideas actually perceived by Sense have not a like dependence on my will. When in broad daylight I open my eyes, it is not in my power to choose whether I shall see or no, or to determine what particular objects shall present themselves to my view; and so likewise as to the hearing and other senses, the ideas imprinted on them are not creatures of my will. There is therefore some *other* Will or Spirit that produces them.

30. The ideas of Sense are more strong, lively, and distinct than those of the Imagination; they have likewise a steadiness, order, and coherence, and are not excited at random, as those which are the effects of human wills often

are, but in a regular train or series—the admirable connexion whereof sufficiently testifies the wisdom and benevolence of its Author. Now the set rules or established methods wherein the Mind we depend on excites in us the ideas of sense, are called the *laws of nature*; and these we learn by experience, which teaches us that such and such ideas are attended with such and such other ideas, in the ordinary course of things.

31. This gives us a sort of foresight which enables us to regulate our actions for the benefit of life. And without this we should be eternally at a loss; we could not know how to act anything that might procure us the least pleasure, or remove the least pain of sense. That food nourishes, sleep refreshes, and fire warms us; that to sow in the seedtime is the way to reap in the harvest; and in general that to obtain such or such ends, such or such means are conducive—all this we know, not by discovering any *necessary connexion* between our ideas, but only by the *observation* of the settled laws of nature, without which we should be all in uncertainty and confusion, and a grown man no more know how to manage himself in the affairs of life than an infant just born.

32. And yet this consistent uniform working, which so evidently displays the goodness and wisdom of that Governing Spirit whose Will constitutes the laws of nature, is so far from leading our thoughts to Him, that it rather sends them wandering after second causes. For, when we perceive certain ideas of Sense constantly followed by other ideas, and we know this is not of our own doing, we forthwith attribute power and agency to the ideas themselves, and make one the cause of another, than which nothing can be more absurd and unintelligible. Thus, for example, having observed that when we perceive by sight a certain round luminous figure we at the same time perceive by touch the idea or sensation called heat, we do from thence conclude the sun to be the *cause* of heat. And in like

manner perceiving the motion and collision of bodies to be attended with sound, we are inclined to think the latter the *effect* of the former.

33. The ideas imprinted on the Senses by the Author of nature are called *real things* : and those excited in the Imagination being less regular, vivid, and constant, are more properly termed *ideas,* or *images of things,* which they copy and represent. But then our sensations, be they never so vivid and distinct, are nevertheless ideas, that is, they exist in the mind, or are perceived by it, as truly as the ideas of its own framing. The ideas of Sense are allowed to have more reality in them, that is, to be more strong, orderly, and coherent than the creatures of the mind; but this is no argument that they exist without the mind. They are also less dependent on the spirit, or thinking substance which perceives them, in that they are excited by the will of another and more powerful Spirit; yet still they are *ideas,* and certainly no idea, whether faint or strong, can exist otherwise than in a mind perceiving it.

34. Before we proceed any farther it is necessary we spend some time in answering Objections which may probably be made against the principles we have hitherto laid down. In doing of which, if I seem too prolix to those of quick apprehensions, I desire I may be excused, since all men do not equally apprehend things of this nature, and I am willing to be understood by every one.

First, then, it will be objected that by the foregoing principles all that is real and substantial in nature is banished out of the world, and instead thereof a chimerical scheme of *ideas* takes place. All things that exist exist only in the mind, that is, they are purely notional. What therefore becomes of the sun, moon, and stars? What must we think of houses, rivers, mountains, trees, stones; nay, even of our own bodies? Are all these but so many chimeras and illusions on the fancy?—To all which, and whatever else of the same sort may be objected, I answer, that by the principles premised we are not deprived of any one thing in nature. Whatever we see, feel, hear, or any wise conceive or understand, remains as secure as ever, and is as real as ever. There is a *rerum natura,* and the distinction between realities and chimeras retains its full force. This is evident from sect. 29, 30, and 33, where we have shewn what is meant by *real things,* in opposition to *chimeras* or ideas of our own framing; but then they both equally exist in the mind, and in that sense are alike *ideas.*

35. I do not argue against the existence of any one thing that we can apprehend either by sense or reflection. That the things I see with my eyes and touch with my hands do exist, really exist, I make not the least question. The only thing whose existence we deny is that which *Philosophers* call Matter or corporeal substance. And in doing of this there is no damage done to the rest of mankind, who, I dare say, will never miss it. The Atheist indeed will want the colour of an empty name to support his impiety; and the Philosophers may possibly find they have lost a great handle for trifling and disputation.

36. If any man thinks this detracts from the existence or reality of things, he is very far from understanding what hath been premised in the plainest terms I could think of. Take here an abstract of what has been said :—There are spiritual substances, minds, or human souls, which will or excite ideas in themselves at pleasure; but these are faint, weak, and unsteady in respect of others they perceive by Sense—which, being impressed upon them according to certain Rules or Laws of Nature, speak themselves the effects of a Mind more powerful and wise than human spirits. These latter are said to have *more reality* in them than the former;—by which is meant that they are more affecting, orderly, and distinct, and that they are not fictions of the mind perceiving them. And in this sense the sun that I see by day is the real sun, and that which I imagine by night is the idea of the former. In the sense here given of *reality,* it is evident that every vegetable, star, mineral, and in general each part of the mundane

system, is as much a *real being* by our principles as by any other. Whether others mean anything by the term *reality* different from what I do, I entreat them to look into their own thoughts and see.

37. It will be urged that thus much at least is true, to wit, that we take away all corporeal substances. To this my answer is, that if the word *substance* be taken in the vulgar sense—for a *combination* of sensible qualities, such as extension, solidity, weight, and the like—this we cannot be accused of taking away; but if it be taken in a philosophic sense—for the support of accidents or qualities without the mind—then indeed I acknowledge that we take it away, if one may be said to take away that which never had any existence, not even in the imagination.

38. But after all, say you, it sounds very harsh to say we eat and drink ideas, and are clothed with ideas. I acknowledge it does so—the word *idea* not being used in common discourse to signify the several combinations of sensible qualities which are called *things*; and it is certain that any expression which varies from the familiar use of language will seem harsh and ridiculous. But this doth not concern the truth of the proposition, which in other words is no more than to say, we are fed and clothed with those things which we perceive immediately by our senses. The hardness or softness, the colour, taste, warmth, figure, or such-like qualities, which, combined together, constitute the several sorts of victuals and apparel, have been shewn to exist only in the mind that perceives them; and this is all that is meant by calling them *ideas*; which word, if it was as ordinarily used as *thing*, would sound no harsher nor more ridiculous than it. I am not for disputing about the propriety, but the truth of the expression. If therefore you agree with me that we eat and drink and are clad with the immediate objects of sense, which cannot exist unperceived or without the mind, I shall readily grant it is more proper or conformable to custom that they should be called *things* rather than *ideas*.

39. If it be demanded why I make use of the word *idea,* and do not rather in compliance with custom call them *things*; I answer, I do it for two reasons :—first, because the term *thing,* in contradistinction to *idea,* is generally supposed to denote somewhat existing without the mind; secondly, because *thing* hath a more comprehensive signification than *idea,* including spirit or thinking things as well as ideas. Since therefore the objects of sense exist only in the mind, and are withal thoughtless and inactive, I choose to mark them by the word *idea,* which implies those properties.

40. But, say what we can, some one perhaps may be apt to reply, he will still believe his senses, and never suffer any arguments, how plausible soever, to prevail over the certainty of them. Be it so; assert the evidence of sense as high as you please, we are willing to do the same. That what I see, hear, and feel doth exist, that is to say, is perceived by me, I no more doubt than I do of my own being. But I do not see how the testimony of *sense* can be alleged as a proof for the existence of anything which is *not* perceived by sense. We are not for having any man turn sceptic and disbelieve his senses; on the contrary, we give them all the stress and assurance imaginable; nor are there any principles more opposite to Scepticism than those we have laid down, as shall be hereafter clearly shewn.

41. *Secondly,* it will be objected that there is a great difference betwixt real fire for instance, and the idea of fire, betwixt dreaming or imagining oneself burnt, and actually being so : if you suspect it to be only the idea of fire which you see, do but put your hand into it and you will be convinced with a witness. This and the like may be urged in opposition to our tenets. To all which the answer is evident from what hath been already said, and I shall only add in this place, that if real fire be very different from the idea of fire, so also is the real pain that it occasions very different from the idea of the same pain; and yet

nobody will pretend that real pain either is, or can possibly be, in an unperceiving thing, or without the mind, any more than its idea.

42. *Thirdly,* it will be objected that we *see* things actually without or at a distance from us, and which consequently do not exist in the mind; it being absurd that those things which are seen at the distance of several miles should be as near to us as our own thoughts. In answer to this, I desire it may be considered that in a dream we do oft perceive things as existing at a great distance off, and yet for all that, those things are acknowledged to have their existence only in the mind.

43. But, for the fuller clearing of this point, it may be worth while to consider *how* it is that we perceive distance and things placed at a distance by sight. For, that we should in truth see external space, and bodies actually existing in it—some nearer, and others farther off—seems to carry with it some opposition to what hath been said of their existing nowhere without the mind. The consideration of this difficulty it was that gave birth to my *Essay towards a New Theory of Vision,* which was published not long since—wherein it is shewn that *distance* or *outness* is neither immediately of itself perceived by sight, nor yet apprehended or judged of by lines and angles, or anything that hath a necessary connexion with it; but that it is only suggested to our thoughts by certain visible ideas and sensations attending vision, which in their own nature have no manner of similitude or relation either with distance or things placed at a distance; but, by a connexion taught us by experience, they come to signify and suggest them to us, after the same manner that words of any language suggest the ideas they are made to stand for; insomuch that a man born blind and afterwards made to see, would not, at first sight, think the things he saw to be without his mind, or at any distance from him. See sect. 41 of the forementioned treatise.

44. The ideas of sight and touch make two species

entirely distinct and heterogeneous. The former are marks and prognostics of the latter. That the proper objects of sight neither exist without the mind, nor are the images of external things, was shewn even in that treatise. Though throughout the same the contrary be supposed true of tangible objects—not that to suppose that vulgar error was necessary for establishing the notion therein laid down, but because it was beside my purpose to examine and refute it in a discourse concerning *Vision*. So that in strict truth the ideas of sight, when we apprehend by them distance and things placed at a distance, do not suggest or mark out to us things actually existing at a distance, but only admonish us what ideas of touch will be imprinted in our minds at such and such distances of time, and in consequence of such and such actions. It is, I say, evident from what has been said in the foregoing parts of this *Treatise,* and in sect. 147 and elsewhere of the *Essay* concerning Vision, that visible ideas are the Language whereby the Governing Spirit on whom we depend informs us what tangible ideas he is about to imprint upon us, in case we excite this or that motion in our own bodies. But for a fuller information on this point I refer to the *Essay* itself.

45. *Fourthly,* it will be objected that from the foregoing principles it follows things are every moment annihilated and created anew. The objects of sense exist only when they are perceived; the trees therefore are in the garden, or the chairs in the parlour, no longer than while there is somebody by to perceive them. Upon shutting my eyes all the furniture in the room is reduced to nothing, and barely upon opening them it is again created.—In answer to all which, I refer the reader to what has been said in sect. 3, 4, &c., and desire he will consider whether he *means* anything by the actual existence of an idea distinct from its being perceived. For my part, after the nicest inquiry I could make, I am not able to discover that anything else is meant by those words; and I once more

entreat the reader to sound his own thoughts, and not suffer himself to be imposed on by words. If he can conceive it possible either for his ideas or their archetypes to exist without being perceived, then I give up the cause; but if he cannot, he will acknowledge it is unreasonable for him to stand up in defence of he knows not what, and pretend to charge on me as an absurdity the not assenting to those propositions which at bottom have no meaning in them.

46. It will not be amiss to observe how far the received principles of philosophy are themselves chargeable with those pretended absurdities. It is thought strangely absurd that upon closing my eyelids all the visible objects around me should be reduced to nothing; and yet is not this what philosophers commonly acknowledge, when they agree on all hands that light and colours, which alone are the proper and immediate objects of sight, are mere sensations that exist no longer than they are perceived? Again, it may to some perhaps seem very incredible that things should be every moment creating, yet this very notion is commonly taught in the schools. For the Schoolmen, though they acknowledge the existence of matter, and that the whole mundane fabric is framed out of it, are nevertheless of opinion that it cannot subsist without the divine conservation, which by them is expounded to be a continual creation.

47. Farther, a little thought will discover to us that though we allow the existence of Matter or corporeal substance, yet it will unavoidably follow, from the principles which are now generally admitted, that the particular bodies, of what kind soever, do none of them exist whilst they are not perceived. For, it is evident, from sect. 11 and the following sections, that the Matter philosophers contend for is an incomprehensible somewhat, which hath none of those particular qualities whereby the bodies falling under our senses are distinguished one from another. But, to make this more plain, it must be remarked that the

infinite divisibility of Matter is now universally allowed, at least by the most approved and considerable philosophers, who, on the received principles, demonstrate it beyond all exception. Hence, it follows there is an infinite number of parts in each particle of Matter which are not perceived by sense. The reason therefore that any particular body seems to be of a finite magnitude, or exhibits only a finite number of parts to sense, is, not because it contains no more, since in itself it contains an infinite number of parts, but because the sense is not acute enough to discern them. In proportion therefore as the sense is rendered more acute, it perceives a greater number of parts in the object, that is, the object appears greater, and its figure varies, those parts in its extremities which were before unperceivable appearing now to bound it in very different lines and angles from those perceived by an obtuser sense. And at length, after various changes of size and shape, when the sense becomes infinitely acute the body shall seem infinite. During all which there is no alteration in the body, but only in the sense. Each body therefore, considered in itself, is infinitely extended, and consequently void of all shape and figure.— From which it follows that, though we should grant the existence of Matter to be never so certain, yet it is withal as certain, the Materialists themselves are by their own principles forced to acknowledge, that neither the particular bodies perceived by sense, nor anything like them, exists without the mind. Matter, I say, and each particle thereof, is according to them infinite and shapeless, and it is the mind that frames all that variety of bodies which compose the visible world, any one whereof does not exist longer than it is perceived.

48. But, after all, if we consider it, the objection proposed in sect. 45 will not be found reasonably charged on the principles we have premised, so as in truth to make any objection at all against our notions. For, though we hold indeed the objects of sense to be nothing else but ideas which cannot exist unperceived, yet we may not hence con-

clude they have no existence except only while they are perceived by us; since there may be some other spirit that perceives them though we do not. Wherever bodies are said to have no existence without the mind, I would not be understood to mean this or that particular mind, but *all minds whatsoever.* It does not therefore follow from the foregoing principles that bodies are annihilated and created every moment, or exist not at all during the intervals between *our* perception of them.

49. *Fifthly,* it may perhaps be objected that if extension and figure exist only in the mind, it follows that the mind is extended and figured; since extension is a mode or attribute which (to speak with the schools) is predicated of the *subject* in which it exists.—I answer, those qualities are in the mind only as they are perceived by it—that is, not by way of *mode* or *attribute,* but only by way of *idea*; and it no more follows the soul or mind is extended, because extension exists in it alone, than it does that it is red or blue, because those colours are on all hands acknowledged to exist in it, and nowhere else. As to what philosophers say of " subject " and " mode," that seems very groundless and unintelligible. For instance, in this proposition—" a die is hard, extended, and square," they will have it that the word *die* denotes a subject or substance, distinct from the hardness, extension, and figure which are predicated of it, and in which they exist. This I cannot comprehend : to me a die seems to be nothing distinct from those things which are termed its modes or accident. And, to say " a die is hard, extended, and square " is not to attribute those qualities to a subject distinct from and supporting them, but only an explication of the meaning of the word *die.*

50. *Sixthly,* you will say there have been a great many things explained by matter and motion; take away these and you destroy the whole corpuscular philosophy, and undermine those mechanical principles which have been

applied with so much success to account for the phenomena. In short, whatever advances have been made, either by ancient or modern philosophers, in the study of Nature do all proceed on the supposition that corporeal substance or Matter doth really exist.—To this I answer that there is not any one phenomenon explained on that supposition which may not as well be explained without it, as might easily be made appear by an induction of particulars. To explain the phenomena, is all one as to shew why, upon such and such occasions, we are affected with such and such ideas. But how Matter should operate on a Spirit, or produce any idea in it, is what no philosopher will pretend to explain; it is therefore evident there can be no use of Matter in Natural Philosophy. Besides, they who attempt to account for things do it not by corporeal substance, but by figure, motion, and other qualities, which are in truth no more than mere ideas, and therefore cannot be the *cause* of anything, as hath been already shewn. See sect. 25.

51. *Seventhly*, it will upon this be demanded whether it does not seem absurd to take away Natural Causes, and ascribe everything to the immediate operation of Spirits? We must no longer say upon these principles that fire heats, or water cools, but that a Spirit heats, and so forth. Would not a man be deservedly laughed at, who should talk after this manner?—I answer, he would so; in such things we ought to "think with the learned, and speak with the vulgar."[8] They who to demonstration are convinced of the truth of the Copernican system do nevertheless say "the sun rises," "the sun sets," or "comes to the meridian"; and if they affected a contrary style in common talk it would without doubt appear very ridiculous. A little reflection on what is here said will make it manifest that the common use of language would receive no manner

[8] Berkeley perhaps quotes this phrase from Bacon's *De Augmentis Scientiarum*.

of alteration or disturbance from the admission of our tenets.

52. In the ordinary affairs of life, any phrases may be retained, so long as they excite in us proper sentiments, or dispositions to act in such a manner as is necessary for our well-being, how false soever they may be if taken in a strict and speculative sense. Nay, this is unavoidable, since, propriety being regulated by custom, language is suited to the received opinions, which are not always the truest. Hence it is impossible—even in the most rigid, philosophic reasonings—so far to alter the bent and genius of the tongue we speak as never to give a handle for cavillers to pretend difficulties and inconsistencies. But a fair and ingenuous reader will collect the sense from the scope and tenor and connexion of a discourse, making allowances for those inaccurate modes of speech which use has made inevitable.

53. As to the opinion that there are no Corporeal Causes, this has been heretofore maintained by some of the Schoolmen, as it is of late by others among the modern philosophers,[4] who, though they allow Matter to exist, yet will have God *alone* to be the immediate efficient cause of all things. These men saw that amongst all the objects of sense there was none which had any power or activity included in it; and that by consequence this was likewise true of whatever bodies *they* supposed to exist without the mind, like unto the immediate objects of sense. But then, that they should suppose an innumerable multitude of created beings, which they acknowledge are not capable of producing any one effect in nature, and which therefore are made to no manner of purpose, since God might have done everything as well without them—this I say, though we should allow it possible, must yet be a very unaccountable and extravagant supposition.

54. In the *eighth* place, the universal concurrent Assent

[4] Malebranche, Geulinx, and other so-called Occasionalists.

of Mankind may be thought by some an invincible argument in behalf of Matter, or the existence of external things. Must we suppose the whole world to be mistaken? And if so, what cause can be assigned of so widespread and predominant an error?—I answer, first, that, upon a narrow inquiry, it will not perhaps be found so many as is imagined do really believe the existence of Matter or things without the mind. Strictly speaking, to believe that which involves a contradiction, or has no meaning in it, is impossible; and whether the foregoing expressions are not of that sort, I refer it to the impartial examination of the reader. In one sense, indeed, men may be said to believe that Matter exists; that is, they act as if the immediate cause of their sensations, which affects them every moment, and is so nearly present to them, were some senseless unthinking being. But, that they should clearly apprehend any *meaning* marked by those words, and form thereof a settled speculative opinion, is what I am not able to conceive. This is not the only instance wherein men impose upon themselves, by imagining they believe those propositions which they have often heard, though at bottom they have no meaning in them.

55. But secondly, though we should grant a notion to be never so universally and stedfastly adhered to, yet this is but a weak argument of its truth to whoever considers what a vast number of prejudices and false opinions are everywhere embraced with the utmost tenaciousness, by the unreflecting (which are the far greater) part of mankind. There was a time when the antipodes and motion of the earth were looked upon as monstrous absurdities even by men of learning : and if it be considered what a small proportion they bear to the rest of mankind, we shall find that at this day those notions have gained but a very inconsiderable footing in the world.

56. But it is demanded that we assign a Cause of this Prejudice, and account for its obtaining in the world.—To

this I answer, that men knowing they perceived several ideas, whereof *they themselves* were not the authors—as not being excited from within nor depending on the operation of *their* wills—*this* made them maintain those ideas or objects of perception had an existence independent of and without the mind, without ever dreaming that a contradiction was involved in those words. But, philosophers having plainly seen that the *immediate objects* of perception do not exist without the mind, they in some degree corrected the mistake of the vulgar, but at the same time run into another which seems no less absurd, to wit, that there are certain objects really existing without the mind, or having a subsistence distinct from being perceived, of which our ideas are only images or resemblances, imprinted by those objects on the mind. And this notion of the philosophers owes its origin to the same cause with the former, namely, their being conscious that *they* were not the authors of their own sensations, which they evidently knew were imprinted from without, and which therefore must have some cause distinct from the minds on which they are imprinted.

57. But why they should suppose the ideas of sense to be excited in us by *things in their likeness,* and not rather have recourse to *Spirit* which alone can act, may be accounted for, first, because they were not aware of the repugnancy there is, as well in supposing things like unto our ideas existing without, as in attributing to them power or activity. Secondly, because the Supreme Spirit which excites those ideas in our minds, is not marked out and limited to our view by any particular finite collection of sensible ideas, as human agents are by their size, complexion, limbs, and motions. And thirdly, because His operations are regular and uniform. Whenever the course of nature is interrupted by a miracle, men are ready to own the presence of a superior agent. But, when we see things go on in the ordinary course they do not excite in us any reflection; their order and concatenation, though it be an

argument of the greatest wisdom, power, and goodness in their Creator, is yet so constant and familiar to us that we do not think them the immediate effects of a FREE SPIRIT; especially since inconsistency and mutability in acting, though it be an imperfection, is looked on as a mark of freedom.

58. *Tenthly*, it will be objected that the notions we advance are inconsistent with several sound truths in Philosophy and Mathematics. For example, the motion of the earth is now universally admitted by astronomers as a truth grounded on the clearest and most convincing reasons. But, on the foregoing principles, there can be no such thing. For, motion being only an idea, it follows that if it be not perceived it *exists* not : but the motion of the earth is not perceived by sense.—I answer, that tenet, if rightly understood, will be found to agree with the principles we have premised; for, the question whether the earth moves or no amounts in reality to no more than this, to wit, whether we have reason to conclude, from what has been observed by astronomers, that if we were placed in such and such circumstances, and such or such a position and distance both from the earth and sun, we should perceive the former to move among the choir of the planets, and appearing in all respects like one of them; and this, by the established rules of nature which we have no reason to mistrust, is reasonably collected from the phenomena.

59. We may, from the experience we have had of the train and succession of ideas in our minds, often make, I will not say uncertain conjectures, but sure and well-grounded predictions concerning the ideas we shall be affected with pursuant to a great train of actions, and be enabled to pass a right judgment of what would have appeared to us, in case we were placed in circumstances very different from those we are in at present. Herein consists the knowledge of nature, which may preserve its use and certainty very consistently with what hath been

said. It will be easy to apply this to whatever objections of the like sort may be drawn from the magnitude of the stars, or any other discoveries in astronomy or nature.

60. In the *eleventh* place, it will be demanded to what purpose serves that curious organization of plants, and the animal mechanism in the parts of animals; might not vegetables grow, and shoot forth leaves and blossoms, and animals perform all their motions as well without as with all that variety of internal parts so elegantly contrived and put together; which, being ideas, have nothing powerful or operative in them, nor have any *necessary* connexion with the effects ascribed to them? If it be a Spirit that immediately produces every effect by a *fiat* or act of his will, we must think all that is fine and artificial in the works, whether of man or nature, to be made in vain. By this doctrine, though an artist has made the spring and wheels, and every movement of a watch, and adjusted them in such a manner as he knew would produce the motions he designed, yet he must think all this is done to no purpose, and that it is an Intelligence which directs the index, and points to the hour of the day. If so, why may not the Intelligence do it without his being at the pains of making the movements and putting them together? Why does not an empty case serve as well as another? And how comes it to pass that whenever there is any fault in the going of a watch, there is some corresponding disorder to be found in the movements, which being mended by a skilful hand all is right again? The like may be said of all the Clockwork of Nature, great part whereof is so wonderfully fine and subtle as scarce to be discerned by the best microscope. In short, it will be asked, how, upon our principles, any tolerable account can be given, or any final cause assigned, of an innumerable multitude of bodies and machines, framed with the most exquisite art, which in the common philosophy have very apposite uses assigned them, and serve to explain abundance of phenomena?

61. To all which I answer, first, that though there were ome difficulties relating to the administration of Pro-idence, and the uses by it assigned to the several parts of ature, which I could not solve by the foregoing prin-iples, yet this objection could be of small weight against he truth and certainty of those things which may be roved *a priori*, with the utmost evidence and rigour of lemonstration. Secondly, but neither are the received rinciples free from the like difficulties; for, it may still be lemanded to what end God should take those roundabout nethods of effecting things by instruments and machines, which no one can deny might have been effected by the nere command of His will without all that apparatus : nay, f we narrowly consider it, we shall find the objection may oe retorted with greater force on those who hold the exist-:nce of those machines without the mind; for it has been nade evident that solidity, bulk, figure, motion, and the ike have no *activity* or *efficacy* in them, so as to be cap-ıble of producing any one effect in nature. See sect. 25. Vhoever therefore supposes *them* to exist (allowing the upposition possible) when they are not perceived does it nanifestly to no purpose; since the only use that is as-igned to them, as they exist unperceived, is that they pro-luce those perceivable effects which in truth cannot be ıscribed to anything but Spirit.

62. But, to come nigher the difficulty, it must be ob-erved that though the fabrication of all those parts and rgans be not absolutely necessary to the producing *any* effect, yet it is necessary to the producing of things *in a onstant regular way according to the laws of nature.* There are certain general laws that run through the whole :hain of natural effects : these are learned by the observa-ion and study of nature, and are by men applied as well o the framing artificial things for the use and ornament of ife as to the explaining the various phenomena—which xplanation consists only in shewing the conformity any ıarticular phenomenon hath to the general laws of nature,

or, which is the same thing, in discovering the *uniformity*
there is in the production of natural effects; as will be
evident to whoever shall attend to the several instances
wherein philosophers pretend to account for appearances.
That there is a great and conspicuous *use* in these regular
constant methods of working observed by the Supreme
Agent hath been shewn in sect. 31. And it is no less visible
that a particular size, figure, motion, and disposition of
parts are necessary, though not absolutely to the producing
any effect, yet to the producing it according to the standing mechanical laws of nature. Thus, for instance, it cannot be denied that God, or the Intelligence that sustains
and rules the ordinary course of things, might, if He were
minded to produce a miracle, cause all the motions on the
dial-plate of a watch, though nobody had ever made the
movements and put them in it : but yet, if He will act
agreeably to the rules of mechanism—by Him for wise
ends established and maintained in the creation—it is necessary that those actions of the watchmaker, whereby he
makes the movements and rightly adjusts them, precede
the production of the aforesaid motions; as also that any
disorder in them be attended with the perception of some
corresponding disorder in the movements, which being
once corrected all is right again.

63. It may indeed on some occasions be necessary that
the Author of nature display His overruling power in producing appearances out of the ordinary series of things.
Such exceptions from the general rules of nature are proper
to surprise and awe men into an acknowledgment of the
Divine Being; but then they are to be used but seldom,
otherwise there is a plain reason why they fail of that
effect. Besides, God seems to choose the convincing our
reason of His attributes by the works of nature, which discover so much harmony and contrivance in their make,
and are such plain indications of wisdom and beneficence
in their Author, rather than to astonish us into a belief of
His Being by anomalous and surprising events.

64. To set this matter in a yet clearer light, I shall observe that what has been objected in sect. 60 amounts in reality to no more than this :—ideas are not anyhow and at random produced, there being a certain order and connexion between them, like to that of cause and effect : there are also several combinations of them made in a very regular and artificial manner, which seem like so many *instruments* in the hand of nature that, being hid as it were behind the scenes, have a secret operation in producing those appearances which are seen on the theatre of the world, being themselves discernible only to the curious eye of the philosopher. But, since one idea cannot be the *cause* of another, to what purpose is that connexion? And, since those instruments—being barely *inefficacious perceptions* in the mind—are not subservient to the production of natural effects, it is demanded why they are made; or, in other words, what reason can be assigned why God should make us, upon a close inspection into His works, behold so great variety of ideas so artfully laid together, and so much according to rule; it not being credible that He would be at any expense (if one may so speak) of all that art and regularity to no purpose?

65. To all which my answer is, first, that the connexion of ideas does not imply the relation of *cause* and *effect,* but only of a *mark* or *sign* with the *thing signified.* The fire which I see is not the cause of the pain I suffer upon my approaching it, but the mark that forewarns me of it. In like manner the noise that I hear is not the effect of this or that motion or collision of the ambient bodies, but the sign thereof. Secondly, the reason why ideas are formed into machines, that is, artificial and regular combinations, is the same with that for combining letters into words. That a few original ideas may be made to signify a great number of effects and actions, it is necessary they be variously combined together. And, to the end their use be permanent and universal, these combinations must be made by *rule,* and with *wise contrivance.* By this means abund-

ance of information is conveyed unto us, concerning what we are to expect from such and such actions, and what methods are proper to be taken for the exciting such and such ideas—which in effect is all that I conceive to be distinctly meant when it is said that, by discerning the figure, texture, and mechanism of the inward parts of bodies, whether natural or artificial, we may attain to know the several uses and properties depending thereon, or the nature of the thing.

66. Hence, it is evident that those things which, under the notion of a cause co-operating or concurring to the production of effects, are altogether inexplicable, and run us into great absurdities, may be very naturally explained, and have a proper and obvious use assigned to them, when they are considered only as marks or signs for our information. And it is the searching after and endeavouring to understand this Language (if I may so call it) of the Author of Nature, that ought to be the employment of the natural philosopher; and not the pretending to explain things by corporeal causes, which doctrine seems to have too much estranged the minds of men from that Active Principle, that supreme and wise Spirit " in whom we live, move, and have our being."

67. In the *twelfth* place, it may perhaps be objected that —though it be clear from what has been said that there can be no such thing as an inert, senseless, extended, solid, figured, moveable substance existing without the mind, such as philosophers describe Matter,—yet, if any man shall leave out of his idea of matter the positive ideas of extension, figure, solidity and motion, and say that he means only by that word an inert, senseless substance, that exists without the mind or unperceived, which is the *occasion* of our ideas, or at the presence whereof God is pleased to excite ideas in us—it doth not appear but that Matter taken in this sense may possibly exist.—In answer to which I say, first, that it seems no less absurd to suppose a sub-

stance without accidents, than it is to suppose accidents without a substance. But secondly, though we should grant this unknown substance may possibly exist, yet *where* can it be supposed to be? That it exists not in the *mind* is agreed; and that it exists not in *place* is no less certain—since all place or extension exists only in the mind, as hath been already proved. It remains therefore that it exists nowhere at all.

68. Let us examine a little the description that is here given us of *Matter*. It neither acts, nor perceives, nor is perceived; for this is all that is meant by saying it is an inert, senseless, unknown substance; which is a definition entirely made up of negatives, excepting only the relative notion of its standing under or supporting. But then it must be observed that it supports nothing at all, and how nearly this comes to the description of a *nonentity* I desire may be considered. But, say you, it is the *unknown occasion,* at the presence of which ideas are excited in us by the will of God. Now, I would fain know how anything can be present to us, which is neither perceivable by sense nor reflection, nor capable of producing any idea in our minds, nor is at all extended, nor hath any form, nor exists in any place. The words "to be present," when thus applied, must needs be taken in some abstract and strange meaning, and which I am not able to comprehend.

69. Again, let us examine what is meant by *occasion*. So far as I can gather from the common use of language, that word signifies either the agent which produces any effect, or else something that is observed to accompany or go before it in the ordinary course of things. But when it is applied to Matter as above described, it can be taken in neither of those senses; for Matter is said to be passive and inert, and so cannot be an agent or efficient cause. It is also unperceivable, as being devoid of all sensible qualities, and so cannot be the occasion of our perceptions in the latter sense—as when the burning my finger is said to be the occasion of the pain that attends it. What therefore

can be meant by calling Matter an *occasion*? This term is either used in no sense at all, or else in some very distant from its received signification.

70. You will perhaps say that Matter, though it be not perceived by us, is nevertheless perceived by God, to whom it is the *occasion* of exciting ideas in our minds. For, say you, since we observe our sensations to be imprinted in an orderly and constant manner, it is but reasonable to suppose that there are certain constant and regular occasions of their being produced. That is to say, that there are certain permanent and distinct parcels of Matter, corresponding to our ideas, which, though they do not excite them in our minds, or anywise immediately affect us, as being altogether passive and unperceivable to *us,* they are nevertheless to God, *by whom they are perceived,* as it were, so many occasions to remind Him when and what ideas to imprint on our minds—that so things may go on in a constant uniform manner.

71. In answer to this, I observe that, as the notion of Matter is here stated, the question is no longer concerning the existence of a thing distinct from *Spirit* and *idea,* from perceiving and being perceived; but whether there are not certain Ideas, of I know not what sort, in the mind of God, which are so many marks or notes that direct Him how to produce sensations in our minds in a constant and regular method—much after the same manner as a musician is directed by the notes of music to produce that harmonious strain and composition of sound which is called a tune, though they who hear the music do not perceive the notes, and may be entirely ignorant of them. But, this notion of Matter (which after all is the only intelligible one that I can pick from what is said of unknown occasions) seems too extravagant to deserve a confutation. Besides, it is in effect no objection against what we have advanced, viz. that there is no *senseless unperceived* substance.

72. If we follow the light of reason, we shall, from the

constant uniform method of our sensations, collect the goodness and wisdom of the Spirit who excites them in our minds; but this is all that I can see reasonably concluded from thence. To me, I say, it is evident that the being of a Spirit infinitely wise, good, and powerful is abundantly sufficient to explain all the appearances of nature. But, as for *inert, senseless Matter,* nothing that I perceive has any the least connexion with it, or leads to the thoughts of it. And I would fain see any one explain any the meanest phenomenon in nature by *it,* or shew any manner of reason, though in the lowest rank of probability, that he can have for its existence, or even make any tolerable sense or meaning of that supposition. For, as to its being an occasion, we have, I think, evidently shewn that with regard to us it is no occasion. It remains therefore that it must be, if at all, the occasion to God of exciting ideas in us; and what this amounts to we have just now seen.

73. It is worth while to reflect a little on the motives which induced men to suppose the existence of *material substance*; that so having observed the gradual ceasing and expiration of those motives or reasons, we may proportionably withdraw the assent that was grounded on them. First, therefore, it was thought that colour, figure, motion, and the rest of the sensible qualities or accidents, did really exist without the mind; and for this reason it seemed needful to suppose some unthinking *substratum* or substance wherein they did exist—since they could not be conceived to exist by themselves. Afterwards, in process of time, men being convinced that colours, sounds, and the rest of the sensible, *secondary* qualities had no existence without the mind, they stripped this *substratum* or material substance of those qualities—leaving only the *primary* ones, figure, motion, and suchlike, which they still conceived to exist without the mind, and consequently to stand in need of a material support. But, it having been shewn that none even of these can possibly exist otherwise than in a Spirit

or Mind which perceives them, it follows that we have no longer any reason to suppose the being of Matter, nay, that it is utterly impossible that there should be any such thing—so long as that word is taken to denote an *unthinking substratum* of qualities or accidents wherein they exist without the mind.

74. But—though it be allowed by the Materialists themselves that Matter was thought of only for the sake of supporting accidents, and, the reason entirely ceasing, one might expect the mind should naturally, and without any reluctance at all, quit the belief of what was solely grounded thereon—yet the prejudice is riveted so deeply in our thoughts, that we can scarce tell how to part with it, and are therefore inclined, since the *thing* itself is indefensible, at least to retain the *name*, which we apply to I know not what abstracted and indefinite notions of Being, or Occasion, though without any show of reason, at least so far as I can see. For, what is there on our part, or what do we perceive, amongst all the ideas, sensations, notions which are imprinted on our minds, either by sense or reflection, from whence may be inferred the existence of an inert, thoughtless, unperceived occasion? and, on the other hand, on the part of an All-sufficient Spirit, what can there be that should make us believe or even suspect He is directed by an inert occasion to excite ideas in our minds?

75. It is a very extraordinary instance of the force of prejudice, and much to be lamented, that the mind of man retains so great a fondness, against all the evidence of reason, for a *stupid thoughtless Somewhat*, by the interposition whereof it would as it were screen itself from the Providence of God, and remove Him farther off from the affairs of the world. But, though we do the utmost we can to secure the belief of Matter; though, when reason forsakes us, we endeavour to support our opinion on the bare possibility of the thing, and though we indulge ourselves in the full scope of an imagination not regulated by reason to make out that poor possibility, yet the upshot of

all is—that there are certain *unknown Ideas in the mind of God*; for this, if anything, is all that I conceive to be meant by *occasion* with regard to God. And this at the bottom is no longer contending for the thing, but for the name.

76. Whether therefore there are such Ideas in the mind of God, and whether *they* may be called by the name *Matter,* I shall not dispute. But, if you stick to the notion of an unthinking substance or support of extension, motion, and other sensible qualities, then to me it is most evidently impossible there should be any such thing; since it is a plain repugnancy that those qualities should exist in or be supported by an unperceiving substance.

77. But, say you, though it be granted that there is no thoughtless support of extension and the other qualities or accidents which we perceive, yet there may perhaps be some inert, unperceiving substance or *substratum* of some other qualities, as incomprehensible to us as colours are to a man born blind, because we have not a sense adapted to them. But, if we had a new sense, we should possibly no more doubt of their existence than a blind man made to see does of the existence of light and colours.—I answer, first, if what you mean by the word *Matter* be only the *unknown* support of *unknown* qualities, it is no matter whether there is such a thing or no, since it no way concerns us; and I do not see the advantage there is in disputing about what we know not *what,* and we know not *why.*

78. But, secondly, if we had a new sense it could only furnish us with new ideas or sensations; and then we should have the same reason against *their* existing in an unperceiving substance that has been already offered with relation to figure, motion, colour, and the like. " Qualities," as hath been shewn, are nothing else but *sensations* or *ideas,* which exist only in a *mind* perceiving them; and this is true not only of the ideas we are acquainted with at present, but likewise of all possible ideas whatsoever.

79. But, you will insist, what if I have no reason to believe the existence of Matter? what if I cannot assign any use to it or explain anything by it, or even conceive what is meant by that word? yet still it is no contradiction to say that Matter exists, and that this Matter is in general a *substance,* or *occasion* of ideas; though indeed to go about to unfold the meaning or adhere to any particular explication of those words may be attended with great difficulties. I answer, when words are used without a meaning, you may put them together as you please without danger of running into a contradiction. You may say, for example, that twice two is equal to seven, so long as you declare you do not take the words of that proposition in their usual acceptation but for marks of you know not what. And, by the same reason, you may say there is *an inert thoughtless substance without accidents* which is the occasion of our ideas. And we shall understand just as much by one proposition as the other.

80. In the *last* place, you will say, what if we give up the cause of material *Substance,* and stand to it that Matter is an unknown *Somewhat*—neither substance nor accident, spirit nor idea, inert, thoughtless, indivisible, immoveable, unextended, existing in no place? For, say you, whatever may be urged against *substance* or *occasion,* or any other positive or relative notion of Matter, hath no place at all, so long as this *negative* definition of Matter is adhered to. —I answer, you may, if so it shall seem good, use the word " Matter " in the same sense as other men use "nothing," and so make those terms convertible in your style. For, after all, this is what appears to me to be the result of that definition—the parts whereof when I consider with attention, either collectively or separate from each other, I do not find that there is any kind of effect or impression made on my mind different from what is excited by the term *nothing*.

81. You will reply, perhaps, that in the aforesaid definition is included what doth sufficiently distinguish it from

nothing—the positive abstract idea of *quiddity, entity,* or *existence.* I own, indeed, that those who pretend to the faculty of framing abstract general ideas do talk as if they had such an idea, which is, say they, the most abstract and general notion of all; that is, to me, the most incomprehensible of all others. That there are a great variety of spirits of different orders and capacities, whose faculties both in number and extent are far exceeding those the Author of my being has bestowed on me, I see no reason to deny. And for me to pretend to determine, by my own few, stinted, narrow inlets of perception, what ideas the inexhaustible power of the Supreme Spirit may imprint upon them were certainly the utmost folly and presumption—since there may be, for aught that I know, innumerable sorts of ideas or sensations, as different from one another, and from all that I have perceived, as colours are from sounds. But, how ready soever I may be to acknowledge the scantiness of my comprehension with regard to the endless variety of spirits and ideas that may possibly exist, yet for any one to pretend to a notion of Entity or Existence, *abstracted* from *spirit* and *idea,* from perceived and being perceived, is, I suspect, a downright repugnancy and trifling with words.

It remains that we consider the objections which may possibly be made on the part of Religion.

82. Some there are who think that, though the arguments for the real existence of bodies which are drawn from Reason be allowed not to amount to demonstration, yet the Holy Scriptures are so clear in the point as will sufficiently convince every good Christian that bodies do really exist, and are something more than mere ideas; there being in Holy Writ innumerable facts related which evidently suppose the reality of timber and stone, mountains and rivers, and cities, and human bodies. To which I answer that no sort of writings whatever, sacred or pro-

fane, which use those and the like words in the vulgar
acceptation, or so as to have a meaning in them, are in
danger of having their truth called in question by our
doctrine. That all those things do really exist, that there
are bodies, even corporeal substances, when taken in the
vulgar sense, has been shewn to be agreeable to our Principles : and the difference betwixt *things* and *ideas,
realities* and *chimeras,* has been distinctly explained. See
sect. 29, 30, 33, 36, &c. And I do not think that either
what philosophers call *Matter,* or the existence of objects
without the mind, is anywhere mentioned in Scripture.

83. Again, whether there be or be not external things, it
is agreed on all hands that the proper use of words is the
marking our conceptions, or things only as they are known
and perceived by us; whence it plainly follows that in the
tenets we have laid down there is nothing inconsistent with
the right use and significancy of language, and that discourse, of what kind soever, so far as it is intelligible, remains undisturbed. But all this seems so very manifest,
from what has been largely set forth in the premises, that it
is needless to insist any farther on it.

84. But, it will be urged that Miracles do, at least, lose
much of their stress and import by our principles. What
must we think of Moses' rod? was it not *really* turned into
a serpent, or was there only a change of *ideas* in the minds
of the spectators? And, can it be supposed that our Saviour
did no more at the marriage-feast in Cana than impose on
the sight, and smell, and taste of the guests, so as to create
in them the appearance or idea only of wine? The same
may be said of all other miracles; which, in consequence of
the foregoing principles, must be looked upon only as so
many cheats, or illusions of fancy.—To this I reply, that
the rod was changed into a real serpent, and the water into
real wine. That this does not in the least contradict what
I have elsewhere said will be evident from sect. 34 and 35.
But this business of *real* and *imaginary* has been already so
plainly and fully explained, and so often referred to, and

the difficulties about it are so easily answered from what has gone before, that it were an affront to the reader's understanding to resume the explication of it in this place. I shall only observe that if at table all who were present should see, and smell, and taste, and drink wine, and find the effects of it, with me there could be no doubt of its reality;—so that at bottom the scruple concerning real miracles has no place at all on ours, but only on the received principles, and consequently makes rather for than against what has been said.

85. Having done with the Objections, which I endeavoured to propose in the clearest light, and gave them all the force and weight I could, we proceed in the next place to take a view of our tenets in their Consequences.

Some of these appear at first sight—as that several difficult and obscure questions, on which abundance of speculation has been thrown away, are entirely banished from philosophy. "Whether corporeal substance can think," "whether Matter be infinitely divisible," and "how it operates on spirit"—these and the like inquiries have given infinite amusement to philosophers in all ages; but, depending on the existence of Matter, they have no longer any place on our principles. Many other advantages there are, as well with regard to religion as the sciences, which it is easy for any one to deduce from what has been premised; but this will appear more plainly in the sequel.

86. From the Principles we have laid down it follows Human Knowledge may naturally be reduced to two heads —that of IDEAS and that of SPIRITS. Of each of these I shall treat in order.

And *first* as to IDEAS or *unthinking things*. Our knowledge of these has been very much obscured and confounded, and we have been led into very dangerous errors, by supposing a two-fold existence of the objects of sense— the one *intelligible* or in the mind; the other *real* and without the mind, whereby unthinking things are thought to have a natural subsistence of their own, distinct from being perceived by spirits. This, which, if I mistake not, hath been shewn to be a most groundless and absurd notion, is the very root of Scepticism; for, so long as men thought that real things subsisted without the mind, and that their knowledge was only so far forth *real* as it was *conformable to real things,* it follows they could not be certain that they had any real knowledge at all. For, how can it be *known* that the things which are perceived are conformable to those which are not perceived, or exist without the mind?

87. Colour, figure, motion, extension, and the like, considered only as so many *sensations* in the mind, are perfectly known, there being nothing in them which is not perceived. But, if they are looked on as notes or images, referred to *things* or *archetypes existing without the mind,* then are we involved all in scepticism. We see only the appearances, and not the real qualities of things. What may be the extension, figure, or motion of anything really and absolutely, or in itself, it is impossible for us to know, but only the proportion or relation they bear to our senses. Things remaining the same, our ideas vary, and which of them, or even whether any of them at all, represent the true quality really existing in the thing, it is out of our reach to determine. So that, for aught we know, all we see, hear, and feel, may be only phantom and vain chimera, and not at all agree with the real things existing *in rerum natura.* All this sceptical cant follows from our supposing a difference between *things* and *ideas,* and that the former had a subsistence without the mind or unperceived. It were easy to dilate on this subject, and shew how the arguments urged by sceptics in all ages depend on the supposition of external objects.

88. So long as we attribute a real existence to unthinking things, distinct from their being perceived, it is not only impossible for us to know with evidence the nature of any real unthinking being, but even that it exists. Hence it is that we see philosophers distrust their senses, and doubt of

the existence of heaven and earth, of everything they see or feel, even of their own bodies. And, after all their labouring and struggle of thought, they are forced to own we cannot attain to any self-evident or demonstrative knowledge of the existence of sensible things. But all this doubtfulness, which so bewilders and confounds the mind and makes philosophy ridiculous in the eyes of the world, vanishes if we annex a meaning to our words, and not amuse ourselves with the terms " absolute," " external," " exist," &c.—signifying we know not what. For my part, I can as well doubt of my own being as of the being of those *things which I actually perceive by sense*; it being a manifest contradiction that any sensible object should be immediately perceived by sight or touch, and at the same time have no existence in nature, since the very *existence* of an unthinking being consists in *being perceived*.

89. Nothing seems of more importance towards erecting a firm system of sound and real knowledge, which may be proof against the assaults of Scepticism, than to lay the beginning in a distinct explication of *what is meant by* THING, REALITY, EXISTENCE; for in vain shall we dispute concerning the " real existence " of things, or pretend to any knowledge thereof, so long as we have not fixed the meaning of those words. THING or BEING is the most general name of all : it comprehends under it two kinds entirely distinct and heterogeneous, and which have nothing common but the name, viz. SPIRITS and IDEAS. The former are active, indivisible substances : the latter are inert, fleeting, or dependent beings, which subsist not by themselves, but are supported by, or exist in minds or spiritual substances. We comprehend our own existence by inward feeling or Reflection, and that of other spirits by Reason.—We may be said to have some knowledge or *notion* of our own minds, of spirits and active beings— whereof in a strict sense we have not ideas. In like manner, we know and have a *notion* of relations between things or ideas—which relations are distinct from the ideas or things

related, inasmuch as the latter may be perceived by us without our perceiving the former. To me it seems that *ideas, spirits,* and *relations* are all, in their respective kinds, the object of human knowledge and subject of discourse, and that the term *idea* would be improperly extended to signify *everything* we know or have any notion of.

90. Ideas imprinted on the senses are "real" things, or do really exist : this we do not deny; but we deny they can subsist without the minds which perceive them, or that they are resemblances of any archetypes existing without the mind; since the very being of a sensation or idea consists in being perceived, and an idea can be like nothing but an idea.—Again, the things perceived by sense may be termed "external," with regard to their origin, in that they are not generated from within by the mind itself, but imprinted by a Spirit distinct from that which perceives them.—Sensible objects may likewise be said to be "without the mind" in another sense, namely when they exist in some other mind; thus, when I shut my eyes, the things I saw may still exist, but it must be in another mind.

91. It were a mistake to think that what is here said derogates in the least from the reality of things. It is acknowledged, on the received principles, that extension, motion, and in a word all sensible qualities, have need of a support, as not being able to subsist by themselves. But the objects perceived by sense are allowed to be nothing but combinations of those qualities, and consequently cannot subsist by themselves. Thus far it is agreed on all hands. So that in denying the things perceived by sense an existence independent of a substance or support wherein they may exist, we detract nothing from the received opinion of their reality, and are guilty of no innovation in that respect. All the difference is that, according to us, the unthinking beings perceived by sense have no existence distinct from being perceived, and cannot therefore exist in any other substance than those unextended indivisible substances or *Spirits* which act and think and perceive

them; whereas philosophers vulgarly hold the sensible qualities do exist in an inert, extended, unperceiving substance which they call *Matter*—to which they attribute a natural subsistence, exterior to all thinking beings, or distinct from being perceived by any mind whatsoever, even the eternal mind of the Creator, wherein they suppose only Ideas of the corporeal substances created by Him: if indeed they allow them to be at all created.

92. For, as we have shewn the doctrine of Matter or Corporeal Substance to have been the main pillar and support of Scepticism, so likewise upon the same foundation have been raised all the impious schemes of Atheism and Irreligion. Nay, so great a difficulty has it been thought to conceive Matter produced out of nothing, that the most celebrated among the ancient philosophers, even of those who maintained the being of a God, have thought Matter to be uncreated and coeternal with Him. How great a friend *material substance* has been to Atheists in all ages were needless to relate. All their monstrous systems have so visible and necessary a dependance on it that, when this corner-stone is once removed, the whole fabric cannot choose but fall to the ground, insomuch that it is no longer worth while to bestow a particular consideration on the absurdities of every wretched sect of Atheists.

93. That impious and profane persons should readily fall in with those systems which favour their inclinations, by deriding immaterial substance, and supposing the soul to be divisible and subject to corruption as the body; which exclude all freedom, intelligence, and design from the formation of things, and instead thereof make a self-existent, stupid, unthinking substance the root and origin of all beings; that they should hearken to those who deny a Providence, or inspection of a Superior Mind over the affairs of the world, attributing the whole series of events either to blind chance or fatal necessity arising from the impulse of one body on another—all this is very natural. And, on the other hand, when men of better principles

observe the enemies of religion lay so great a stress on *unthinking Matter,* and all of them use so much industry and artifice to reduce everything to it, methinks they should rejoice to see them deprived of their grand support, and driven from that only fortress, without which your Epicureans, Hobbists, and the like, have not even the shadow of a pretence, and become the most cheap and easy triumph in the world.

94. The existence of Matter, or bodies unperceived, has not only been the main support of Atheists and Fatalists, but on the same principle doth Idolatry likewise in all its various forms depend. Did men but consider that the sun, moon, and stars, and every other object of the senses, are *only* so many sensations in their minds, which have no other existence but barely being perceived, doubtless they would never fall down and worship their own *ideas*—but rather address their homage to that Eternal Invisible Mind which produces and sustains all things.

95. The same absurd principle, by mingling itself with the articles of our faith, has occasioned no small difficulties to Christians. For example, about the Resurrection, how many scruples and objections have been raised by Socinians and others? But do not the most plausible of them depend on the supposition that a body is denominated the *same,* with regard not to the *form,* or that which is perceived by sense, but the *material substance,* which remains the same under several forms? Take away this *material substance*—about the *identity* whereof all the dispute is—and mean by *body* what every plain ordinary person means by that word, to wit, *that which is immediately seen and felt,* which is only a combination of sensible qualities or ideas, and then their most unanswerable objections come to nothing.

96. Matter being once expelled out of nature drags with it so many sceptical and impious notions, such an incredible number of disputes and puzzling questions, which have been thorns in the sides of divines as well as philosophers,

and made so much fruitless work for mankind, that if the arguments we have produced against it are not found equal to demonstration (as to me they evidently seem), yet I am sure all friends to knowledge, peace, and religion have reason to wish they were.

97. Beside the external existence of the objects of perception, another great source of errors and difficulties with regard to *ideal* knowledge is the doctrine of " abstract ideas," such as it hath been set forth in the Introduction. The plainest things in the world, those we are most intimately acquainted with and perfectly know, when they are considered in an abstract way, appear strangely difficult and incomprehensible. Time, Place, and Motion, taken in particular or concrete, are what everybody knows; but, having passed through the hands of a metaphysician, they become too abstract and fine to be apprehended by men of ordinary sense. Bid your servant to meet you at such a *time* in such a *place,* and he shall never stay to deliberate on the meaning of those words; in conceiving that particular time and place, or the motion by which he is to get thither, he finds not the least difficulty. But if Time be taken exclusive of all those *particular* actions and ideas that diversify the day, merely for the continuation of existence, or duration in abstract, then it will perhaps gravel even a philosopher to comprehend it.

98. For my own part, whenever I attempt to frame a simple idea of Time, abstracted from the succession of ideas in my mind, which flows uniformly and is participated by all beings, I am lost and embrangled in inextricable difficulties. I have no notion of it at all : only I hear others say it is infinitely divisible, and speak of it in such a manner as leads me to harbour odd thoughts of my existence;—since that doctrine lays one under an absolute necessity of thinking, either that he passes away innumerable ages without a thought, or else that he is annihilated every moment of his life, both which seem equally absurd. Time therefore being *nothing,* abstracted from the succes-

sion of ideas in our minds, it follows that the duration of
any finite spirit must be estimated by the number of
ideas or actions succeeding each other in that same spirit
or mind. Hence, it is a plain consequence that *the soul
always thinks*; and in truth whoever shall go about to
divide in his thoughts, or abstract the *existence* of a spirit
from its *cogitation,* will, I believe, find it no easy task.

99. So likewise when we attempt to abstract Extension
and Motion from all other qualities, and consider them by
themselves, we presently lose sight of them, and run into
great extravagances. All which depend on a twofold abstraction;—first, it is supposed that extension, for example,
may be abstracted from all other sensible qualities; and
secondly, that the entity of extension may be abstracted
from its being perceived. But, whoever shall reflect, and
take care to understand what he says, will, if I mistake not,
acknowledge that all sensible qualities are alike *sensations*
and alike *real*—that where the extension is, there is the
colour too, *i.e.* in *his* mind; that their archetypes can exist
only in *some other* mind; and that the objects of sense *are*
nothing but those sensations combined, blended, or (if one
may so speak) concreted together—none of all which can
be supposed to exist unperceived.

100. What is it for a man to be happy, or an object
good, every one may think he knows. But to frame an
abstract idea of happiness, prescinded from all particular
pleasure, or of goodness from everything that is good, this
is what few can pretend to. So likewise a man may be just
and virtuous without having precise ideas of justice and
virtue. The opinion that those and the like words stand
for general notions, abstracted from all particular persons
and actions, seems to have rendered Morality very difficult, and the study thereof of small use to mankind. And
in effect one may make a great progress in school-ethics
without ever being the wiser or better man for it, or
knowing how to behave himself in the affairs of life more
to the advantage of himself or his neighbours than he did

before. This hint may suffice to let any one see the doctrine of *abstraction* has not a little contributed towards spoiling the most useful parts of knowledge.

101. The two great provinces of speculative science conversant about *ideas received from Sense,* are Natural Philosophy and Mathematics; with regard to each of these I shall make some observations.

And first I shall say somewhat of Natural Philosophy. On this subject it is that the sceptics triumph. All that stock of arguments they produce to depreciate our faculties and make mankind appear ignorant and low, are drawn principally from this head, namely, that we are under an invincible blindness as to the *true* and *real* nature of things. This they exaggerate, and love to enlarge on. We are miserably bantered, say they, by our senses, and amused only with the outside and show of things. The real essence —the internal qualities and constitution—of every the meanest object, is hid from our view; something there is in every drop of water, every grain of sand, which it is beyond the power of human understanding to fathom or comprehend. But, it is evident from what has been shewn that all this complaint is groundless, and that we are influenced by false principles to that degree as to mistrust our senses, and think we know nothing of those things which we perfectly comprehend.

102. One great inducement to our pronouncing ourselves ignorant of the nature of things is the current opinion that everything includes within itself the cause of its properties; or that there is in each object an inward *essence* which is the source whence its discernible qualities flow, and whereon they depend.[5] Some have pretended to account for appearances by occult qualities : but of late they are mostly resolved into mechanical causes, to wit, the figure, motion, weight, and suchlike qualities, of insensible particles;—whereas, in truth, there is no other agent or efficient cause than *spirit,* it being evident that motion, as

[5] See Locke, *Essay,* Bk. III, ch. 3, and Bk. IV, ch. 6.

well as all other *ideas,* is perfectly inert. See sect. 2
Hence, to endeavour to explain the production of colour
or sounds, by figure, motion, magnitude and the like, mus
needs be labour in vain. And accordingly we see the at
tempts of that kind are not at all satisfactory. Which ma
be said in general of those instances wherein one idea o
quality is assigned for the cause of another. I need not sa
how many hypotheses and speculations are left out, and
how much the study of nature is abridged by this doctrine

103. The great *mechanical* principle now in vogue i
Attraction. That a stone falls to the earth, or the se;
swells towards the moon, may to some appear sufficientl
explained thereby. But how are we enlightened by being
told this is done by attraction? Is it that that word signi
fies the manner of the tendency, and that it is by the
mutual drawing of bodies or their being impelled or pro
truded towards each other? But nothing is determined o
the manner of action, and it may as truly (for aught we
know) be termed " impulse," or " protrusion," as " attrac
tion." Again, the parts of steel we see cohere firmly to
gether, and this also is accounted for by attraction; but, i
this as in the other instances, I do not perceive that any
thing is signified besides the effect itself; for as to th
manner of the action whereby it is produced, or the caus
which produces it, these are not so much as aimed at.

104. Indeed, if we take a view of the several pheno
mena, and compare them together, we may observe som
likeness and conformity between them. For example, i
the falling of a stone to the ground, in the rising of the se
towards the moon, in cohesion, crystallization, &c., there i
something alike, namely, an union or mutual approach o
bodies. So that any one of these or the like phenomen
may not seem strange or surprising to a man who ha
nicely observed and compared the effects of nature. Fo
that only is thought so which is uncommon, or a thing b
itself, and out of the ordinary course of our observation
That bodies should tend towards the centre of the earth i

not thought strange, because it is what we perceive every moment of our lives. But that they should have a like gravitation towards the centre of the moon may seem odd and unaccountable to most men, because it is discerned only in the tides. But a philosopher, whose thoughts take in a larger compass of nature, having observed a certain similitude of appearances, as well in the heavens as the earth, that argue innumerable bodies to have a mutual tendency towards each other, which he denotes by the general name " attraction," whatever can be reduced to *that* he thinks justly accounted for. Thus he explains the tides by the attraction of the terraqueous globe towards the moon, which to him does not appear odd or anomalous, but only a particular example of a general rule or law of nature.

105. If therefore we consider the difference there is betwixt natural philosophers and other men, with regard to their knowledge of the phenomena, we shall find it consists not in an exacter knowledge of the *efficient cause* that produces them—for *that* can be no other than the *will of a spirit*—but only in a greater largeness of comprehension, whereby analogies, harmonies, and agreements are discovered in the works of nature, and the particular effects explained, that is, *reduced to general rules*, see sect. 62; which rules, grounded on the analogy and uniformness observed in the production of natural effects, are most agreeable and sought after by the mind; for that they extend our prospect beyond what is present and near to us, and enable us to make very probable conjectures touching things that may have happened at very great distances of time and place, as well as to predict things to come; which sort of endeavour towards Omniscience is much affected by the mind.

106. But we should proceed warily in such things, for we are apt to lay too great a stress on analogies, and, to the prejudice of truth, humour that eagerness of the mind whereby it is carried to extend its knowledge into general

theorems. For example, in the business of gravitation or mutual attraction, because it appears in many instances, some are straightway for pronouncing it *universal*; and that to attract and be attracted by every other body is an essential quality inherent in all bodies whatsoever. Whereas it is evident the fixed stars have no such tendency towards each other; and, so far is that gravitation from being *essential* to bodies that in some instances a quite contrary principle seems to shew itself; as in the perpendicular growth of plants, and the elasticity of the air. There is nothing necessary or essential in the case, but it depends entirely on the Will of the Governing Spirit, who causes certain bodies to cleave together or tend towards each other according to various laws, whilst He keeps others at a fixed distance; and to some he gives a quite contrary tendency to fly asunder just as He sees convenient.

107. After what has been premised, I think we may lay down the following conclusions.—First, it is plain philosophers amuse themselves in vain, when they enquire for *any* natural efficient cause, distinct from a *Mind* or *Spirit*. Secondly, considering the whole creation is the workmanship of a *wise and good Agent,* it should seem to become philosophers to employ their thoughts (contrary to what some hold) about the final causes of things; and I must confess I see no reason why pointing out the various ends to which natural things are adapted, and for which they were originally with unspeakable wisdom contrived, should not be thought one good way of accounting for them, and altogether worthy a philosopher. Thirdly, from what has been premised no reason can be drawn why the history of nature should not still be studied, and observations and experiments made—which, that they are of use to mankind, and enable us to draw any general conclusions, is not the result of any immutable habitudes or relations between things themselves, but only of God's goodness and kindness to men in the administration of the world. See sect. 30 and 31. Fourthly, by a diligent observation of the

phenomena within our view, we may discover the general laws of nature, and from them deduce the other phenomena; I do not say *demonstrate*, for all deductions of that kind depend on a supposition that the Author of Nature always operates uniformly, and in a constant observance of those rules we take for principles—which we cannot evidently know.

108. Those men who frame general rules for the phenomena, and afterwards derive the phenomena from those rules, seem to consider Signs rather than Causes. A man may well understand natural signs without knowing their analogy, or being able to say by what rule a thing is so or so. And, as it is very possible to write improperly, through too strict an observance of general grammar-rules; so, in arguing from general laws of nature, it is not impossible we may extend the analogy too far, and by that means run into mistakes.

109. As in reading other books a wise man will choose to fix his thoughts on the sense and apply it to use, rather than lay them out in grammatical remarks on the language; so, in perusing the Volume of Nature, methinks it is beneath the dignity of the mind to affect an exactness in reducing each particular phenomenon to general rules, or shewing how it follows from them. We should propose to ourselves nobler views, namely, to recreate and exalt the mind with a prospect of the beauty, order, extent, and variety of natural things : hence, by proper inferences, to enlarge our notions of the grandeur, wisdom, and beneficence of the Creator; and lastly, to make the several parts of the creation, so far as in us lies, subservient to the ends they were designed for—God's glory, and the sustentation and comfort of ourselves and fellow-creatures.

110. The best key for the aforesaid Analogy or Natural Science will be easily acknowledged to be a certain celebrated Treatise of *Mechanics*.[6] In the entrance of which justly admired treatise, Time, Space, and Motion are dis-

[6] Newton's *Principia*, published in 1687.

tinguished into *absolute* and *relative, true* and *apparent, mathematical* and *vulgar;*—which distinction, as it is at large explained by the author, does suppose those Quantities to have an existence without the mind, and that they are ordinarily conceived with relation to sensible things, to which nevertheless in their own nature they bear no relation at all.

111. As for *Time,* as it is there taken in an absolute or abstracted sense, for the duration or perseverance of the existence of things, I have nothing more to add concerning it after what has been already said on that subject. Sect. 97 and 98. For the rest, this celebrated author holds there is an *Absolute Space,* which, being unperceivable to sense, remains in itself similar and immoveable; and *relative space* to be the measure thereof, which being moveable, and defined by its situation in respect of sensible bodies, is vulgarly taken for immoveable space. *Place* he defines to be that part of space which is occupied by any body; and according as the space is absolute or relative so also is the place. *Absolute Motion* is said to be the translation of a body from absolute place to absolute place, as *relative motion* is from one relative place to another. And, because the parts of Absolute Space do not fall under our senses, instead of them we are obliged to use their sensible measures, and so define both place and motion with respect to bodies which we regard as immoveable. But, it is said in philosophical matters we must abstract from our senses, since it may be that none of those bodies which seem to be quiescent are truly so, and the same thing which is moved relatively may be really at rest; as likewise one and the same body may be in relative rest and motion, or even moved with contrary relative motions at the same time, according as its place is variously defined. All which ambiguity is to be found in the apparent motions, but not at all in the true or absolute, which should therefore be alone regarded in philosophy. And the true we are told are distinguished from apparent or relative motions by the fol-

lowing properties.—First, in true or absolute motion all parts which preserve the same position with respect of the whole, partake of the motions of the whole. Secondly, the place being moved, that which is placed therein is also moved; so that a body moving in a place which is in motion doth participate the motion of its place. Thirdly, true motion is never generated or changed otherwise than by force impressed on the body itself. Fourthly, true motion is always changed by force impressed on the body moved. Fifthly, in circular motion barely relative there is no centrifugal force, which nevertheless, in that which is true or absolute, is proportional to the quantity of motion.

112. But, notwithstanding what has been said, I must confess it does not appear to me that there can be any motion other than *relative*; so that to conceive motion there must be at least conceived two bodies, whereof the distance or position in regard to each other is varied. Hence, if there was one only body in being it could not possibly be moved. This to me seems very evident, in that the idea I have of motion does necessarily include relation.

113. But, though in every motion it be necessary to conceive more bodies than one, yet it may be that one only is moved, namely, that on which the force causing the change in the distance or situation of the bodies is impressed. For, however some may define relative motion, so as to term that body *moved* which changes its distance from some other body, whether the force or action causing that change were impressed on *it* or no, yet as relative motion is that which is perceived by sense, and regarded in the ordinary affairs of life, it follows that every man of common sense knows what it is as well as the best philosopher. Now, I ask any one whether, in his sense of motion as he walks along the streets, the stones he passes over may be said to *move*, because they change distance with his feet? To me it appears that though motion includes a relation of one thing to another, yet it is not necessary that each term of

the relation be denominated from it. As a man may think of somewhat which does not think, so a body may be moved to or from another body which is not therefore *itself* in motion.—I mean relative motion, for other I am not able to conceive.

114. As the place happens to be variously defined, the motion which is related to it varies. A man in a ship may be said to be quiescent with relation to the sides of the vessel, and yet move with relation to the land. Or he may move eastward in respect of the one, and westward in respect of the other. In the common affairs of life men never go beyond the Earth to define the place of any body; and what is quiescent *in respect of that* is accounted *absolutely* to be so. But philosophers, who have a greater extent of thought, and juster notions of the system of things, discover even the Earth itself to be moved. In order therefore to fix their notions, they seem to conceive the Corporeal World as finite, and the utmost unmoved walls or shell thereof to be the place where they estimate true motions. If we sound our own conceptions, I believe we may find all the absolute motion we can frame an idea of to be at bottom no other than relative motion thus defined. For, as has been already observed, absolute motion, exclusive of all external relation, is incomprehensible; and to this kind of relative motion all the above-mentioned properties, causes, and effects ascribed to absolute motion will, if I mistake not, be found to agree. As to what is said of the centrifugal force, that it does not at all belong to circular relative motion, I do not see how this follows from the experiment which is brought to prove it. See *Philosophiæ Naturalis Principia Mathematica, in Schol. Def. VIII.* For the water in the vessel at that time wherein it is said to have the greatest relative circular motion, has, I think, no motion at all; as is plain from the foregoing section.

115. For, to denominate a body *moved* it is requisite, first, that it changes its distance or situation with regard to

some other body; secondly, that the force occasioning that change be impressed on *it*. If either of these be wanting, I do not think that, agreeably to the sense of mankind, or the propriety of language, a body can be said to be in motion. I grant indeed that it is possible for us to think a body which we see change its distance from some other to be moved, though it have no force applied to it (in which sense there may be apparent motion); but then it is because the force causing the change of distance is imagined by us to be applied or impressed on that body thought to move; which indeed shews we are capable of mistaking a thing to be in motion which is not, and that is all.

116. From what has been said it follows that the philosophic consideration of motion does not imply the being of an Absolute Space, distinct from that which is perceived by sense and related to bodies; which that *it* cannot exist without the mind is clear upon the same principles that demonstrate the like of all other objects of sense.—And perhaps, if we inquire narrowly, we shall find we cannot even frame an idea of Pure Space exclusive of all body. This I must confess seems impossible, as being a most abstract idea. When I excite a motion in some part of my body, if it be free or without resistance, I say there is *Space*; but if I find a resistance, then I say there is *Body*: and in proportion as the resistance to motion is lesser or greater, I say the space is more or less *pure*. So that when I speak of pure or empty space, it is not to be supposed that the word " space " stands for an idea distinct from or conceivable without body and motion—though indeed we are apt to think every noun substantive stands for a distinct idea that may be separated from all others; which has occasioned infinite mistakes. When, therefore, supposing all the world to be annihilated besides my own body, I say there still remains *Pure Space*, thereby nothing else is meant but only that I conceive it possible for the limbs of my body to be moved on all sides without the least resistance; but if that too were annihilated then there could be

no motion, and consequently no Space. Some, perhaps, may think the sense of seeing does furnish them with the idea of Pure Space; but it is plain from what we have else-where shewn, that the ideas of Space and Distance are not obtained by that sense. See the *Essay concerning Vision*.

117. What is here laid down seems to put an end to all those disputes and difficulties that have sprung up amongst the learned concerning the nature of Pure Space. But the chief advantage arising from it is that we are freed from that dangerous dilemma, to which several who have em-ployed their thoughts on that subject imagine themselves reduced, viz. of thinking either that Real Space is God, or else that there is something beside God which is eternal, uncreated, infinite, indivisible, immutable. Both which may justly be thought pernicious and absurd notions. It is certain that not a few divines, as well as philosophers of great note, have, from the difficulty they found in conceiv-ing either limits or annihilation of space, concluded it must be Divine. And some of late have set themselves parti-cularly to shew the incommunicable attributes of God agree to it. Which doctrine, how unworthy soever it may seem of the Divine Nature, yet I must confess I do not see how we can get clear of it, so long as we adhere to the received opinions.

118. Hitherto of Natural Philosophy: we come now to make some inquiry concerning that other great branch of speculative knowledge, to wit, Mathematics. These, how celebrated soever they may be for their clearness and cer-tainty of demonstration, which is hardly anywhere else to be found, cannot nevertheless be supposed altogether free from mistakes, if so be that in their principles there lurks some secret error which is common to the professors of those sciences with the rest of mankind. Mathemati-cians, though they deduce their theorems from a great height of evidence, yet their first principles are limited by the consideration of Quantity: and they do not ascend

into any inquiry concerning those transcendental maxims which influence all the particular sciences, each part whereof, Mathematics not excepted, does consequently participate of the errors involved in them. That the principles laid down by mathematicians are true, and their way of deduction from those principles clear and incontestible, we do not deny; but, we hold there may be certain erroneous maxims of greater extent than the object of Mathematics, and for that reason not expressly mentioned, though tacitly supposed throughout the whole progress of that science; and that the ill effects of those secret unexamined errors are diffused through all the branches thereof. To be plain, we suspect the mathematicians are no less deeply concerned than other men in the errors arising from the doctrine of abstract general ideas, and the existence of objects without the mind.

119. Arithmetic has been thought to have for its object *abstract* ideas of *Number*; of which to understand the properties and mutual habitudes, is supposed no mean part of speculative knowledge. The opinion of the pure and intellectual nature of numbers in abstract has made them in esteem with those philosophers who seem to have affected an uncommon fineness and elevation of thought. It hath set a price on the most trifling numerical speculations, which in practice are of no use, but serve only for amusement; and hath heretofore so far infected the minds of some, that they have dreamed of mighty mysteries involved in numbers, and attempted the explication of natural things by them. But, if we narrowly inquire into our own thoughts, and consider what has been premised, we may perhaps entertain a low opinion of those high flights and abstractions, and look on all inquiries about numbers only as so many *difficiles nugæ,* so far as they are not subservient to practice, and promote the benefit of life.

120. Unity in abstract we have before considered, in sect. 13, from which, and what has been said in the Introduction, it plainly follows there is not any such idea. But,

number being defined a "collection of units," we may conclude that, if there be no such thing as unity or unit in
abstract, there are no ideas of number in abstract denoted
by the numeral names and figures. The theories therefore
in Arithmetic, if they are abstracted from the names and
figures, as likewise from all use and practice, as well as from
the particular things numbered, can be supposed to have
nothing at all for their object; hence we may see how
entirely the science of numbers is subordinate to practice,
and how jejune and trifling it becomes when considered as
a matter of mere speculation.

121. However, since there may be some who, deluded by
the specious show of discovering abstracted verities, waste
their time in arithmetical theorems and problems which
have not any use, it will not be amiss if we more fully consider and expose the vanity of that pretence; and this will
plainly appear by taking a view of Arithmetic in its infancy,
and observing what it was that originally put men on the
study of that science, and to what scope they directed it.
It is natural to think that at first, men, for ease of memory
and help of computation, made use of counters, or in
writing of single strokes, points, or the like, each whereof
was made to signify an unit, *i.e.* some one thing of whatever kind they had occasion to reckon. Afterwards they
found out the more compendious ways of making one
character stand in place of several strokes or points. And,
lastly, the notation of the Arabians or Indians came into
use, wherein, by the repetition of a few characters or
figures, and varying the signification of each figure according to the place it obtains, all numbers may be most aptly
expressed; which seems to have been done in imitation of
language, so that an exact analogy is observed betwixt the
notation by figures and names, the nine simple figures
answering the nine first numeral names and places in the
former, corresponding to denominations in the latter. And
agreeably to those conditions of the simple and local value

of figures, were contrived methods of finding, from the given figures or marks of the parts, what figures and how placed are proper to denote the whole, or *vice versa*. And having found the sought figures, the same rule or analogy being observed throughout, it is easy to read them into words; and so the number becomes perfectly known. For then the number of any particular things is said to be known, when we know the name or figures (with their due arrangement) that according to the standing analogy belong to them. For, these signs being known, we can, by the operations of arithmetic, know the signs of any part of the particular sums signified by them; and, thus computing in signs, (because of the connexion established betwixt them and the distinct multitudes of things whereof one is taken for an unit), we may be able rightly to sum up, divide, and proportion the things themselves that we intend to number.

122. In Arithmetic, therefore, we regard not the *things* but the *signs,* which nevertheless are not regarded for their own sake, but because they direct us how to act with relation to things, and dispose rightly of them. Now, agreeably to what we have before observed of words in general (sect. 19, Introd.) it happens here likewise that *abstract ideas* are thought to be signified by numeral names or characters, while they do not suggest *ideas of particular things* to our minds. I shall not at present enter into a more particular dissertation on this subject, but only observe that it is evident, from what has been said, those things which pass for *abstract* truths and theorems concerning numbers, are in reality conversant about no object distinct from *particular numberable things,* except only names and characters, which originally came to be considered on no other account but their being signs, or capable to represent aptly whatever particular things men had need to compute. Whence it follows that to study them for their own sake would be just as wise, and to as good purpose, as if a man, neglecting the true use or original

intention and subserviency of language, should spend his time in impertinent criticisms upon words, or reasonings and controversies purely verbal.

123. From numbers we proceed to speak of *Extension*, which is the object of Geometry. The *infinite* divisibility of *finite* extension, though it is not expressly laid down either as an axiom or theorem in the elements of that science, yet is throughout the same everywhere supposed and thought to have so inseparable and essential a connexion with the principles and demonstrations in Geometry, that mathematicians never admit it into doubt, or make the least question of it. And, as this notion is the source from whence do spring all those amusing geometrical paradoxes which have such a direct repugnancy to the plain common sense of mankind, and are admitted with so much reluctance into a mind not yet debauched by learning; so is it the principal occasion of all that nice and extreme subtlety which renders the study of Mathematics so very difficult and tedious. Hence, if we can make it appear that *no finite extension contains innumerable parts, or is infinitely divisible,* it follows that we shall at once clear the science of Geometry from a great number of difficulties and contradictions which have ever been esteemed a reproach to human reason, and withal make the attainment thereof a business of much less time and pains than it hitherto has been.

124. Every particular finite extension which may possibly be the object of our thought is an *idea* existing only in the mind, and consequently each part thereof must be perceived. If, therefore, I cannot perceive innumerable parts in any finite extension that I consider, it is certain they are not contained in it; but, it is evident that I cannot distinguish innumerable parts in any particular line, surface, or solid, which I either perceive by sense, or figure to myself in my mind : wherefore I conclude they are not contained in it. Nothing can be plainer to me than that the extensions I have in view are no other than my own ideas;

and it is no less plain that I cannot resolve any one of my ideas into an infinite number of other ideas, that is, that they are not infinitely divisible. If by finite extension be meant something distinct from a finite idea, I declare I do not know what that is, and so cannot affirm or deny anything of it. But if the terms " extension," " parts," &c., are taken in any sense conceivable, that is, for ideas, then to say a finite quantity or extension consists of parts infinite in number is so manifest and glaring a contradiction, that every one at first sight acknowledges it to be so; and it is impossible it should ever gain the assent of any reasonable creature who is not brought to it by gentle and slow degrees, as a converted Gentile to the belief of transubstantiation. Ancient and rooted prejudices do often pass into principles; and those propositions which once obtain the force and credit of a *principle,* are not only themselves, but likewise whatever is deducible from them, thought privileged from all examination. And there is no absurdity so gross, which, by this means, the mind of man may not be prepared to swallow.

125. He whose understanding is prepossessed with the doctrine of *abstract* general ideas may be persuaded that (whatever be thought of the *ideas of sense*) extension in *abstract* is infinitely divisible. And any one who thinks the objects of sense exist without the mind will perhaps in virtue thereof be brought to admit that a line but an inch long may contain innumerable parts—really existing, though too small to be discerned. These errors are grafted as well in the minds of geometricians as of other men, and have a like influence on their reasonings; and it were no difficult thing to shew how the arguments from Geometry made use of to support the infinite divisibility of extension are bottomed on them. At present we shall only observe in general whence it is the mathematicians are all so fond and tenacious of that doctrine.

126. It has been observed in another place that the theorems and demonstrations in Geometry are conversant

about *universal ideas* (sect. 15. Introd.); where it is explained in what sense this ought to be understood, to wit, the *particular* lines and figures included in the diagram are supposed to stand for innumerable others of different sizes; or, in other words, the geometer considers *them* abstracting from their magnitude—which does not imply that he forms an abstract idea, but only that he cares not what the particular magnitude is, whether great or small, but looks on that as a thing indifferent to the demonstration. Hence it follows that a line in the scheme but an inch long must be spoken of as though *it* contained ten thousand parts, since it is regarded not in itself, but as it is universal; and it is universal only in its signification, whereby it represents innumerable lines greater than itself, in which may be distinguished ten thousand parts or more, though there may not be above an inch in it. After this manner, the properties of the lines signified are (by a very usual figure) transferred to the sign, and thence, through mistake, thought to appertain to it considered in its own nature.

127. Because there is no number of parts so great but it is possible there may be *a* line containing more, the *inch*-line is said to contain parts more than any assignable number; which is true, not of the inch taken absolutely, but only for the things signified by it. But men, not retaining that distinction in their thoughts, slide into a belief that the small particular line described on paper contains in itself parts innumerable. There is no such thing as the ten thousandth part of an inch; but there is of a mile or diameter of the earth, which may be signified by that inch. When therefore I delineate a triangle on paper, and take one side not above an inch, for example, in length to be the radius, this I consider as divided into 10,000 or 100,000 parts or more; for, though the ten thousandth part of *that* line considered in itself is nothing at all, and consequently may be neglected without any error or inconveniency, yet these described lines, being only marks standing for greater quantities, whereof it may be the ten thousandth part is

very considerable, it follows that, to prevent notable errors in practice, the radius must be taken of 10,000 parts or more.

128. From what has been said the reason is plain why, to the end any theorem become universal in its use, it is necessary we speak of the lines described on paper as though they contained parts which really they do not. In doing of which, if we examine the matter thoroughly, we shall perhaps discover that we cannot conceive an inch itself as consisting of, or being divisible into, a thousand parts, but only some other line which is far greater than an inch, and represented by it; and that when we say a line is infinitely divisible, we must mean a line which is infinitely great. What we have here observed seems to be the chief cause why, to suppose the infinite divisibility of finite extension has been thought necessary in geometry.

129. The several absurdities and contradictions which flowed from this false principle might, one would think, have been esteemed so many demonstrations against it. But, by I know not what logic, it is held that proofs *a posteriori* are not to be admitted against propositions relating to infinity—as though it were not impossible even for an infinite mind to reconcile contradictions; or as if anything absurd and repugnant could have a necessary connexion with truth or flow from it. But, whoever considers the weakness of this pretence will think it was contrived on purpose to humour the laziness of the mind which had rather acquiesce in an indolent scepticism than be at the pains to go through with a severe examination of those principles it has ever embraced for true.

130. Of late the speculations about Infinities have run so high, and grown to such strange notions, as have occasioned no small scruples and disputes among the geometers of the present age. Some there are of great note who, not content with holding that finite lines may be divided into an infinite number of parts, do yet farther maintain that each of those infinitesimals is itself subdivisible into an infinity

of other parts or infinitesimals of a second order, and so on *ad infinitum*. These, I say, assert there are infinitesimals of infinitesimals of infinitesimals, &c., without ever coming to an end : so that according to them an inch does not barely contain an infinite number of parts, but an infinity of an infinity of an infinity *ad infinitum* of parts. Others there be who hold all order of infinitesimals below the first to be nothing at all; thinking it with good reason absurd to imagine there is any positive quantity or part of extension which, though multiplied infinitely, can never equal the smallest given extension. And yet on the other hand it seems no less absurd to think the square, cube, or other power of a positive real root, should itself be nothing at all; which they who hold infinitesimals of the first order, denying all of the subsequent orders, are obliged to maintain.

131. Have we not therefore reason to conclude they are *both* in the wrong, and that there is in effect no such thing as parts infinitely small, or an infinite number of parts contained in any finite quantity? But you will say that if this doctrine obtains it will follow the very foundations of Geometry are destroyed, and those great men who have raised that science to so astonishing a height, have been all the while building a castle in the air. To this it may be replied that whatever is useful in geometry, and promotes the benefit of human life, does still remain firm and unshaken on our principles—that science considered as practical will rather receive advantage than any prejudice from what has been said. But to set this in a due light, and shew how lines and figures may be measured, and their properties investigated, without supposing finite extension to be infinitely divisible, may be the proper business of another place. For the rest, though it should follow that some of the more intricate and subtle parts of Speculative Mathematics may be pared off without any prejudice to truth, yet I do not see what damage will be thence derived to mankind. On the contrary, I think it were highly to be

wished that men of great abilities and obstinate application would draw off their thoughts from those amusements, and employ them in the study of such things as lie nearer the concerns of life, or have a more direct influence on the manners.

132. If it be said that several theorems undoubtedly true are discovered by methods in which Infinitesimals are made use of, which could never have been if their existence included a contradiction in it—I answer that upon a thorough examination it will not be found that in any instance it is necessary to make use of or conceive infinitesimal parts of finite lines, or even quantities less than the *minimum sensibile*; nay, it will be evident this is never done, it being impossible.

133. By what we have hitherto said, it is plain that very numerous and important errors have taken their rise from those false Principles which were impugned in the foregoing parts of this treatise; and the opposites of those erroneous tenets at the same time appear to be most fruitful Principles, from whence do flow innumerable consequences highly advantageous to true philosophy, as well as to religion. Particularly *Matter*, or the *absolute* existence of corporeal objects, hath been shewn to be that wherein the most avowed and pernicious enemies of all knowledge, whether human or divine, have ever placed their chief strength and confidence. And surely if by distinguishing the *real* existence of unthinking things from their *being perceived*, and allowing them a subsistence of their own out of the minds of spirits, no one thing is explained in nature, but on the contrary a great many inexplicable difficulties arise; if the supposition of Matter is barely precarious, as not being grounded on so much as one single reason; if its consequences cannot endure the light of examination and free inquiry, but screen themselves under the dark and general pretence of Infinites being incompre-

hensible; if withal the removal of this Matter be not attended with the least evil consequence; if it be not even missed in the world, but everything as well, nay much easier, conceived without it; if, lastly, both Sceptics and Atheists are for ever silenced upon supposing only SPIRITS and IDEAS, and this scheme of things is perfectly agreeable both to Reason and Religion—methinks we may expect it should be admitted and firmly embraced, though it were proposed only as an *hypothesis,* and the existence of Matter had been allowed possible—which yet I think we have evidently demonstrated that it is not.

134. True it is that, in consequence of the foregoing Principles, several disputes and speculations which are esteemed no mean parts of learning, are rejected as useless. But, how great a prejudice soever against our notions this may give to those who have already been deeply engaged and made large advances in studies of that nature, yet by others we hope it will not be thought any just ground of dislike to the principles and tenets herein laid down—that they abridge the labour of study, and make human Sciences far more clear, compendious, and attainable than they were before.

135. Having despatched what we intended to say concerning the knowledge of IDEAS, the method we proposed leads us in the next place to treat of SPIRITS—with regard to which, perhaps, human knowledge is not so deficient as is vulgarly imagined. The great reason that is assigned for our being thought ignorant of the nature of Spirit is—our not having an *idea* of it. But, surely it ought not to be looked on as a defect in a human understanding that it does not perceive the idea of spirit, if it is manifestly impossible there should be any such idea. And this if I mistake not has been demonstrated in section 27; to which I shall here add—that a spirit has been shewn to be the only substance or support wherein unthinking beings or ideas can exist; but that this *substance* which supports or per-

ceives ideas should itself be an idea or like an idea is
evidently absurd.

136. It will perhaps be said that we want a *sense* (as
some have imagined) proper to know substances withal,
which, if we had, we might know our own soul as we do a
triangle. To this I answer, that, in case we had a new
sense bestowed upon us, we could only receive thereby
some new sensations or ideas of sense. But I believe nobody will say that what he means by the terms *soul* and
substance is only some particular sort of idea or sensation.
We may therefore infer that, all things duly considered, it
is not more reasonable to think our faculties defective, in
that they do not furnish us with an *idea* of spirit or active
thinking substance, than it would be if we should blame
them for not being able to comprehend a *round square*.

137. From the opinion that spirits are to be known after
the manner of an idea or sensation have risen many absurd
and heterodox tenets, and much scepticism about the
nature of the soul. It is even probable that this opinion
may have produced a doubt in some whether they had any
soul at all distinct from their body, since upon inquiry
they could not find they had an idea of it. That an *idea,*
which is inactive and the existence whereof consists in being
perceived, should be the image or likeness of an agent
subsisting by itself, seems to need no other refutation
than barely attending to what is meant by those words.
But perhaps you will say that though an idea cannot resemble a spirit in its thinking, acting, or subsisting by itself,
yet it may in some other respects; and it is not necessary
that an idea or image be in all respects like the original.

138. I answer, if it does not in those mentioned, it is
impossible it should represent it in any other thing. Do
but leave out the power of willing, thinking, and perceiving ideas, and there remains nothing else wherein the idea
can be like a spirit. For, by the word *spirit* we mean only
that which thinks, wills, and perceives; this, and this alone,
constitutes the signification of that term. If therefore it is

impossible that any degree of those powers should be represented in an idea, it is evident there can be no idea of a spirit.

139. But it will be objected that, if there is no *idea* signified by the terms "soul," "spirit," and "substance," they are wholly insignificant, or have no meaning in them. I answer, those words do mean or signify a real thing—which is neither an idea nor like an idea, but that which perceives ideas, and wills, and reasons about them. What I am myself—that which I denote by the term *I*—is the same with what is meant by *soul* or *spiritual substance*. But if I should say that *I* was nothing, or that *I* was an idea, nothing could be more evidently absurd than either of these propositions. If it be said that this is only quarrelling at a word, and that, since the *immediate* significations of other names are by common consent called *ideas,* no reason can be assigned why that which is signified by the name *spirit* or *soul* may not partake in the same appellation, I answer—All the unthinking objects of the mind agree in that they are entirely passive, and their existence consists only in being perceived; whereas a soul or spirit is an active being, whose existence consists, not in being perceived, but in perceiving ideas and thinking. It is therefore necessary—in order to prevent equivocation and confounding natures perfectly disagreeing and unlike—that we distinguish between SPIRIT and IDEA. See sect. 27.

140. In a large sense indeed, we may be said to have an idea or rather a notion of *spirit*; that is, we understand the meaning of the word, otherwise we could not affirm or deny anything of it. Moreover, as we conceive the ideas that are in the minds of other spirits by means of our own, which we suppose to be resemblances of them; so we know *other* spirits by means of *our own soul*—which in that sense is *the image or idea of them*; it having a like respect to other spirits that blueness or heat by me perceived has to those ideas perceived by another.

141. The Natural Immortality of the Soul is a necessary

consequence of the foregoing doctrine. But before we attempt to prove this, it is fit that we explain the meaning of that tenet. It must not be supposed that they who assert the natural immortality of the soul are of opinion that it is absolutely incapable of annihilation even by the infinite power of the Creator who first gave it being, but only that it is not liable to be broken or dissolved by the ordinary laws of nature or motion. They indeed who hold the soul of man to be only a thin vital flame, or system of animal spirits, make it perishing and corruptible as the body; since there is nothing more easily dissipated than such a being, which it is naturally impossible should survive the ruin of the tabernacle wherein it is enclosed. And this notion has been greedily embraced and cherished by the worst part of mankind, as the most effectual antidote against all impressions of virtue and religion. But it has been made evident that *bodies,* of what frame and texture soever, are barely passive ideas in the *mind*—which is more distant and heterogeneous from them than light is from darkness. We have shewn that the soul is indivisible, incorporeal, unextended, and it is consequently incorruptible. Nothing can be plainer than that the motions, changes, decays, and dissolutions which we hourly see befall natural bodies (and which is what we mean by the *course of nature*) cannot possibly affect an active, simple, uncompounded substance : such a being therefore is indissoluble by the force of nature; that is to say—the soul of man is *naturally* immortal.

142. After what has been said, it is, I suppose, plain that our souls are not to be known in the same manner as senseless, inactive objects, or by way of *idea*. *Spirits* and *ideas* are things so wholly different, that when we say "they exist," "they are known," or the like, these words must not be thought to signify anything common to both natures. There is nothing alike or common in them; and to expect that by any multiplication or enlargement of our faculties we may be enabled to know a spirit as we do a

triangle, seems as absurd as if we should hope to see a sound. This is inculcated because I imagine it may be of moment towards clearing several important questions, and preventing some very dangerous errors concerning the Nature of the Soul. We may not, I think, strictly be said to have an *idea* of an active being, or of an action, although we may be said to have a *notion* of them. I have some knowledge or notion of my mind, and its acts about ideas—inasmuch as I know or understand what is meant by these words. What I know, that I have some notion of. I will not say that the terms *idea* and *notion* may not be used convertibly, if the world will have it so; but yet it conduceth to clearness and propriety that we distinguish things very different by different names. It is also to be remarked that, all *relations* including an act of the mind, we cannot so properly be said to have an idea, but rather a notion of the relations and habitudes between things. But if, in the modern way, the word *idea* is extended to *spirits*, and *relations* and *acts*, this is, after all, an affair of verbal concern.

143. It will not be amiss to add, that the doctrine of *abstract* ideas has had no small share in rendering those sciences intricate and obscure which are particularly conversant about spiritual things. Men have imagined they could frame abstract notions of the *powers* and *acts* of the mind, and consider them prescinded as well from the mind or spirit itself, as from their respective objects and effects. Hence a great number of dark and ambiguous terms, presumed to stand for abstract notions, have been introduced into metaphysics and morality, and from these have grown infinite distractions and disputes among the learned.

144. But, nothing seems more to have contributed towards engaging men in controversies and mistakes with regard to the nature and operations of the mind, than the being used to speak of those things in terms borrowed from sensible ideas. For example, the will is termed the *motion* of the soul : this infuses a belief that the mind of man is as

a ball in motion, impelled and determined by the objects of sense, as necessarily as that is by the stroke of a racket. Hence arise endless scruples and errors of dangerous consequence in morality. All which, I doubt not, may be cleared, and truth appear plain, uniform, and consistent, could but philosophers be prevailed on to depart from some received prejudices and modes of speech, and retire into themselves, and attentively consider their own meaning.

145. From what has been said, it is plain that we cannot know the existence of *other spirits* otherwise than by their operations, or the ideas by them excited in us. I perceive several motions, changes, and combinations of ideas, that inform me there are certain particular agents, like myself, which accompany them and concur in their production. Hence, the knowledge I have of other spirits is not immediate, as is the knowledge of my ideas; but depending on the intervention of ideas, by me referred to agents or spirits distinct from myself, as effects or concomitant signs.

146. But, though there be some things which convince us *human* agents are concerned in producing them, yet it is evident to every one that those things which are called the Works of Nature—that is, the far greater part of the ideas or sensations perceived by us—are not produced by, or dependent on, the wills of men. There is therefore some other Spirit that causes them; since it is repugnant that they should subsist by themselves. See sect. 29. But, if we attentively consider the constant regularity, order, and concatenation of natural things, the surprising magnificence, beauty and perfection of the larger, and the exquisite contrivance of the smaller parts of the creation, together with the exact harmony and correspondence of the whole; but above all the never-enough-admired laws of pain and pleasure, and the instincts or natural inclinations, appetites, and passions of animals—I say if we consider all these things, and at the same time attend to the meaning and import of the attributes One, Eternal, In-

finitely Wise, Good, and Perfect, we shall clearly perceive that they belong to the aforesaid Spirit, " who works all in all," and " by whom all things consist."

147. Hence, it is evident that God is known as certainly and immediately as any other mind or spirit whatsoever distinct from ourselves. We may even assert that the existence of God is far more evidently perceived than the existence of men; because the effects of Nature are infinitely more numerous and considerable than those ascribed to human agents. There is not any one mark that denotes a man, or effect produced by him, which does not more strongly evince the being of that Spirit who is the Author of Nature. For, it is evident that in affecting other persons the will of man has no other object than barely the motion of the limbs of his body; but that such a motion should be attended by, or excite any idea in the mind of another, depends wholly on the will of the Creator. He alone it is who, " upholding all things by the word of His power," maintains that intercourse between spirits whereby they are able to perceive the existence of each other. And yet this pure and clear light which enlightens every one is itself invisible.

148. It seems to be a general pretence of the unthinking herd that they cannot *see* God. Could we but see Him, say they, as we see a man, we should believe that He is, and believing obey His commands. But alas, we need only open our eyes to see the Sovereign Lord of all things, with a more full and clear view than we do any one of our fellow-creatures. Not that I imagine we see God (as some will have it) by a direct and immediate view; or see corporeal things, not by themselves, but by seeing that which represents them in the essence of God, which doctrine is, I must confess, to me incomprehensible. But I shall explain my meaning:—A human spirit or person is not perceived by sense, as not being an idea; when therefore we see the colour, size, figure, and motions of a man, we perceive only

certain sensations or ideas excited in our own minds; and these being exhibited to our view in sundry distinct collections, serve to mark out unto us the existence of finite and created spirits like ourselves. Hence it is plain we do not *see* a man—if by *man* is meant that which lives, moves, perceives, and thinks as we do—but only such a certain collection of ideas as directs us to think there is a distinct principle of thought and motion, like to ourselves, accompanying and represented by it. And after the same manner we *see* God; all the difference is that, whereas some one finite and narrow assemblage of ideas denotes a particular human mind, whithersoever we direct our view, we do at all times and in all places perceive manifest tokens of the Divinity—everything we see, hear, feel, or anywise perceive by Sense, being a *sign* or *effect* of the power of God; as is our perception of those very motions which are produced by men.

149. It is therefore plain that nothing can be more evident to any one that is capable of the least reflection than the existence of God, or a Spirit who is intimately present to our minds—producing in them all that variety of ideas or sensations which continually affect us, on whom we have an absolute and entire dependence, in short " in whom we live, and move, and have our being." That the discovery of this great truth, which lies so near and obvious to the mind, should be attained to by the reason of so very few, is a sad instance of the stupidity and inattention of men, who, though they are surrounded with such clear manifestations of the Deity, are yet so little affected by them that they seem, as it were, blinded with excess of light.

150. But you will say, Hath Nature no share in the production of natural things, and must they be all ascribed to the immediate and sole operation of God? I answer, if by *Nature* is meant only the *visible series* of *effects or sensations* imprinted on our minds, according to certain fixed and general laws, then it is plain that Nature, taken in this

sense, cannot produce anything at all. But, if by *Nature* is meant some being distinct from God, as well as from the laws of nature, and things perceived by sense, I must confess that word is to me an empty sound without any intelligible meaning annexed to it. Nature, in this acceptation, is a vain chimera, introduced by those heathens who had not just notions of the omnipresence and infinite perfection of God. But, it is more unaccountable that it should be received among Christians, professing belief in the Holy Scriptures, which constantly ascribe those effects to the immediate hand of God that heathen philosophers are wont to impute to Nature. "The Lord He causeth the vapours to ascend; He maketh lightnings with rain; He bringeth forth the wind out of His treasures." Jerem. **x.** 13. "He turneth the shadow of death into the morning, and maketh the day dark with night." Amos v. 8. "He visiteth the earth, and maketh it soft with showers: He blesseth the springing thereof, and crowneth the year with His goodness; so that the pastures are clothed with flocks, and the valleys are covered over with corn." See Psal. lxv. But, notwithstanding that this is the constant language of Scripture, yet we have I know not what aversion from believing that God concerns Himself so nearly in our affairs. Fain would we suppose Him at a great distance off, and substitute some *blind unthinking* deputy in His stead, though (if we may believe Saint Paul) "He be not far from every one of us."

151. It will, I doubt not, be objected that the slow, gradual, and roundabout methods observed in the production of natural things do not seem to have for their cause the *immediate* hand of an Almighty Agent. Besides, monsters, untimely births, fruits blasted in the blossom, rains falling in desert places, miseries incident to human life, and the like, are so many arguments that the whole frame of nature is not immediately actuated and superintended by a Spirit of infinite wisdom and goodness. But the answer to this objection is in a good measure plain

from sect. 62; it being visible that the aforesaid Methods of Nature are absolutely necessary, in order to working by the most simple and general rules, and after a steady and consistent manner; which argues both the wisdom and goodness of God. Such is the artificial contrivance of this mighty Machine of Nature that, whilst its motions and various phenomena strike on our senses, the hand which actuates the whole is itself unperceivable to men of flesh and blood. " Verily " (saith the prophet) " thou art a God that hidest thyself." Isaiah xlv. 15. But, though the Lord conceal Himself from the eyes of the sensual and lazy, who will not be at the least expense of thought, yet to an unbiased and attentive mind nothing can be more plainly legible than the intimate presence of an All-wise Spirit, who fashions, regulates and sustains the whole system of beings. It is clear, from what we have elsewhere observed, that the operating according to general and stated laws is so necessary for our guidance in the affairs of Life, and letting us into the secret of Nature, that without it all reach and compass of thought, all human sagacity and design, could serve to no manner of purpose; it were even impossible there should be any such faculties or powers in the mind. See sect. 31. Which one consideration abundantly outbalances whatever particular inconveniences may thence arise.

152. But we should further consider that the very blemishes and defects of Nature are not without their use, in that they make an agreeable sort of variety, and augment the beauty of the rest of the creation, as shades in a picture serve to set off the brighter and more enlightened parts. We would likewise do well to examine whether our taxing the waste of seeds and embryos, and accidental destruction of plants and animals, before they come to full maturity, as an imprudence in the Author of Nature, be not the effect of prejudice contracted by our familiarity with impotent and saving mortals. In man indeed a thrifty management of those things which he cannot procure without much

pains and industry may be esteemed wisdom. But, we must not imagine that the inexplicably fine machine of an animal or vegetable costs the great Creator any more pains or trouble in its production than a pebble does; nothing being more evident than that an Omnipotent Spirit can indifferently produce everything by a mere *fiat* or act of his will. Hence, it is plain that the splendid profusion of natural things should not be interpreted weakness or prodigality in the agent who produces them, but rather be looked on as an argument of the riches of his power.

153. As for the mixture of pain or uneasiness which is in the world, pursuant to the general Laws of Nature, and the actions of finite, imperfect spirits, this, in the state we are in at present, is indispensably necessary to our well-being. But our prospects are too narrow. We take, for instance, the idea of some one particular pain into our thoughts, and account *it* evil; whereas, if we enlarge our view, so as to comprehend the various ends, connexions, and dependencies of things, on what occasions and in what proportions we are affected with pain and pleasure, the nature of human freedom, and the design with which we are put into the world; we shall be forced to acknowledge that those particular things which, considered in themselves, appear to be evil, have the nature of good, when considered as linked with the whole system of beings.

154. From what has been said, it will be manifest to any considering person, that it is merely for want of attention and comprehensiveness of mind that there are any favourers of Atheism or the Manichæan Heresy to be found. Little and unreflecting souls may indeed burlesque the works of Providence—the beauty and order whereof they have not capacity, or will not be at the pains, to comprehend; but those who are masters of any justness and extent of thought, and are withal used to reflect, can never sufficiently admire the divine traces of Wisdom and Goodness that shine throughout the Economy of Nature. But what truth is there which glares so strongly on the mind

that, by an aversion of thought—a wilful shutting of the eyes—we may not escape seeing it, at least with a full and direct view? Is it therefore to be wondered at, if the generality of men, who are ever intent on business or pleasure, and little used to fix or open the eye of their mind, should not have all that conviction and evidence of the Being of God which might be expected in reasonable creatures?

155. We should rather wonder that men can be found so stupid as to neglect, than that neglecting they should be unconvinced of such an evident and momentous truth. And yet it is to be feared that too many of parts and leisure, who live in Christian countries, are, merely through a supine and dreadful negligence, sunk into Atheism. They cannot say there is not a God, but neither are they convinced that there is. Since it is downright impossible that a soul pierced and enlightened with a thorough sense of the omnipresence, holiness, and justice of that Almighty Spirit should persist in a remorseless violation of His laws. We ought, therefore, earnestly to meditate and dwell on those important points; that so we may attain conviction without all scruple " that the eyes of the Lord are in every place beholding the evil and the good; that He is with us and keepeth us in all places whither we go, and giveth us bread to eat and raiment to put on "; that He is present and conscious to our innermost thoughts; in fine, that we have a most absolute and immediate dependence on Him. A clear view of which great truths cannot choose but fill our hearts with an awful circumspection and holy fear, which is the strongest incentive to VIRTUE and the best guard against VICE.

156. For, after all, what deserves the first place in our studies is the consideration of GOD and our DUTY; which to promote, as it was the main drift and design of my labours, so shall I esteem them altogether useless and ineffectual if, by what I have said, I cannot inspire my readers with a pious Sense of the Presence of God; and, having

shewn the falseness or vanity of those barren speculations which make the chief employment of learned men, the better dispose them to reverence and embrace the salutary truths of the Gospel, which to know and to practise is the highest perfection of human nature.

THREE DIALOGUES
BETWEEN HYLAS AND PHILONOUS,

IN OPPOSITION TO SCEPTICS
AND ATHEISTS

THE FIRST DIALOGUE

Philonous. Good morrow, Hylas: I did not expect to find you abroad so early.

Hylas. It is indeed something unusual: but my thoughts were so taken up with a subject I was discoursing of last night, that finding I could not sleep, I resolved to rise and take a turn in the garden.

Phil. It happened well, to let you see what innocent and agreeable pleasures you lose every morning. Can there be a pleasanter time of the day, or a more delightful season of the year? That purple sky, those wild but sweet notes of birds, the fragrant bloom upon the trees and flowers, the gentle influence of the rising sun, these and a thousand nameless beauties of nature inspire the soul with secret transports; its faculties too being at this time fresh and lively, are fit for these meditations, which the solitude of a garden and tranquillity of the morning naturally dispose us to. But I am afraid I interrupt your thoughts; for you seemed very intent on something.

Hyl. It is true, I was, and shall be obliged to you if you will permit me to go on in the same vein; not that I would by any means deprive myself of your company, for my thoughts always flow more easily in conversation with a friend, than when I am alone: but my request is, that you would suffer me to impart my reflections to you.

Phil. With all my heart, it is what I should have requested myself, if you had not prevented me.

Hyl. I was considering the odd fate of those men who have in all ages, through an affectation of being distinguished from the vulgar, or some unaccountable turn of thought, pretended either to believe nothing at all, or believe the most extravagant things in the world. This however might be borne, if their paradoxes and scepticism did not draw after them some consequences of general disadvantage to mankind. But the mischief lieth here, that when men of less leisure see them who are supposed to have spent their whole time in the pursuits of knowledge, professing an entire ignorance of all things, or advancing such notions as are repugnant to plain and commonly received principles, they will be tempted to entertain suspicions concerning the most important truths, which they had hitherto held sacred and unquestionable.

Phil. I entirely agree with you, as to the ill tendency of the affected doubts of some philosophers, and fantastical conceits of others. I am even so far gone of late in this way of thinking, that I have quitted several of the sublime notions I had got in their schools for vulgar opinions. And I give it you on my word, since this revolt from metaphysical notions to the plain dictates of nature and common sense, I find my understanding strangely enlightened, so that I can now easily comprehend a great many things which before were all mystery and riddle.

Hyl. I am glad to find there was nothing in the accounts I heard of you.

Phil. Pray, what were those?

Hyl. You were represented in last night's conversation, as one who maintained the most extravagant opinion that ever entered into the mind of man, to wit, that there is no such thing as *material substance* in the world.

Phil. That there is no such thing as what philosophers call *material substance,* I am seriously persuaded : but if I were made to see any thing absurd or sceptical in this, I should then have the same reason to renounce this, that I imagine I have now to reject the contrary opinion.

Hyl. What! can any thing be more fantastical, more repugnant to common sense, or a more manifest piece of scepticism, than to believe there is no such thing as *matter*?

Phil. Softly, good Hylas. What if it should prove, that

you who hold there is, are by virtue of that opinion a greater sceptic, and maintain more paradoxes and repugnancies to common sense, than I who believe no such thing?

Hyl. You may as soon persuade me, the part is greater than the whole, as that, in order to avoid absurdity and scepticism, I should ever be obliged to give up my opinion in this point.

Phil. Well then, are you content to admit that opinion for true, which upon examination shall appear most agreeable to common sense, and remote from scepticism?

Hyl. With all my heart. Since you are for raising disputes about the plainest things in nature, I am content for once to hear what you have to say.

Phil. Pray, Hylas, what do you mean by a *sceptic*?

Hyl. I mean what all men mean, one that doubts of every thing.

Phil. He then who entertains no doubt concerning some particular point, with regard to that point cannot be thought a *sceptic*.

Hyl. I agree with you.

Phil. Whether doth doubting consist in embracing the affirmative or negative side of a question?

Hyl. In neither; for whoever understands English, cannot but know that *doubting* signifies a suspense between both.

Phil. He then that denieth any point, can no more be said to doubt of it than he who affirmeth it with the same degree of assurance.

Hyl. True.

Phil. And consequently, for such his denial is no more to be esteemed a *sceptic* than the other.

Hyl. I acknowledge it.

Phil. How cometh it to pass then, Hylas, that you pronounce me a *sceptic*, because I deny what you affirm, to wit, the existence of matter? Since, for aught you can tell,

I am as peremptory in my denial, as you in your affirmation.

Hyl. Hold, Philonous, I have been a little out in my definition; but every false step a man makes in discourse is not to be insisted on. I said, indeed, that a *sceptic* was one who doubted of every thing; but I should have added, or who denies the reality and truth of things.

Phil. What things? Do you mean the principles and theorems of sciences? but these you know are universal intellectual notions, and consequently independent of matter; the denial therefore of this doth not imply the denying them.

Hyl. I grant it. But are there no other things? What think you of distrusting the senses, of denying the real existence of sensible things, or pretending to know nothing of them? Is not this sufficient to denominate a man a *sceptic*?

Phil. Shall we therefore examine which of us it is that denies the reality of sensible things, or professes the greatest ignorance of them; since, if I take you rightly, he is to be esteemed the greatest *sceptic*?

Hyl. That is what I desire.

Phil. What mean you by sensible things?

Hyl. Those things which are perceived by the senses. Can you imagine that I mean any thing else?

Phil. Pardon me, Hylas, if I am desirous clearly to apprehend your notions, since this may much shorten our inquiry. Suffer me then to ask you this further question. Are those things only perceived by the senses which are perceived immediately? or may those things properly be said to be *sensible*, which are perceived mediately, or not without the intervention of others?

Hyl. I do not sufficiently understand you.

Phil. In reading a book, what I immediately perceive are the letters, but mediately, or by means of these, are suggested to my mind the notions of God, virtue, truth, &c. Now that the letters are truly sensible things, or perceived by sense, there is no doubt: but I would know whether you take the things suggested by them to be so too.

Hyl. No, certainly, it were absurd to think *God* or *virtue* sensible things, though they may be signified and suggested to the mind by sensible marks, with which they have an arbitrary connexion.

Phil. It seems then, that by *sensible things* you mean those only which can be perceived immediately by sense.

Hyl. Right.

Phil. Doth it not follow from this, that though I see one part of the sky red, and another blue, and that my reason doth thence evidently conclude there must be some cause of that diversity of colours, yet that cause cannot be said to be a sensible thing, or perceived by the sense of seeing?

Hyl. It doth.

Phil. In like manner, though I hear variety of sounds, yet I cannot be said to hear the causes of those sounds.

Hyl. You cannot.

Phil. And when by my touch I perceive a thing to be hot and heavy, I cannot say with any truth or propriety, that I feel the cause of its heat or weight.

Hyl. To prevent any more questions of this kind, I tell you once for all, that by *sensible things* I mean those only which are perceived by sense, and that in truth the senses perceive nothing which they do not perceive immediately: for they make no inferences. The deducing therefore of causes or occasions from effects and appearances, which alone are perceived by sense, entirely relates to reason.

Phil. This point then is agreed between us, that *sensible things are those only which are immediately perceived by sense*. You will further inform me, whether we immediately perceive by sight any thing beside light, and colours, and figures: or by hearing any thing but sounds: by the palate, any thing besides tastes: by the smell, besides odours: or by the touch, more than tangible qualities.

Hyl. We do not.

Phil. It seems therefore, that if you take away all sensible qualities, there remains nothing sensible.

Hyl. I grant it.

Phil. Sensible things therefore are nothing else but so many sensible qualities, or combinations of sensible qualities.

Hyl. Nothing else.

Phil. Heat then is a sensible thing.

Hyl. Certainly.

Phil. Doth the reality of sensible things consist in being perceived? or is it something distinct from their being perceived, and that bears no relation to the mind?

Hyl. To *exist* is one thing, and to be *perceived* is another.

Phil. I speak with regard to sensible things only; and of these I ask, whether by their real existence you mean a subsistence exterior to the mind, and distinct from their being perceived?

Hyl. I mean a real absolute being, distinct from, and without any relation to their being perceived.

Phil. Heat, therefore, if it be allowed a real being, must exist without the mind.

Hyl. It must.

Phil. Tell me, Hylas, is this real existence equally compatible to all degrees of heat, which we perceive : or is there any reason why we should attribute it to some, and deny it others? and if there be, pray let me know that reason.

Hyl. Whatever degree of heat we perceive by sense, we may be sure the same exists in the object that occasions it.

Phil. What, the greatest as well as the least?

Hyl. I tell you, the reason is plainly the same in respect of both : they are both perceived by sense; nay, the greater degree of heat is more sensibly perceived; and consequently, if there is any difference, we are more certain of its real existence than we can be of the reality of a lesser degree.

Phil. But is not the most vehement and intense degree of heat a very great pain?

Hyl. No one can deny it.

Phil. And is any unperceiving thing capable of pain or pleasure?

Hyl. No, certainly.

Phil. Is your material substance a senseless being, or a being endowed with sense and perception?

Hyl. It is senseless without doubt.

Phil. It cannot therefore be the subject of pain.

Hyl. By no means.

Phil. Nor consequently of the greatest heat perceived by sense, since you acknowledge this to be no small pain.

Hyl. I grant it.

Phil. What shall we say then of your external object; is it a material substance, or no?

Hyl. It is a material substance with the sensible qualities inhering in it.

Phil. How then can a great heat exist in it, since you own it cannot in a material substance? I desire you would clear this point.

Hyl. Hold, Philonous; I fear I was out in yielding intense heat to be a pain. It should seem rather, that pain is something distinct from heat, and the consequence or effect of it.

Phil. Upon putting your hand near the fire, do you perceive one simple uniform sensation, or two distinct sensations?

Hyl. But one simple sensation.

Phil. Is not the heat immediately perceived?

Hyl. It is.

Phil. And the pain?

Hyl. True.

Phil. Seeing therefore they are both immediately perceived at the same time, and the fire affects you only with one simple, or uncompounded idea, it follows that this same simple idea is both the intense heat immediately perceived, and the pain; and consequently, that the intense heat immediately perceived, is nothing distinct from a particular sort of pain.

Hyl. It seems so.

Phil. Again, try in your thoughts, Hylas, if you can conceive a vehement sensation to be without pain, or pleasure.

Hyl. I cannot.

Phil. Or can you frame to yourself an idea of sensible pain or pleasure in general, abstracted from every particular idea of heat, cold, tastes, smells, &c.?

Hyl. I do not find that I can.

Phil. Doth it not therefore follow, that sensible pain is nothing distinct from those sensations or ideas, in an intense degree?

Hyl. It is undeniable; and to speak the truth, I begin to suspect a very great heat cannot exist but in a mind perceiving it.

Phil. What! are you then in that *sceptical* state of suspense, between affirming and denying?

Hyl. I think I may be positive in the point. A very violent and painful heat cannot exist without the mind.

Phil. It hath not therefore, according to you, any real being.

Hyl. I own it.

Phil. Is it therefore certain, that there is no body in nature really hot?

Hyl. I have not denied there is any real heat in bodies. I only say, there is no such thing as an intense real heat.

Phil. But did you not say before, that all degrees of heat were equally real: or if there was any difference, that the greater were more undoubtedly real than the lesser?

Hyl. True: but it was, because I did not then consider the ground there is for distinguishing between them, which I now plainly see. And it is this: because intense heat is nothing else but a particular kind of painful sensation; and pain cannot exist but in a perceiving being; it follows that no intense heat can really exist in an unperceiving corporeal substance. But this is no reason why we should deny heat in an inferior degree to exist in such a substance.

Phil. But how shall we be able to discern those degrees of heat which exist only in the mind, from those which exist without it?

Hyl. That is no difficult matter. You know, the least pain cannot exist unperceived; whatever therefore degree of heat is a pain, exists only in the mind. But as for all other degrees of heat, nothing obliges us to think the same of them.

Phil. I think you granted before, that no unperceiving being was capable of pleasure, any more than of pain.

Hyl. I did.

Phil. And is not warmth, or a more gentle degree of heat than what causes uneasiness, a pleasure?

Hyl. What then?

Phil. Consequently it cannot exist without the mind in any unperceiving substance, or body.

Hyl. So it seems.

Phil. Since therefore, as well those degrees of heat that are not painful, as those that are, can exist only in a thinking substance; may we not conclude that external bodies are absolutely incapable of any degree of heat whatsoever?

Hyl. On second thoughts, I do not think it so evident that warmth is a pleasure, as that a great degree of heat is a pain.

Phil. I do not pretend that warmth is as great a pleasure as heat is a pain. But if you grant it to be even a small pleasure, it serves to make good my conclusion.

Hyl. I could rather call it an *indolence*. It seems to be nothing more than a privation of both pain and pleasure. And that such a quality or state as this may agree to an unthinking substance, I hope you will not deny.

Phil. If you are resolved to maintain that warmth, or a

gentle degree of heat, is no pleasure, I know not how to convince you otherwise, than by appealing to your own sense. But what think you of cold?

Hyl. The same that I do of heat. An intense degree of cold is a pain; for to feel a very great cold, is to perceive a great uneasiness : it cannot therefore exist without the mind; but a lesser degree of cold may, as well as a lesser degree of heat.

Phil. Those bodies therefore, upon whose application to our own we perceive a moderate degree of heat, must be concluded to have a moderate degree of heat or warmth in them; and those, upon whose application we feel a like degree of cold, must be thought to have cold in them.

Hyl. They must.

Phil. Can any doctrine be true that necessarily leads a man into an absurdity?

Hyl. Without doubt it cannot.

Phil. Is it not an absurdity to think that the same thing should be at the same time both cold and warm?

Hyl. It is.

Phil. Suppose now one of your hands hot, and the other cold, and that they are both at once put into the same vessel of water, in an intermediate state; will not the water seem cold to one hand, and warm to the other?

Hyl. It will.

Phil. Ought we not therefore by your principles to conclude, it is really both cold and warm at the same time, that is, according to your own concession, to believe an absurdity?

Hyl. I confess it seems so.

Phil. Consequently, the principles themselves are false, since you have granted that no true principle leads to an absurdity.

Hyl. But after all, can any thing be more absurd than to say, *there is no heat in the fire*?

Phil. To make the point still clearer; tell me, whether

in two cases exactly alike, we ought not to make the same judgment?

Hyl. We ought.

Phil. When a pin pricks your finger, doth it not rend and divide the fibres of your flesh?

Hyl. It doth.

Phil. And when a coal burns your finger, doth it any more?

Hyl. It doth not.

Phil. Since therefore you neither judge the sensation itself occasioned by the pin, nor any thing like it to be in the pin; you should not, conformably to what you have now granted, judge the sensation occasioned by the fire, or any thing like it, to be in the fire.

Hyl. Well, since it must be so, I am content to yield this point, and acknowledge, that heat and cold are only sensations existing in our minds : but there still remain qualities enough to secure the reality of external things.

Phil. But what will you say, Hylas, if it shall appear that the case is the same with regard to all other sensible qualities, and that they can no more be supposed to exist without the mind, than heat and cold?

Hyl. Then indeed you will have done something to the purpose; but that is what I despair of seeing proved.

Phil. Let us examine them in order. What think you of tastes, do they exist without the mind, or no?

Hyl. Can any man in his senses doubt whether sugar is sweet, or wormwood bitter?

Phil. Inform me, Hylas. Is a sweet taste a particular kind of pleasure or pleasant sensation, or is it not?

Hyl. It is.

Phil. And is not bitterness some kind of uneasiness or pain?

Hyl. I grant it.

Phil. If therefore sugar and wormwood are unthinking corporeal substances existing without the mind, how can sweetness and bitterness, that is, pleasure and pain, agree to them?

Hyl. Hold, Philonous; I now see what it was deluded me all this time. You asked whether heat and cold, sweetness and bitterness, were not particular sorts of pleasure and pain; to which I answered simply, that they were. Whereas I should have thus distinguished : those qualities, as perceived by us, are pleasures or pains, but not as existing in the external objects. We must not therefore conclude absolutely, that there is no heat in the fire, or sweetness in the sugar, but only that heat or sweetness, as perceived by us, are not in the fire or sugar. What say you to this?

Phil. I say it is nothing to the purpose. Our discourse proceeded altogether concerning sensible things, which you defined to be the things we *immediately perceive by our senses*. Whatever other qualities therefore you speak of, as distinct from these, I know nothing of them, neither do they at all belong to the point in dispute. You may indeed pretend to have discovered certain qualities which you do not perceive, and assert those insensible qualities exist in fire and sugar. But what use can be made of this to your present purpose, I am at a loss to conceive. Tell me then once more, do you acknowledge that heat and cold, sweetness and bitterness (meaning those qualities which are perceived by the senses), do not exist without the mind?

Hyl. I see it is to no purpose to hold out, so I give up the cause as to those mentioned qualities. Though I profess it sounds oddly, to say that sugar is not sweet.

Phil. But for your further satisfaction, take this along with you : that which at other times seems sweet, shall to a distempered palate appear bitter. And nothing can be plainer, than that divers persons perceive different tastes in the same food, since that which one man delights in, another abhors. And how could this be, if the taste was something really inherent in the food?

Hyl. I acknowledge I know not how.

Phil. In the next place, odours are to be considered.

And with regard to these, I would fain know, whether what hath been said of tastes doth not exactly agree to them? Are they not so many pleasing or displeasing sensations?

Hyl. They are.

Phil. Can you then conceive it possible that they should exist in an unperceiving thing?

Hyl. I cannot.

Phil. Or can you imagine, that filth and ordure affect those brute animals that feed on them out of choice, with the same smells which we perceive in them?

Hyl. By no means.

Phil. May we not therefore conclude of smells, as of the other forementioned qualities, that they cannot exist in any but a perceiving substance or mind?

Hyl. I think so.

Phil. Then as to sounds, what must we think of them: are they accidents really inherent in external bodies, or not?

Hyl. That they inhere not in the sonorous bodies, is plain from hence; because a bell struck in the exhausted receiver of an air-pump, sends forth no sound. The air therefore must be thought the subject of sound.

Phil. What reason is there for that, Hylas?

Hyl. Because when any motion is raised in the air, we perceive a sound greater or lesser, in proportion to the air's motion; but without some motion in the air, we never hear any sound at all.

Phil. And granting that we never hear a sound but when some motion is produced in the air, yet I do not see how you can infer from thence, that the sound itself is in the air.

Hyl. It is this very motion in the external air, that produces in the mind the sensation of *sound*. For striking on the drum of the ear, it causeth a vibration, which by the auditory nerves being communicated to the brain, the soul is thereupon affected with the sensation called *sound*.

Phil. What! is sound then a sensation?

Hyl. I tell you, as perceived by us, it is a particular sensation in the mind.

Phil. And can any sensation exist without the mind?

Hyl. No, certainly.

Phil. How then can sound, being a sensation, exist in the air, if by the *air* you mean a senseless substance existing without the mind.

Hyl. You must distinguish, Philonous, between sound, as it is perceived by us, and as it is in itself; or, (which is the same thing) between the sound we immediately perceive, and that which exists without us. The former indeed is a particular kind of sensation, but the latter is merely a vibrative or undulatory motion in the air.

Phil. I thought I had already obviated that distinction by the answer I gave when you were applying it in a like case before. But to say no more of that: are you sure then that sound is really nothing but motion?

Hyl. I am.

Phil. Whatever therefore agrees to real sound, may with truth be attributed to motion.

Hyl. It may.

Phil. It is then good sense to speak of *motion*, as of a thing that is *loud, sweet, acute,* or *grave.*

Hyl. I see you are resolved not to understand me. Is it not evident, those accidents or modes belong only to sensible sound, or *sound* in the common acceptation of the word, but not to *sound* in the real and philosophic sense, which, as I just now told you, is nothing but a certain motion of the air?

Phil. It seems then there are two sorts of sound, the one vulgar, or that which is heard, the other philosophical and real.

Hyl. Even so.

Phil. And the latter consists in motion.

Hyl. I told you so before.

Phil. Tell me, Hylas, to which of the senses, think you, the idea of motion belongs : to the hearing?

Hyl. No, certainly, but to the sight and touch.

Phil. It should follow then, that according to you, real sounds may possibly be *seen* or *felt,* but never *heard.*

Hyl. Look you, Philonous, you may if you please make a jest of my opinion, but that will not alter the truth of things. I own, indeed, the inferences you draw me into sound something oddly : but common language, you know, is framed by, and for the use of the vulgar : we must not therefore wonder, if expressions adapted to exact philosophic notions, seem uncouth and out of the way.

Phil. Is it come to that? I assure you, I imagine myself to have gained no small point, since you make so light of departing from common phrases and opinions; it being a main part of our inquiry, to examine whose notions are widest of the common road, and most repugnant to the general sense of the world. But can you think it no more than a philosophical paradox, to say that *real sounds are never heard,* and that the idea of them is obtained by some other sense. And is there nothing in this contrary to nature and the truth of things?

Hyl. To deal ingenuously, I do not like it. And after the concessions already made, I had as well grant that sounds too have no real being without the mind.

Phil. And I hope you will make no difficulty to acknowledge the same of colours.

Hyl. Pardon me; the case of colours is very different. Can any thing be plainer, than that we see them on the objects?

Phil. The objects you speak of are, I suppose, corporeal substances existing without the mind.

Hyl. They are.

Phil. And have true and real colours inhering in them?

Hyl. Each visible object hath that colour which we see in it.

Phil. How! is there any thing visible but what we perceive by sight?

Hyl. There is not.

Phil. And do we perceive any thing by sense, which we do not perceive immediately?

Hyl. How often must I be obliged to repeat the same thing? I tell you, we do not.

Phil. Have patience, good Hylas; and tell me once more whether there is any thing immediately perceived by the senses, except sensible qualities. I know you asserted there was not: but I would now be informed, whether you still persist in the same opinion.

Hyl. I do.

Phil. Pray, is your corporeal substance either a sensible quality or made up of sensible qualities?

Hyl. What a question that is! who ever thought it was?

Phil. My reason for asking was, because in saying, *each visible object hath that colour which we see in it,* you make visible objects to be corporeal substances; which implies either that corporeal substances are sensible qualities, or else that there is something beside sensible qualities perceived by sight: but as this point was formerly agreed between us, and is still maintained by you, it is a clear consequence, that your corporeal substance is nothing distinct from sensible qualities.

Hyl. You may draw as many absurd consequences as you please, and endeavour to perplex the plainest things; but you shall never persuade me out of my senses. I clearly understand my own meaning.

Phil. I wish you would make me understand it too. But since you are unwilling to have your notion of corporeal substance examined, I shall urge that point no further. Only be pleased to let me know, whether the same colours which we see, exist in external bodies, or some other.

Hyl. The very same.

Phil. What! are then the beautiful red and purple we see on yonder clouds, really in them? Or do you imagine they have in themselves any other form than that of a dark mist or vapour?

Hyl. I must own, Philonous, those colours are not really in the clouds as they seem to be at this distance. They are only apparent colours.

Phil. *Apparent* call you them? how shall we distinguish these apparent colours from real?

Hyl. Very easily. Those are to be thought apparent, which, appearing only at a distance, vanish upon a nearer approach.

Phil. And those I suppose are to be thought real, which are discovered by the most near and exact survey.

Hyl. Right.

Phil. Is the nearest and exactest survey made by the help of a microscope, or by the naked eye?

Hyl. By a microscope, doubtless.

Phil. But a microscope often discovers colours in an object different from those perceived by the unassisted sight. And in case we had microscopes magnifying to any assigned degree; it is certain, that no object whatsoever viewed through them, would appear in the same colour which it exhibits to the naked eye.

Hyl. And what will you conclude from all this? You cannot argue that there are really and naturally no colours on objects; because by artificial managements they may be altered, or made to vanish.

Phil. I think it may evidently be concluded from your own concessions, that all the colours we see with our naked eyes, are only apparent as those on the clouds, since they vanish upon a more close and accurate inspection, which is afforded us by a microscope. Then as to what you say by way of prevention; I ask you, whether the real and natural state of an object is better discovered by a very sharp and piercing sight, or by one which is less sharp.

Hyl. By the former without doubt.

Phil. Is it not plain from *dioptrics*, that microscopes make the sight more penetrating, and represent objects as

they would appear to the eye, in case it were naturally
endowed with a most exquisite sharpness?

Hyl. It is.

Phil. Consequently the microscopical representation is
to be thought that which best sets forth the real nature of
the thing, or what it is in itself. The colours therefore by it
perceived, are more genuine and real, than those perceived
otherwise.

Hyl. I confess there is something in what you say.

Phil. Besides, it is not only possible but manifest, that
there actually are animals, whose eyes are by nature framed
to perceive those things, which by reason of their minute-
ness escape our sight. What think you of those inconceiv-
ably small animals perceived by glasses? Must we suppose
they are all stark blind? Or, in case they see, can it be
imagined their sight hath not the same use in preserving
their bodies from injuries, which appears in that of all other
animals? And if it hath, is it not evident they must see
particles less than their own bodies, which will present
them with a far different view in each object, from that
which strikes our senses? Even our own eyes do not
always represent objects to us after the same manner. In
the *jaundice*, every one knows that all things seem yellow.
Is it not therefore highly probable, those animals in whose
eyes we discern a very different texture from that of ours,
and whose bodies abound with different humours, do not
see the same colours in every object that we do? From all
of which, should it not seem to follow that all colours are
equally apparent, and that none of those which we perceive are really inherent in any outward object?

Hyl. It should.

Phil. The point will be past all doubt, if you consider,
that in case colours were real properties or affections inherent in external bodies, they could admit of no alteration,
without some change wrought in the very bodies themselves; but is it not evident from what hath been said, that
upon the use of microscopes, upon a change happening in

the humours of the eye, or a variation of distance, without any manner of real alteration in the thing itself, the colours of any object are either changed, or totally disappear? Nay, all other circumstances remaining the same, change but the situation of some objects, and they shall present different colours to the eye. The same thing happens upon viewing an object in various degrees of light. And what is more known, than that the same bodies appear differently coloured by candle-light from what they do in the open day? Add to these the experiments of a prism, which, separating the heterogeneous rays of light, alters the colour of any object; and will cause the whitest to appear of a deep blue or red to the naked eye. And now tell me, whether you are still of opinion, that every body hath its true, real colour inhering in it; and if you think it hath, I would fain know further from you, what certain distance and position of the object, what peculiar texture and formation of the eye, what degree or kind of light is necessary for ascertaining that true colour, and distinguishing it from apparent ones.

Hyl. I own myself entirely satisfied, that they are all equally apparent; and that there is no such thing as colour really inhering in external bodies, but that it is altogether in the light. And what confirms me in this opinion, is, that in proportion to the light, colours are still more or less vivid; and if there be no light, then are there no colours perceived. Besides, allowing there are colours on external objects, yet how is it possible for us to perceive them? For no external body affects the mind, unless it act first on our organs of sense. But the only action of bodies is motion; and motion cannot be communicated otherwise than by impulse. A distant object therefore cannot act on the eye, nor consequently make itself or its properties perceivable to the soul. Whence it plainly follows, that it is immediately some contiguous substance, which operating on the eye occasions a perception of colours: and such is light.

Phil. How! is light then a substance?

Hyl. I tell you, Philonous, external light is nothing but a thin fluid substance, whose minute particles being agitated with a brisk motion, and in various manners reflected from the different surfaces of outward objects to the eyes, communicate different motions to the optic nerves; which being propagated to the brain, cause therein various impressions : and these are attended with the sensations of red, blue, yellow, &c.

Phil. It seems, then, the light doth no more than shake the optic nerves.

Hyl. Nothing else.

Phil. And consequent to each particular motion of the nerves the mind is affected with a sensation, which is some particular colour.

Hyl. Right.

Phil. And these sensations have no existence without the mind.

Hyl. They have not.

Phil. How then do you affirm that colours are in the light, since by *light* you understand a corporeal substance external to the mind?

Hyl. Light and colours, as immediately perceived by us, I grant cannot exist without the mind. But in themselves they are only the motions and configurations of certain insensible particles of matter.

Phil. Colours then, in the vulgar sense, or taken for the immediate objects of sight, cannot agree to any but a perceiving substance.

Hyl. That is what I say.

Phil. Well then, since you give up the point as to those sensible qualities, which are alone thought colours by all mankind beside, you may hold what you please with regard to those invisible ones of the philosophers. It is not my business to dispute about them; only I would advise you to bethink yourself, whether, considering the inquiry we are upon, it be prudent for you to affirm *the red and blue which we see are not real colours, but certain un-known motions and figures which no man ever did or can see, are truly so.* Are not these shocking notions, and are not they subject to as many ridiculous inferences, as those you were obliged to renounce before in the case of sounds?

Hyl. I frankly own, Philonous, that it is in vain to stand out any longer. Colours, sounds, tastes, in a word, all those termed *secondary qualities,* have certainly no exist-ence without the mind. But by this acknowledgment I must not be supposed to derogate any thing from the reality of matter or external objects, seeing it is no more than several philosophers maintain, who nevertheless are the furthest imaginable from denying matter. For the clearer understanding of this, you must know sensible qualities are by philosophers divided into *primary* and *secondary.* The former are extension, figure, solidity, gravity, motion, and rest. And these they hold exist really in bodies. The latter are those above enumerated; or briefly, all sensible qualities beside the primary, which they assert are only so many sensations or ideas existing no where but in the mind. But all this, I doubt not, you are already apprised of. For my part, I have been a long time sensible there was such an opinion current among philosophers, but was never thoroughly convinced of its truth till now.

Phil. You are still then of opinion, that extension and figures are inherent in external unthinking substances.

Hyl. I am.

Phil. But what if the same arguments which are brought against secondary qualities, will hold proof against these also?

Hyl. Why then I shall be obliged to think, they too exist only in the mind.

Phil. Is it your opinion, the very figure and extension which you perceive by sense, exist in the outward object or material substance?

Hyl. It is.

Phil. Have all other animals as good grounds to think the same of the figure and extension which they see and feel?

Hyl. Without doubt, if they have any thought at all.

Phil. Answer me, Hylas. Think you the senses were bestowed upon all animals for their preservation and well-being in life? or were they given to men alone for this end?

Hyl. I make no question but they have the same use in all other animals.

Phil. If so, is it not necessary they should be enabled by them to perceive their own limbs, and those bodies which are capable of harming them?

Hyl. Certainly.

Phil. A mite therefore must be supposed to see his own foot, and things equal or even less than it, as bodies of some considerable dimension; though at the same time they appear to you scarce discernible, or at best as so many visible points.

Hyl. I cannot deny it.

Phil. And to creatures less than the mite they will seem yet larger.

Hyl. They will.

Phil. Insomuch that what you can hardly discern, will to another extremely minute animal appear as some huge mountain.

Hyl. All this I grant.

Phil. Can one and the same thing be at the same time in itself of different dimensions?

Hyl. That were absurd to imagine.

Phil. But from what you have laid down it follows, that both the extension by you perceived, and that perceived by the mite itself, as likewise all those perceived by lesser animals, are each of them the true extension of the mite's foot, that is to say, by your own principles you are led into an absurdity.

Hyl. There seems to be some difficulty in the point.

Phil. Again, have you not acknowledged that no real inherent property of any object can be changed, without some change in the thing itself?

Hyl. I have.

Phil. But as we approach to or recede from an object, the visible extension varies, being at one distance ten or a hundred times greater than at another. Doth it not therefore follow from hence likewise, that it is not really inherent in the object?

Hyl. I own I am at a loss what to think.

Phil. Your judgment will soon be determined, if you will venture to think as freely concerning this quality, as you have done concerning the rest. Was it not admitted as a good argument, that neither heat nor cold was in the water, because it seemed warm to one hand, and cold to the other?

Hyl. It was.

Phil. Is it not the very same reasoning to conclude, there is no extension or figure in an object, because to one eye it shall seem little, smooth, and round, when at the same time it appears to the other, great, uneven, and angular?

Hyl. The very same. But doth this latter fact ever happen?

Phil. You may at any time make the experiment, by looking with one eye bare, and with the other through a microscope.

Hyl. I know not how to maintain it, and yet I am loath to give up *extension,* I see so many odd consequences following upon such a concession.

Phil. Odd, say you? After the concessions already made, I hope you will stick at nothing for its oddness. But on the other hand should it not seem very odd, if the general reasoning which includes all other sensible qualities did not also include extension? If it be allowed that no idea nor any thing like an idea can exist in an unperceiving substance, then surely it follows, that no figure or mode of extension, which we can either perceive or imagine, or have any idea of, can be really inherent in matter; not to mention the peculiar difficulty there must be, in conceiving a material substance, prior to and distinct from extension, to be the *substratum* of extension. Be the sensible quality what it will, figure, or sound, or colour; it seems alike impossible it should subsist in that which doth not perceive it.

Hyl. I give up the point for the present, reserving still a right to retract my opinion, in case I shall hereafter discover any false step in my progress to it.

Phil. That is a right you cannot be denied. Figures and extension being despatched, we proceed next to *motion.* Can a real motion in any external body be at the same time both very swift and very slow?

Hyl. It cannot.

Phil. Is not the motion of a body swift in a reciprocal proportion to the time it takes up in describing any given space? Thus a body that describes a mile in an hour, moves three times faster than it would in case it described only a mile in three hours.

Hyl. I agree with you.

Phil. And is not time measured by the succession of ideas in our minds?

Hyl. It is.

Phil. And is it not possible ideas should succeed one another twice as fast in your mind, as they do in mine, or in that of some spirit of another kind?

Hyl. I own it.

Phil. Consequently the same body may to another seem to perform its motion over any space in half the time that it doth to you. And the same reasoning will hold as to any other proportion : that is to say, according to your principles (since the motions perceived are both really in the object) it is possible one and the same body shall be really moved the same way at once, both very swift and very slow. How is this consistent either with common sense, or with what you just now granted?

Hyl. I have nothing to say to it.

Phil. Then as for *solidity* : either you do not mean any sensible quality by that word, and so it is beside our inquiry : or if you do, it must be either hardness or resistance. But both the one and the other are plainly relative to our senses : it being evident, that what seems hard to one animal, may appear soft to another, who hath greater force and firmness of limbs. Nor is it less plain, that the resistance I feel is not in the body.

Hyl. I own the very sensation of resistance, which is all you immediately perceive, is not in the *body,* but the cause of that sensation is.

Phil. But the causes of our sensations are not things immediately perceived, and therefore not sensible. This point I thought had been already determined.

Hyl. I own it was; but you will pardon me if I seem a little embarrassed : I know not how to quit my old notions.

Phil. To help you out, do but consider, that if extension be once acknowledged to have no existence without the mind, the same must necessarily be granted of motion, solidity, and gravity, since they all evidently suppose extension. It is therefore superfluous to inquire particularly concerning each of them. In denying extension, you have denied them all to have any real existence.

Hyl. I wonder, Philonous, if what you say be true, why those philosophers who deny the secondary qualities any real existence, should yet attribute it to the primary. If there is no difference between them, how can this be accounted for?

Phil. It is not my business to account for every opinion of the philosophers. But among other reasons which may be assigned for this, it seems probable, that pleasure and pain being rather annexed to the former than the latter, may be one. Heat and cold, tastes and smells, have something more vividly pleasing or disagreeable than the

ideas of extension, figure, and motion, affect us with. And
it being too visibly absurd to hold, that pain or pleasure
can be in an unperceiving substance, men are more easily
weaned from believing the external existence of the
secondary, than the primary qualities. You will be satisfied there is something in this, if you recollect the difference you made between an intense and more moderate
degree of heat, allowing the one a real existence, while
you denied it to the other. But after all, there is no
rational ground for that distinction; for surely an indifferent sensation is as truly *a sensation,* as one more pleasing
or painful; and consequently should not any more than
they be supposed to exist in an unthinking object.

Hyl. It is just come into my head, Philonous, that I
have somewhere heard of a distinction between absolute
and sensible extension. Now though it be acknowledged
that *great* and *small,* consisting merely in the relation
which other extended beings have to the parts of our
own bodies, do not really inhere in the substances themselves; yet nothing obliges us to hold the same with regard
to *absolute extension,* which is something abstracted from
great and *small,* from this or that particular magnitude or
figure. So likewise as to motion, *swift* and *slow* are altogether relative to the succession of ideas in our own minds.
But it doth not follow, because those modifications of
motion exist not without the mind, that therefore absolute
motion abstracted from them doth not.

Phil. Pray what is it that distinguishes one motion, or
one part of extension from another? Is it not something
sensible, as some degree of swiftness or slowness, some
certain magnitude or figure peculiar to each?

Hyl. I think so.

Phil. These qualities therefore, stripped of all sensible
properties, are without all specific and numerical differences, as the schools call them.

Hyl. They are.

Phil. That is to say, they are extension in general, and motion in general.

Hyl. Let it be so.

Phil. But it is a universally received maxim, that *every thing which exists is particular.* How then can motion in general, or extension in general, exist in any corporeal substance?

Hyl. I will take time to solve your difficulty.

Phil. But I think the point may be speedily decided. Without doubt you can tell, whether you are able to frame this or that idea. Now I am content to put our dispute on this issue. If you can frame in your thoughts a distinct abstract idea of motion or extension, divested of all those sensible modes, as swift and slow, great and small, round and square, and the like, which are acknowledged to exist only in the mind, I will then yield the point you contend for. But if you cannot, it will be unreasonable on your side to insist any longer upon what you have no notion of.

Hyl. To confess ingenuously, I cannot.

Phil. Can you even separate the ideas of extension and motion, from the ideas of all those qualities which they who make the distinction term *secondary*?

Hyl. What! is it not an easy matter, to consider extension and motion by themselves, abstracted from all other sensible qualities? Pray how do the mathematicians treat of them?

Phil. I acknowledge, Hylas, it is not difficult to form general propositions and reasonings about those qualities, without mentioning any other; and in this sense to consider or treat of them abstractedly. But how doth it follow that because I can pronounce the word *motion* by itself, I can form the idea of it in my mind exclusive of body? Or because theorems may be made of extension and figures, without any mention of *great* or *small*, or any other sensible mode or quality; that therefore it is possible such an abstract idea of extension, without any particular size or figure, or sensible quality, should be distinctly formed, and apprehended by the mind? Mathematicians treat of quantity, without regarding what other sensible qualities it is attended with, as being altogether indifferent to their demonstrations. But when laying aside the words, they contemplate the bare ideas, I believe you will find, they are not the pure abstracted ideas of extension.

Hyl. But what say you to *pure intellect*? May not abstracted ideas be framed by that faculty?

Phil. Since I cannot frame abstract ideas at all, it is plain, I cannot frame them by the help of *pure intellect,* whatsoever faculty you understand by those words. Besides—not to inquire into the nature of pure intellect and its spiritual objects, as *virtue, reason, God,* or the like— thus much seems manifest, that sensible things are only to be perceived by sense, or represented by the imagination. Figures therefore and extension, being originally perceived by sense, do not belong to pure intellect. But for your further satisfaction, try if you can frame the idea of any figure, abstracted from all particularities of size, or even from other sensible qualities.

Hyl. Let me think a little——I do not find that I can.

Phil. And can you think it possible, that should really exist in nature, which implies a repugnancy in its conception?

Hyl. By no means.

Phil. Since therefore it is impossible even for the mind to disunite the ideas of extension and motion from all other sensible qualities, doth it not follow, that where the one exist, there necessarily the other exist likewise?

Hyl. It should seem so.

Phil. Consequently the very same arguments which you admitted, as conclusive against the secondary qualities, are without any further application of force against the primary too. Besides, if you will trust your senses, is it not plain all sensible qualities co-exist, or to them appear as being in the same place? Do they ever represent a motion, or figure, as being divested of all other visible and tangible qualities?

Hyl. You need say no more on this head. I am free to own, if there be no secret error or oversight in our proceedings hitherto, that all sensible qualities are alike to be denied existence without the mind. But my fear is, that I have been too liberal in my former concessions, or overlooked some fallacy or other. In short, I did not take time to think.

Phil. For that matter, Hylas, you may take what time you please in reviewing the progress of our inquiry. You are at liberty to recover any slips you might have made, or offer whatever you have omitted, which makes for your first opinion.

Hyl. One great oversight I take to be this: that I did not sufficiently distinguish the *object* from the *sensation*. Now though this latter may not exist without the mind, yet it will not thence follow that the former cannot.

Phil. What object do you mean? The object of the senses?

Hyl. The same.

Phil. It is then immediately perceived?

Hyl. Right.

Phil. Make me to understand the difference between what is immediately perceived, and a sensation.

Hyl. The sensation I take to be an act of the mind perceiving; beside which, there is something perceived; and this I call the *object*. For example, there is red and yellow on that tulip. But then the act of perceiving those colours is in me only, and not in the tulip.

Phil. What tulip do you speak of? it is that which you see?

Hyl. The same.

Phil. And what do you see beside colour, figure, and extension?

Hyl. Nothing.

Phil. What you would say then is, that the red and yellow are co-existent with the extension; is it not?

Hyl. That is not all : I would say, they have a real existence without the mind, in some unthinking substance.

Phil. That the colours are really in the tulip which I see, is manifest. Neither can it be denied, that this tulip may exist independent of your mind or mine; but that any immediate object of the senses, that is, any idea, or combination of ideas, should exist in an unthinking substance, or exterior to all minds, is in itself an evident contradiction. Nor can I imagine how this follows from what you said just now, to wit that the red and yellow were on the tulip *you saw,* since you do not pretend to *see* that unthinking substance.

Hyl. You have an artful way, Philonous, of diverting our inquiry from the subject.

Phil. I see you have no mind to be pressed that way. To return then to your distinction between *sensation* and *object*; if I take you right, you distinguish in every perception two things, the one an action of the mind, the other not.

Hyl. True.

Phil. And this action cannot exist in, or belong to any unthinking thing; but whatever beside is implied in a perception, may.

Hyl. That is my meaning.

Phil. So that if there was a perception without any act of the mind, it were impossible such a perception should exist in an unthinking substance.

Hyl. I grant it. But it is impossible there should be such a perception.

Phil. When is the mind said to be active?

Hyl. When it produces, puts an end to, or changes any thing.

Phil. Can the mind produce, discontinue, or change any thing but by an act of the will?

Hyl. It cannot.

Phil. The mind therefore is to be accounted active in its perceptions, so far forth as volition is included in them.

Hyl. It is.

Phil. In plucking this flower, I am active, because I do it by the motion of my hand, which was consequent upon my volition; so likewise in applying it to my nose. But is either of these smelling?

Hyl. No.

Phil. I act too in drawing the air through my nose; because my breathing so rather than otherwise, is the effect of my volition. But neither can this be called *smelling*: for if it were, I should smell every time I breathed in that manner.

Hyl. True.

Phil. Smelling then is somewhat consequent to all this.

Hyl. It is.

Phil. But I do not find my will concerned any further. Whatever more there is, as that I perceive such a particular smell or any smell at all, this is independent of my will, and therein I am altogether passive. Do you find it otherwise with you, Hylas?

Hyl. No, the very same.

Phil. Then as to seeing, is it not in your power to open your eyes, or keep them shut; to turn them this or that way?

Hyl. Without doubt.

Phil. But doth it in like manner depend on your will, that in looking on this flower, you perceive *white* rather than any other colour? Or directing your open eyes towards yonder part of the heaven, can you avoid seeing the sun? Or is light or darkness the effect of your volition?

Hyl. No, certainly.

Phil. You are then in these respects altogether passive.

Hyl. I am.

Phil. Tell me now, whether *seeing* consists in perceiving light and colours, or in opening and turning the eyes?

Hyl. Without doubt, in the former.

Phil. Since, therefore you are in the very perception of light and colours altogether passive, what is become of that action you were speaking of, as an ingredient in every sensation? And doth it not follow from your own concessions, that the perception of light and colours, including no action in it, may exist in an unperceiving substance? And is not this a plain contradiction?

Hyl. I know not what to think of it.

Phil. Besides, since you distinguish the *active* and *passive* in every perception, you must do it in that of pain. But how is it possible that pain, be it as little active as you please, should exist in an unperceiving substance? In short, do but consider the point, and then confess ingenuously, whether light and colours, tastes, sounds, &c., are not equally passions or sensations in the soul. You may indeed call them *external objects,* and give them in words what subsistence you please. But examine your own thoughts, and then tell me whether it be not as I say?

Hyl. I acknowledge, Philonous, that upon a fair observation of what passes in my mind, I can discover nothing else, but that I am a thinking being, affected with variety of sensations; neither is it possible to conceive how a sensation should exist in an unperceiving substance. But then on the other hand, when I look on sensible things in a different view, considering them as so many modes and qualities, I find it necessary to suppose a material *substratum,* without which they cannot be conceived to exist.

Phil. *Material substratum* call you it? Pray, by which of your senses came you acquainted with that being?

Hyl. It is not itself sensible; its modes and qualities only being perceived by the senses.

Phil. I presume then, it was by reflection and reason you obtained the idea of it.

Hyl. I do not pretend to any proper positive idea of it. However I conclude it exists, because qualities cannot be conceived to exist without a support.

Phil. It seems then you have only a relative notion of it, or that you conceive it not otherwise than by conceiving the relation it bears to sensible qualities.

Hyl. Right.

Phil. Be pleased therefore to let me know wherein that relation consists.

Hyl. Is it not sufficiently expressed in the term *substratum*, or *substance*?

Phil. If so, the word *substratum* should import, that it is spread under the sensible qualities or accidents.

Hyl. True.

Phil. And consequently under extension.

Hyl. I own it.

Phil. It is therefore somewhat in its own nature entirely distinct from extension.

Hyl. I tell you, extension is only a mode, and matter is something that supports modes. And is it not evident the thing supported is different from the thing supporting?

Phil. So that something distinct from, and exclusive of extension, is supposed to be the *substratum* of extension?

Hyl. Just so.

Phil. Answer me, Hylas. Can a thing be spread without extension? or is not the idea of extension necessarily included in *spreading*?

Hyl. It is.

Phil. Whatsoever therefore you suppose spread under any thing, must have in itself an extension distinct from the extension of that thing under which it is spread.

Hyl. It must.

Phil. Consequently every corporeal substance being the *substratum* of extension must have in itself another extension by which it is qualified to be a *substratum*; and so on to infinity. And I ask whether this be not absurd in itself, and repugnant to what you granted just now, to wit, that the *substratum* was something distinct from, and exclusive of extension.

Hyl. Aye but Philonous, you take me wrong. I do not

mean that matter is *spread* in a gross literal sense under extension. The word *substratum* is used only to express in general the same thing with *substance*.

Phil. Well then, let us examine the relation implied in the term *substance*. Is it not that it stands under accidents?

Hyl. The very same.

Phil. But that one thing may stand under or support another, must it not be extended?

Hyl. It must.

Phil. Is not therefore this supposition liable to the same absurdity with the former?

Hyl. You still take things in a strict literal sense: that is not fair, Philonous.

Phil. I am not for imposing any sense on your words: you are at liberty to explain them as you please. Only I beseech you, make me understand something by them. You tell me, matter supports or stands under accidents. How! is it as your legs support your body?

Hyl. No; that is the literal sense.

Phil. Pray let me know any sense, literal or not literal, that you understand it in.——How long must I wait for an answer, Hylas?

Hyl. I declare I know not what to say. I once thought I understood well enough what was meant by matter's supporting accidents. But now the more I think on it, the less can I comprehend it; in short, I find that I know nothing of it.

Phil. It seems then you have no idea at all, neither relative nor positive, of matter; you know neither what it is in itself, nor what relation it bears to accidents.

Hyl. I acknowledge it.

Phil. And yet you asserted, that you could not conceive how qualities or accidents should really exist, without conceiving at the same time a material support of them.

Hyl. I did.

Phil. That is to say, when you conceive the real existence of qualities, you do withal conceive something which you cannot conceive.

Hyl. It was wrong, I own. But still I fear there is some fallacy or other. Pray what think you of this? It is just come into my head, that the ground of all our mistake lies in your treating of each quality by itself. Now, I grant that each quality cannot singly subsist without the mind. Colour cannot without extension, neither can figure without some other sensible quality. But as the several qualities united or blended together form entire sensible things, nothing hinders why such things may not be supposed to exist without the mind.

Phil. Either, Hylas, you are jesting, or have a very bad memory. Though indeed we went through all the qualities by name one after another; yet my arguments, or rather your concessions no where tended to prove, that the secondary qualities did not subsist each alone by itself: but that they were not *at all* without the mind. Indeed in treating of figure and motion, we concluded they could not exist without the mind, because it was impossible even in thought to separate them from all secondary qualities, so as to conceive them existing by themselves. But then this was not the only argument made use of upon that occasion. But (to pass by all that hath been hitherto said, and reckon it for nothing, if you will have it so) I am content to put the whole upon this issue. If you can conceive it possible for any mixture or combination of qualities, or any sensible object whatever, to exist without the mind, then I will grant it actually to be so.

Hyl. If it comes to that, the point will soon be decided. What more easy than to conceive a tree or house existing by itself, independent of, and unperceived by any mind whatsoever? I do at this present time conceive them existing after that manner.

Phil. How say you, Hylas, can you see a thing which is at the same time unseen?

Hyl. No, that were a contradiction.

Phil. Is it not as great a contradiction to talk of *conceiving* a thing which is *unconceived*?

Hyl. It is.

Phil. The tree or house therefore which you think of, is conceived by you.

Hyl. How should it be otherwise?

Phil. And what is conceived is surely in the mind.

Hyl. Without question, that which is conceived is in the mind.

Phil. How then came you to say, you conceived a house or tree existing independent and out of all minds whatsoever?

Hyl. That was, I own, an oversight; but stay, let me consider what led me into it.—It is a pleasant mistake enough. As I was thinking of a tree in a solitary place, where no one was present to see it, methought that was to conceive a tree as existing unperceived or unthought of, not considering that I myself conceived it all the while. But now I plainly see, that all I can do is to frame ideas in my own mind. I may indeed conceive in my own thoughts the idea of a tree, or a house, or a mountain, but that is all. And this is far from proving, that I can conceive them *existing out of the minds of all spirits.*

Phil. You acknowledge then that you cannot possibly conceive how any one corporeal sensible thing should exist otherwise than in a mind.

Hyl. I do.

Phil. And yet you will earnestly contend for the truth of that which you cannot so much as conceive.

Hyl. I profess I know not what to think, but still there are some scruples remain with me. Is it not certain I see things at a distance? Do we not perceive the stars and moon, for example, to be a great way off? Is not this, I say, manifest to the senses?

Phil. Do you not in a dream too perceive those or the like objects?

Hyl. I do.

Phil. And have they not then the same appearance of being distant?

Hyl. They have.

Phil. But you do not thence conclude the apparitions in a dream to be without the mind?

Hyl. By no means.

Phil. You ought not therefore to conclude that sensible objects are without the mind, from their appearance or manner wherein they are perceived.

Hyl. I acknowledge it. But doth not my sense deceive me in those cases?

Phil. By no means. The idea or thing which you immediately perceive, neither sense nor reason inform you that it actually exists without the mind. By sense you only know that you are affected with such certain sensations of light and colours, &c. And these you will not say are without the mind.

Hyl. True: but beside all that, do you not think the sight suggests something of *outness* or *distance*?

Phil. Upon approaching a distant object, do the visible size and figure change perpetually, or do they appear the same at all distances?

Hyl. They are in a continual change.

Phil. Sight therefore doth not suggest or in any way inform you, that the visible object you immediately perceive, exists at a distance, or will be perceived when you advance further onward, there being a continued series of visible objects succeeding each other, during the whole time of your approach.

Hyl. It doth not; but still I know, upon seeing an object, what object I shall perceive after having passed over a certain distance: no matter whether it be exactly the same or no: there is still something of distance suggested in the case.

Phil. Good Hylas, do but reflect a little on the point, and then tell me whether there be any more in it than this. From the ideas you actually perceive by sight, you have by experience learned to collect what other ideas you will (according to the standing order of nature) be affected with after such a certain succession of time and motion.

Hyl. Upon the whole, I take it to be nothing else.

Phil. Now is it not plain, that if we suppose a man born blind was on a sudden made to see, he could at first have no experience of what may be suggested by sight?

Hyl. It is.

Phil. He would not then, according to you, have any notion of distance annexed to the things he saw; but would take them for a new set of sensations existing only in his mind.

Hyl. It is undeniable.

Phil. But to make it still more plain: is not *distance* a line turned endwise to the eye?

Hyl. It is.

Phil. And can a line so situated be perceived by sight?

Hyl. It cannot.

Phil. Doth it not therefore follow that distance is not properly and immediately perceived by sight?

Hyl. It should seem so.

Phil. Again, is it your opinion that colours are at a distance?

Hyl. It must be acknowledged, they are only in the mind.

Phil. But do not colours appear to the eye as co-existing in the same place with extension and figures?

Hyl. They do.

Phil. How can you then conclude from sight, that figures exist without, when you acknowledge colours do not; the sensible appearance being the very same with regard to both?

Hyl. I know not what to answer.

Phil. But allowing that distance was truly and immediately perceived by the mind, yet it would not thence follow it existed out of the mind. For whatever is immediately perceived is an idea : and can any *idea* exist out of the mind?

Hyl. To suppose that were absurd : but inform me, Philonous, can we perceive or know nothing beside our ideas?

Phil. As for the rational deducing of causes from effects, that is beside our inquiry. And by the senses you can best tell, whether you perceive any thing which is not immediately perceived. And I ask you, whether the things immediately perceived, are other than your own sensations or ideas? You have indeed more than once, in the course of this conversation, declared yourself on those points; but you seem, by this last question, to have departed from what you then thought.

Hyl. To speak the truth, Philonous, I think there are two kinds of objects, the one perceived immediately, which are likewise called *ideas*; the other are real things or external objects perceived by the mediation of ideas, which are their images and representations. Now I own, ideas do not exist without the mind; but the latter sort of objects do. I am sorry I did not think of this distinction sooner; it would probably have cut short your discourse.

Phil. Are those external objects perceived by sense, or by some other faculty?

Hyl. They are perceived by sense.

Phil. How! is there any thing perceived by sense, which is not immediately perceived?

Hyl. Yes, Philonous, in some sort there is. For example, when I look on a picture or statue of Julius Cæsar, I may be said, after a manner, to perceive him (though not immediately) by my senses.

Phil. It seems, then, you will have our ideas, which alone are immediately perceived, to be pictures of external things : and that these also are perceived by sense, inasmuch as they have a conformity or resemblance to our ideas.

Hyl. That is my meaning.

Phil. And in the same way that Julius Cæsar, in himself invisible, is nevertheless perceived by sight; real things, in themselves imperceptible, are perceived by sense.

Hyl. In the very same.

Phil. Tell me, Hylas, when you behold the picture of Julius Cæsar, do you see with your eyes any more than some colours and figures, with a certain symmetry and composition of the whole?

Hyl. Nothing else.

Phil. And would not a man, who had never known any thing of Julius Cæsar, see as much?

Hyl. He would.

Phil. Consequently he hath his sight, and the use of it, in as perfect a degree as you.

Hyl. I agree with you.

Phil. Whence comes it then that your thoughts are directed to the Roman emperor and his are not? This cannot proceed from the sensations or ideas of sense by you then perceived; since you acknowledge you have no advantage over him in that respect. It should seem therefore to proceed from reason and memory: should it not?

Hyl. It should.

Phil. Consequently it will not follow from that instance, that any thing is perceived by sense which is not immediately perceived. Though I grant we may in one acceptation be said to perceive sensible things mediately by sense: that is, when from a frequently perceived connexion, the immediate perception of ideas by one sense suggests to the mind others perhaps belonging to another sense, which are wont to be connected with them. For instance, when I hear a coach drive along the streets, immediately I perceive only the sound; but from the experience I have had that such a sound is connected with a coach, I am said to hear the coach. It is nevertheless evident, that in truth and strictness, nothing can be *heard* but *sound* : and the coach is not then properly perceived by sense, but suggested from experience. So likewise when we are said to see a red-hot bar of iron; the solidity and heat of the iron are not the objects of sight, but suggested to the imagination by the colour and figure, which are properly perceived by that sense. In short, those things alone are actually and strictly perceived by any sense, which would have been perceived, in case that same sense had then been first conferred on us. As for other things, it is plain they are only suggested to the mind by experience grounded on former perceptions. But to return to your comparison of Cæsar's picture, it is plain, if you keep to that, you must hold the real things or archetypes of our ideas are not perceived by sense, but by some internal faculty of the soul, as reason or memory. I would therefore fain know, what arguments you can draw from reason for the existence of what you call *real things* or *material objects*; or whether you remember to have seen them formerly as they are in themselves; or if you have heard or read of any one that did.

Hyl. I see, Philonous, you are disposed to raillery; but that will never convince me.

Phil. My aim is only to learn from you the way to come at the knowledge of *material beings*. Whatever we perceive, is perceived either immediately or mediately: by sense, or by reason and reflection. But as you have excluded sense, pray show me what reason you have to believe their existence; or what *medium* you can possibly make use of to prove it, either to mine or your own understanding.

Hyl. To deal ingenuously, Philonous, now I consider the point, I do not find I can give you any good reason for it. But thus much seems pretty plain, that it is at least possible such things may really exist; and as long as there is no absurdity in supposing them, I am resolved to believe as I did, till you bring good reasons to the contrary.

Phil. What! is it come to this, that you only believe the existence of material objects, and that your belief is founded barely on the possibility of its being true? Then you will have me bring reasons against it : though another would think it reasonable, the proofs should lie on him who holds the affirmative. And after all, this very point which you are now resolved to maintain without any reason, is, in effect, what you have more than once, during this discourse, seen good reason to give up. But to pass over all this; if I understand you rightly, you say our ideas do not exist without the mind; but that they are copies, images, or representations of certain originals that do.

Hyl. You take me right.

Phil. They are then like external things.

Hyl. They are.

Phil. Have those things a stable and permanent nature independent of our senses; or are they in a perpetual change, upon our producing any motions in our bodies, suspending, exerting, or altering our faculties or organs of sense?

Hyl. Real things, it is plain, have a fixed and real nature, which remains the same, notwithstanding any change in our senses, or in the posture and motion of our bodies; which, indeed, may affect the ideas in our minds, but it were absurd to think they had the same effect on things existing without the mind.

Phil. How then is it possible, that things perpetually fleeting and variable as our ideas, should be copies or images of any thing fixed and constant? or in other words, since all sensible qualities, as size, figure, colour, &c., that is, our ideas, are continually changing upon every alteration in the distance, medium, or instruments of sensation; how can any determinate material objects be properly represented or painted forth by several distinct things, each of which is so different from and unlike the rest? Or if you say it resembles some one only of our ideas, how shall we be able to distinguish the true copy from all the false ones?

Hyl. I profess, Philonous, I am at a loss. I know not what to say to this.

Phil. But neither is this all. Which are material objects in themselves, perceptible or imperceptible?

Hyl. Properly and immediately nothing can be perceived but ideas. All material things therefore are in themselves insensible, and to be perceived only by their ideas.

Phil. Ideas then are sensible, and their archetypes or originals insensible.

Hyl. Right.

Phil. But how can that which is sensible be like that which is insensible? Can a real thing in itself *invisible* be like a *colour*; or a real thing which is not *audible*, be like a *sound*? In a word, can any thing be like a sensation or idea, but another sensation or idea?

Hyl. I must own, I think not.

Phil. Is it possible there should be any doubt in the point? Do you not perfectly know your own ideas?

Hyl. I know them perfectly; since what I do not perceive or know, can be no part of my idea.

Phil. Consider therefore, and examine them, and then tell me if there be any thing in them which can exist without the mind: or if you can conceive any thing like them existing without the mind.

Hyl. Upon inquiry, I find it is impossible for me to conceive or understand how any thing but an idea can be like an idea. And it is most evident, that *no idea can exist without the mind.*

Phil. You are therefore by your principles forced to deny the reality of sensible things, since you made it to consist in an absolute existence exterior to the mind. That is to say, you are a downright sceptic. So I have gained my point, which was to show your principles led to scepticism.

Hyl. For the present I am, if not entirely convinced, at least silenced.

Phil. I would fain know what more you would require in order to a perfect conviction. Have you not had the liberty of explaining yourself all manner of ways? Were any little slips in discourse laid hold and insisted on? Or were you not allowed to retract or reinforce any thing you had offered, as best served your purpose? Hath not every thing you could say been heard and examined with all the fairness imaginable? In a word, have you not in every point been convinced out of your own mouth? And if you can at present discover any flaw in any of your former concessions or think of any remaining subterfuge, any new distinction, colour, or comment whatsoever, why do you not produce it?

Hyl. A little patience, Philonous. I am at present so amazed to see myself ensnared, and as it were imprisoned in the labyrinths you have drawn me into, that on the sudden it cannot be expected I should find my way out. You must give me time to look about me, and recollect myself.

Phil. Hark; is not this the college-bell?

Hyl. It rings for prayers.

Phil. We will go in then if you please, and meet here again to-morrow morning. In the mean time you may employ your thoughts on this morning's discourse, and try if you can find any fallacy in it, or invent any new means to extricate yourself.

Hyl. Agreed.

THE SECOND DIALOGUE

Hylas. I beg your pardon, Philonous, for not meeting you sooner. All this morning my head was so filled with our late conversation, that I had not leisure to think of the time of the day, or indeed of any thing else.

Philonous. I am glad you were so intent upon it, in hopes if there were any mistakes in your concessions, or fallacies in my reasonings from them, you will now discover them to me.

Hyl. I assure you, I have done nothing ever since I saw you, but search after mistakes and fallacies, and with that view have minutely examined the whole series of yesterday's discourse : but all in vain, for the notions it led me into, upon review appear still more clear and evident; and the more I consider them, the more irresistibly do they force my assent.

Phil. And is not this, think you, a sign that they are genuine, that they proceed from nature, and are conformable to right reason? Truth and beauty are in this alike, that the strictest survey sets them both off to advantage. While the false lustre of error and disguise cannot endure being reviewed, or too nearly inspected.

Hyl. I own there is a great deal in what you say. Nor can any one be more entirely satisfied of the truth of those odd consequences, so long as I have in view the reasonings that led to them. But when these are out of my thoughts, there seems on the other hand something so satisfactory, so natural and intelligible in the modern way of explaining things, that I profess I know not how to reject it.

Phil. I know not what way you mean.

Hyl. I mean the way of accounting for our sensations or ideas.

Phil. How is that?

Hyl. It is supposed the soul makes her residence i
some part of the brain, from which the nerves take thei
rise, and are thence extended to all parts of the body : an
that outward objects, by the different impressions the
make on the organs of sense, communicate certain vibra
tive motions to the nerves; and these being filled wit
spirits, propagate them to the brain or seat of the sou
which according to the various impressions or trace
thereby made in the brain, is variously affected with ideas

Phil. And call you this an explication of the manne
whereby we are affected with ideas?

Hyl. Why not, Philonous? have you any thing to objec
against it?

Phil. I would first know whether I rightly understan
your hypothesis. You make certain traces in the brain t
be the causes or occasions of our ideas. Pray tell me
whether by the *brain* you mean any sensible thing?

Hyl. What else think you I could mean?

Phil. Sensible things are all immediately perceivable
and those things which are immediately perceivable, ar
ideas; and these exist only in the mind. Thus much yo
have, if I mistake not, long since agreed to.

Hyl. I do not deny it.

Phil. The brain therefore you speak of, being a sensibl
thing, exists only in the mind. Now, I would fain know
whether you think it reasonable to suppose, that one ide
or thing existing in the mind, occasions all other ideas
And if you think so, pray how do you account for th
origin of that primary idea or brain itself?

Hyl. I do not explain the origin of our ideas by tha
brain which is perceivable to sense, this being itself only
combination of sensible ideas, but by another which
imagine.

Phil. But are not things imagined as truly in the min
as things perceived?

Hyl. I must confess they are.

Phil. It comes therefore to the same thing; and you have been all this while accounting for ideas, by certain motions or impressions in the brain, that is, by some alterations in an idea, whether sensible or imaginable, it matters not.

Hyl. I begin to suspect my hypothesis.

Phil. Beside spirits, all that we know or conceive are our own ideas. When therefore you say, all ideas are occasioned by impressions in the brain, do you conceive this brain or no? If you do, then you talk of ideas imprinted in an idea, causing that same idea, which is absurd. If you do not conceive it, you talk unintelligibly, instead of forming a reasonable hypothesis.

Hyl. I now clearly see it was a mere dream. There is nothing in it.

Phil. You need not be much concerned at it; for after all, this way of explaining things, as you called it, could never have satisfied any reasonable man. What connexion is there between a motion in the nerves, and the sensations of sound or colour in the mind? Or how is it possible these should be the effect of that?

Hyl. But I could never think it had so little in it, as now it seems to have.

Phil. Well then, are you at length satisfied that no sensible things have a real existence; and that you are in truth an arrant *sceptic*?

Hyl. It is too plain to be denied.

Phil. Look! are not the fields covered with a delightful verdure? Is there not something in the woods and groves, in the rivers and clear springs, that soothes, that delights, that transports the soul? At the prospect of the wide and deep ocean, or some huge mountain whose top is lost in the clouds, or of an old gloomy forest, are not our minds filled with a pleasing horror? Even in rocks and deserts, is there not an agreeable wildness? How sincere a pleasure is it to behold the natural beauties of the earth! to preserve and renew our relish for them, is not the veil

of night alternately drawn over her face, and doth she
not change her dress with the seasons? How aptly are the
elements disposed! What variety and use in the meanest
production of nature! What delicacy, what beauty, what
contrivance in animal and vegetable bodies! How ex
quisitely are all things suited as well to their particular
ends, as to constitute opposite parts of the whole! and
while they mutually aid and support, do they not also set
off and illustrate each other? Raise now your thoughts
from this ball of earth, to all those glorious luminaries
that adorn the high arch of heaven. The motion and
situation of the planets, are they not admirable for use and
order? Were those (miscalled *erratic*) globes ever known
to stray, in their repeated journeys through the pathless
void? Do they not measure areas round the sun ever
proportioned to the times? So fixed, so immutable are the
laws by which the unseen Author of nature actuates the
universe. How vivid and radiant is the lustre of the fixed
stars! how magnificent and rich that negligent profusion,
with which they appear to be scattered throughout the
whole azure vault! yet if you take the telescope, it brings
into your sight a new host of stars that escape the naked
eye. Here they seem contiguous and minute, but to a
nearer view immense orbs of light at various distances, far
sunk in the abyss of space. Now you must call imagination to your aid. The feeble narrow sense cannot descry
innumerable worlds revolving round the central fires; and
in those worlds the energy of an all-perfect mind displayed in endless forms. But neither sense nor imagination
are big enough to comprehend the boundless extent with
all its glittering furniture. Though the labouring mind
exert and strain each power to its utmost reach, there still
stands out ungrasped a surplusage immeasurable. Yet all
the vast bodies that compose this mighty frame, how dis-
stant and remote soever, are by some secret mechanism,
some divine art and force, linked in a mutual dependence
and intercourse with each other, even with this earth,

which was almost slipped from my thoughts, and lost in the crowd of worlds. Is not the whole system immense, beautiful, glorious beyond expression and beyond thought? What treatment then do those philosophers deserve, who would deprive these noble and delightful scenes of all reality? How should those principles be entertained, that lead us to think all the visible beauty of the creation a false imaginary glare? To be plain, can you expect this scepticism of yours will not be thought extravagantly absurd by all men of sense?

Hyl. Other men may think as they please: but for your part you have nothing to reproach me with. My comfort is, you are as much a *sceptic* as I am.

Phil. There, Hylas, I must beg leave to differ from you.

Hyl. What! have you all along agreed to the premises, and do you now deny the conclusion, and leave me to maintain those paradoxes by myself which you led me into? This surely is not fair.

Phil. I deny that I agreed with you in those notions that led to scepticism. You indeed said, the reality of sensible things consisted in an *absolute existence* out of the minds of spirits, or distinct from their being perceived. And pursuant to this notion of reality, you are obliged to deny sensible things any real existence: that is, according to your own definition, you profess yourself a *sceptic*. But I neither said nor thought the reality of sensible things was to be defined after that manner. To me it is evident, for the reasons you allow of, that sensible things cannot exist otherwise than in a mind or spirit. Whence I conclude, not that they have no real existence, but that seeing they depend not on my thought, and have an existence distinct from being perceived by me, *there must be some other mind wherein they exist.* As sure therefore as the sensible world really exists, so sure is there an infinite, omnipresent Spirit who contains and supports it.

Hyl. What! this is no more than I and all Christians

hold; nay, and all others too who believe there is a God, and that he knows and comprehends all things.

Phil. Ay, but here lies the difference. Men commonly believe that all things are known or perceived by God, because they believe the being of a God, whereas I, on the other side, immediately and necessarily conclude the being of a God, because all sensible things must be perceived by him.

Hyl. But so long as we all believe the same thing, what matter is it how we come by that belief?

Phil. But neither do we agree in the same opinion. For philosophers, though they acknowledge all corporeal beings to be perceived by God, yet they attribute to them an absolute subsistence distinct from their being perceived by any mind whatever, which I do not. Besides, is there no difference between saying, *there is a God, therefore he perceives all things* : and saying, *sensible things do really exist: and if they really exist, they are necessarily perceived by an infinite mind: therefore there is an infinite mind, or God.* This furnishes you with a direct and immediate demonstration, from a most evident principle, of the *being of a God*. Divines and philosophers had proved beyond all controversy, from the beauty and usefulness of the several parts of the creation, that it was the workmanship of God. But that setting aside all help of astronomy and natural philosophy, all contemplation of the contrivance, order, and adjustment of things, an infinite mind should be necessarily inferred from the bare existence of the sensible world, is an advantage peculiar to them only who have made this easy reflection : that the sensible world is that which we perceive by our several senses; and that nothing is perceived by the senses beside ideas; and that no idea or archetype of an idea can exist otherwise than in a mind. You may now, without any laborious search into the sciences, without any subtility of reason, or tedious length of discourse, oppose and baffle the most strenuous advocate for atheism. Those miserable refuges, whether in an eternal succession of unthinking causes and effects, or in a fortuitous concourse of atoms; those wild imaginations of Vanini,[1] Hobbes, and Spinoza; in a word, the whole system of atheism, is it not entirely overthrown by this single reflection on the repugnancy included in supposing the whole, or any part, even the most rude and shapeless of the visible world, to exist without a mind? Let any one of those abettors of impiety but look into his own thoughts, and there try if he can conceive how so much as a rock, a desert, a chaos, or confused jumble of atoms; how any thing at all, either sensible or imaginable, can exist independent of a mind, and he need go no further to be convinced of his folly. Can any thing be fairer than to put a dispute on such an issue, and leave it to a man himself to see if he can conceive, even in thought, what he holds to be true in fact, and from a notional to allow it a real existence?

Hyl. It cannot be denied, there is something highly serviceable to religion in what you advance. But do you not think it looks very like a notion entertained by some eminent moderns, of *seeing all things in God*?

Phil. I would gladly know that opinion; pray explain it to me.

Hyl. They conceive that the soul being immaterial, is incapable of being united with material things, so as to perceive them in themselves, but that she perceives them by her union with the substance of God, which being spiritual is therefore purely intelligible, or capable of being the immediate object of a spirit's thought. Besides, the divine essence contains in it perfections correspondent to each created being; and which are, for that reason, proper to exhibit or represent them to the mind.

Phil. I do not understand how our ideas, which are things altogether passive and inert, can be the essence, or any part (or like any part) of the essence or substance of

[1] Lucilio Vanini, a Neapolitan priest, burned at the stake in 1619 on the charge of atheism.

God, who is an impassive, indivisible, purely active being. Many more difficulties and objections there are, which occur at first view against this hypothesis; but I shall only add, that it is liable to all the absurdities of the common hypotheses, in making a created world exist otherwise than in the mind of a spirit. Beside all which it hath this peculiar to itself, that it makes that material world serve to no purpose. And if it pass for a good argument against other hypotheses in the sciences, that they suppose nature or the Divine Wisdom to make something in vain, or do that by tedious roundabout methods, which might have been performed in a much more easy and compendious way, what shall we think of that hypothesis which supposes the whole world made in vain?

Hyl. But what say you, are not you too of opinion that we see all things in God? If I mistake not, what you advance comes near it.

Phil. Few men think, yet all will have opinions. Hence men's opinions are superficial and confused. It is nothing strange that tenets, which in themselves are ever so different, should nevertheless be confounded with each other by those who do not consider them attentively. I shall not therefore be surprised, if some men imagine that I run into the enthusiasm of Malebranche, though in truth I am very remote from it. He builds on the most abstract general ideas, which I entirely disclaim. He asserts an absolute external world, which I deny. He maintains that we are deceived by our senses, and know not the real natures, or the true forms and figures of extended beings; of all which I hold the direct contrary. So that, upon the whole, there are no principles more fundamentally opposite than his and mine. It must be owned I entirely agree with what the holy scripture saith, that " in God we live, and move, and have our being." But that we see things in his essence, after the manner above set forth, I am far from believing. Take here in brief my meaning. It is evident that the things I perceive are my own ideas, and that no idea can exist unless it be in a mind. Nor is it less plain that these ideas, or things by me perceived, either themselves or their archetypes, exist independently of my mind, since I know myself not to be their author, it being out of my power to determine at pleasure, what particular ideas I shall be affected with upon opening my eyes or ears. They must therefore exist in some other mind, whose will it is they should be exhibited to me. The things, I say, immediately perceived, are ideas or sensations, call them which you will. But how can any idea or sensation exist in, or be produced by, any thing but a mind or spirit? This indeed is inconceivable; and to assert that which is inconceivable, is to talk nonsense : is it not?

Hyl. Without doubt.

Phil. But on the other hand, it is very conceivable that they should exist in, and be produced by, a spirit : since this is no more than I daily experience in myself, inasmuch as I perceive numberless ideas : and by an act of my will can form a great variety of them, and raise them up in my imagination : though it must be confessed, these creatures of the fancy are not altogether so distinct, so strong, vivid, and permanent, as those perceived by my senses, which latter are called *real things*. From all which I conclude, *there is a mind which affects me every moment with all the sensible impressions I perceive.* And from the variety, order, and manner of these, I conclude the author of them to be *wise, powerful, and good, beyond comprehension.* Mark it well : I do not say, I see things by perceiving that which represents them in the intelligible substance of God. This I do not understand; but I say, the things by me perceived are known by the understanding, and produced by the will, of an infinite Spirit. And is not all this most plain and evident? Is there any more in it, than what a little observation of our own minds, and that which passes in them, not only enableth us to conceive, but also obligeth us to acknowledge?

Hyl. I think I understand you very clearly; and own

the proof you give of a Deity seems no less evident, than it is surprising. But allowing that God is the supreme and universal cause of all things, yet may not there be still a third nature besides spirits and ideas? May we not admit a subordinate and limited cause of our ideas? In a word, may there not for all that be *matter*?

Phil. How often must I inculcate the same thing? You allow the things immediately perceived by sense to exist nowhere without the mind; but there is nothing perceived by sense, which is not perceived immediately: therefore there is nothing sensible that exists without the mind. The matter therefore which you still insist on, is something intelligible, I suppose; something that may be discovered by reason, and not by sense.

Hyl. You are in the right.

Phil. Pray let me know what reasoning your belief of matter is grounded on; and what this matter is in your present sense of it.

Hyl. I find myself affected with various ideas, whereof I know I am not the cause; neither are they the cause of themselves or of one another, or capable of subsisting by themselves, as being altogether inactive, fleeting, dependent beings. They have therefore some cause distinct from me and them: of which I pretend to know no more, than that it is *the cause of my ideas*. And this thing, whatever it be, I call matter.

Phil. Tell me, Hylas, hath every one a liberty to change the current proper signification annexed to a common name in any language? For example, suppose a traveller should tell you, that in a certain country men might pass unhurt through the fire; and, upon explaining himself, you found he meant by the word *fire* that which others call *water*: or if he should assert there are trees which walk upon two legs, meaning men by the term *trees*. Would you think this reasonable?

Hyl. No; I should think it very absurd. Common custom is the standard of propriety in language. And for any man to affect speaking improperly, is to pervert the use of speech, and can never serve to a better purpose, than to protract and multiply disputes where there is no difference in opinion.

Phil. And doth not *matter,* in the common current acceptation of the word, signify an extended, solid, moveable, unthinking, inactive substance?

Hyl. It doth.

Phil. And hath it not been made evident, that no such substance can possibly exist? And though it should be allowed to exist, yet how can that which is *inactive* be a *cause*; or that which is *unthinking* be a *cause of thought*? You may indeed, if you please, annex to the word *matter* a contrary meaning to what is vulgarly received; and tell me you understand by it an unextended, thinking, active being, which is the cause of our ideas. But what else is this, than to play with words, and run into that very fault you just now condemned with so much reason? I do by no means find fault with your reasoning, in that you collect a cause from the phenomena: but I deny that the cause deducible by reason can properly be termed *matter.*

Hyl. There is indeed something in what you say. But I am afraid you do not thoroughly comprehend my meaning. I would by no means be thought to deny that God, or an infinite spirit, is the supreme cause of all things. All I contend for, is that subordinate to the supreme agent there is a cause of a limited and inferior nature, which concurs in the production of our ideas, not by any act of will or spiritual efficiency, but by that kind of action which belongs to matter, viz. *motion.*

Phil. I find, you are at every turn relapsing into your old exploded conceit, of a moveable and consequently an extended substance existing without the mind. What! have you already forgot you were convinced, or are you willing I should repeat what has been said on that head? In truth this is not fair dealing in you, still to suppose the being of that which you have so often acknowledged

to have no being. But not to insist further on what ha
been so largely handled, I ask whether all your ideas ar
not perfectly passive and inert, including nothing of action
in them?

Hyl. They are.

Phil. And are sensible qualities any thing else but ideas

Hyl. How often have I acknowledged that they are
not?

Phil. But is not motion a sensible quality?

Hyl. It is.

Phil. Consequently it is no action.

Hyl. I agree with you. And indeed it is very plain
that when I stir my finger, it remains passive; but my
will which produced the motion, is active.

Phil. Now I desire to know in the first place, whether
motion being allowed to be no action, you can conceive
any action besides volition : and in the second place,
whether to say something and conceive nothing be not to
talk nonsense : and lastly, whether having considered the
premises, you do not perceive that to suppose any efficient
or active cause of our ideas, other than *spirit,* is highly
absurd and unreasonable?

Hyl. I give up the point entirely. But though matter
may not be a cause, yet what hinders it being an *instrument* subservient to the supreme agent in the production
of our ideas?

Phil. An instrument, say you; pray what may be the
figure, springs, wheels, and motions of that instrument?

Hyl. Those I pretend to determine nothing of, both
the substance and its qualities being entirely unknown to
me.

Phil. What? You are then of opinion, it is made up of
unknown parts, that it hath unknown motions, and an
unknown shape.

Hyl. I do not believe it hath any figure or motion at
all, being already convinced, that no sensible qualities can
exist in an unperceiving substance.

Phil. But what notion is it possible to frame of an instrument void of all sensible qualities, even extension itself?

Hyl. I do not pretend to have any notion of it.

Phil. And what reason have you to think, this unknown, this inconceivable somewhat doth exist? Is it that you imagine God cannot act as well without it, or that you find by experience the use of some such thing, when you form ideas in your own mind?

Hyl. You are always teazing me for reasons of my belief. Pray what reasons have you not to believe it?

Phil. It is to me a sufficient reason not to believe the existence of any thing, if I see no reason for believing it. But not to insist on reasons for believing, you will not so much as let me know what it is you would have me believe, since you say you have no manner of notion of it. After all, let me entreat you to consider whether it be like a philosopher, or even like a man of common sense, to pretend to believe you know not what and you know not why.

Hyl. Hold, Philonous. When I tell you matter is an *instrument,* I do not mean altogether nothing. It is true, I know not the particular kind of instrument : but however I have some notion of *instrument in general,* which I apply to it.

Phil. But what if it should prove that there is something, even in the most general notion of *instrument,* as taken in a distinct sense from *cause,* which makes the use of it inconsistent with the divine attributes?

Hyl. Make that appear, and I shall give up the point.

Phil. What mean you by the general nature or notion of *instrument*?

Hyl. That which is common to all particular instruments, composeth the general notion.

Phil. Is it not common to all instruments, that they are applied to the doing those things only, which cannot be performed by the mere act of our wills? Thus for in-

stance, I never use an instrument to move my finger
because it is done by a volition. But I should use one, if
I were to remove part of a rock, or tear up a tree by the
roots. Are you of the same mind? Or can you show any
example where an instrument is made use of in producing an effect immediately depending on the will of the
agent?

Hyl. I own, I cannot.

Phil. How therefore can you suppose, that an all-perfect
Spirit, on whose will all things have an absolute and
immediate dependence, should need an instrument in his
operations, or not needing it make use of it? Thus it
seems to me that you are obliged to own the use of a
lifeless inactive instrument, to be incompatible with the
infinite perfection of God; that is, by your own confession
to give up the point.

Hyl. It doth not readily occur what I can answer you.

Phil. But methinks you should be ready to own the
truth, when it hath been fairly proved to you. We indeed,
who are beings of finite powers, are forced to make use of
instruments. And the use of an instrument showeth the
agent to be limited by rules of another's prescription, and
that he cannot obtain his end, but in such a way and by
such conditions. Whence it seems a clear consequence,
that the supreme unlimited agent useth no tool or instrument at all. The will of an omnipotent Spirit is no sooner
exerted than executed, without the application of means,
which, if they are employed by inferior agents, it is not
upon account of any real efficacy that is in them, or
necessary aptitude to produce any effect, but merely in
compliance with the laws of nature, or those conditions
prescribed to them by the first cause, who is himself above
all limitation or prescription whatsoever.

Hyl. I will no longer maintain that matter is an instrument. However, I would not be understood to give up its
existence neither; since, notwithstanding what hath been
said, it may still be an *occasion*.

Phil. How many shapes is your matter to take? Or how often must it be proved not to exist, before you are content to part with it? But to say no more of this (though by all the laws of disputation I may justly blame you for so frequently changing the signification of the principal term) I would fain know what you mean by affirming that matter is an occasion, having already denied it to be a cause. And when you have shown in what sense you understand *occasion,* pray in the next place be pleased to show me what reason induceth you to believe there is such an occasion of our ideas.

Hyl. As to the first point: by *occasion* I mean an inactive, unthinking being, at the presence whereof God excites ideas in our minds.

Phil. And what may be the nature of that inactive, unthinking being?

Hyl. I know nothing of its nature.

Phil. Proceed then to the second point, and assign some reason why we should allow an existence to this inactive, unthinking, unknown thing.

Hyl. When we see ideas produced in our minds after an orderly and constant manner, it is natural to think they have some fixed and regular occasions, at the presence of which they are excited.

Phil. You acknowledge then God alone to be the cause of our ideas, and that he causes them at the presence of those occasions.

Hyl. That is my opinion.

Phil. Those things which you say are present to God, without doubt he perceives.

Hyl. Certainly; otherwise they could not be to him an occasion of acting.

Phil. Not to insist now on your making sense of this hypothesis, or answering all the puzzling questions and difficulties it is liable to: I only ask whether the order and regularity observable in the series of our ideas, or the course of nature, be not sufficiently accounted for by the wisdom and power of God; and whether it doth not dero gate from those attributes, to suppose he is influenced directed, or put in mind, when and what he is to act, b any unthinking substance. And lastly, whether in case granted all you contend for, it would make any thing to your purpose, it not being easy to conceive how the ex ternal or absolute existence of an unthinking substance distinct from its being perceived, can be inferred from my allowing that there are certain things perceived by the mind of God, which are to him the occasion of producing ideas in us.

Hyl. I am perfectly at a loss what to think, this notion of *occasion* seeming now altogether as groundless as the rest.

Phil. Do you not at length perceive, that in all these different acceptations of *matter,* you have been only sup posing you know not what, for no manner of reason, and to no kind of use?

Hyl. I freely own myself less fond of my notions, since they have been so accurately examined. But still, me thinks I have some confused perception that there is such a thing as *matter*.

Phil. Either you perceive the being of matter imme diately, or mediately. If immediately, pray inform me by which of the senses you perceive it. If mediately, let me know by what reasoning it is inferred from those things which you perceive immediately. So much for the per ception. Then for the matter itself, I ask whether it is object, substratum, cause, instrument, or occasion? You have already pleaded for each of these, shifting your notions, and making matter to appear sometimes in one shape, then in another. And what you have offered hath been disapproved and rejected by yourself. If you have any thing new to advance, I would gladly hear it.

Hyl. I think I have already offered all I had to say on those heads. I am at a loss what more to urge.

Phil. And yet you are loath to part with your old prejudice. But to make you quit it more easily, I desire that, besides what has been hitherto suggested, you will further consider whether, upon supposition that matter exists, you can possibly conceive how you should be affected by it? Or supposing it did not exist, whether it be not evident you might for all that be affected with the same ideas you now are, and consequently have the very same reasons to believe its existence that you now can have?

Hyl. I acknowledge it is possible we might perceive all things just as we do now, though there was no matter in the world; neither can I conceive, if there be matter, how it should produce any idea in our minds. And I do further grant, you have entirely satisfied me, that it is impossible there should be such a thing as matter in any of the fore-going acceptations. But still I cannot help supposing that there is *matter* in some sense or other. What that is I do not indeed pretend to determine.

Phil. I do not expect you should define exactly the nature of that unknown being. Only be pleased to tell me, whether it is a substance : and if so, whether you can suppose a substance without accidents : or in case you suppose it to have accidents or qualities, I desire you will let me know what those qualities are, at least what is meant by matter's supporting them.

Hyl. We have already argued on those points. I have no more to say to them. But to prevent any further questions, let me tell you, I at present understand by *matter* neither substance nor accident, thinking or extended being, neither cause, instrument, nor occasion, but something entirely unknown, distinct from all these.

Phil. It seems then you include in your present notion of matter, nothing but the general abstract idea of *entity*.

Hyl. Nothing else, save only that I superadd to this general idea the negation of all those particular things, qualities, or ideas that I perceive, imagine, or in any wise apprehend.

Phil. Pray where do you suppose this unknown matter to exist?

Hyl. Oh Philonous! now you think you have entangled me; for if I say it exists in place, then you will infer that it exists in the mind, since it is agreed, that place or extension exists only in the mind: but I am not ashamed to own my ignorance. I know not where it exists; only I am sure it exists not in place. There is a negative answer for you: and you must expect no other to all the questions you put for the future about matter.

Phil. Since you will not tell me where it exists, be pleased to inform me after what manner you suppose it to exist, or what you mean by its *existence*.

Hyl. It neither thinks nor acts, neither perceives, nor is perceived.

Phil. But what is there positive in your abstracted notion of its existence?

Hyl. Upon a nice observation, I do not find I have any positive notion or meaning at all. I tell you again I am not ashamed to own my ignorance. I know not what is meant by its *existence*, or how it exists.

Phil. Continue, good Hylas, to act the same ingenuous part, and tell me sincerely whether you can frame a distinct idea of entity in general, prescinded from and exclusive of all thinking and corporeal beings, all particular things whatsoever.

Hyl. Hold, let me think a little——I profess, Philonous, I do not find that I can. At first glance methought I had some dilute and airy notion of pure entity in abstract; but upon closer attention it hath quite vanished out of sight. The more I think on it, the more am I confirmed in my prudent resolution of giving none but negative answers, and not pretending to the least degree of any positive knowledge or conception of matter, its *where*, its *how*, its *entity*, or any thing belonging to it.

Phil. When therefore you speak of the existence of matter, you have not any notion in your mind.

Hyl. None at all.

Phil. Pray tell me if the case stands not thus: at first, from a belief of material substance you would have it that the immediate objects existed without the mind; then that their archetypes; then causes; next instruments; then occasions: lastly, *something in general,* which being interpreted proves *nothing.* So matter comes to nothing. What think you, Hylas? is not this a fair summary of your whole proceeding?

Hyl. Be that as it will, yet I still insist upon it, that our not being able to conceive a thing, is no argument against its existence.

Phil. That from a cause, effect, operation, sign, or other circumstance, there may reasonably be inferred the existence of a thing not immediately perceived, and that it were absurd for any man to argue against the existence of that thing, from his having no direct and positive notion of it, I freely own. But where there is nothing of all this; where neither reason nor revelation induces us to believe the existence of a thing; where we have not even a relative notion of it; where an abstraction is made from perceiving and being perceived, from spirit and idea: lastly, where there is not so much as the most inadequate or faint idea pretended to: I will not indeed thence conclude against the reality of any notion or existence of any thing: but my inference shall be, that you mean nothing at all: that you imply words to no manner of purpose, without any design or signification whatsoever. And I leave it to you to consider how mere jargon should be treated.

Hyl. To deal frankly with you, Philonous, your arguments seem in themselves unanswerable, but they have not so great an effect on me as to produce that entire conviction, that hearty acquiescence which attends demonstration. I find myself still relapsing into an obscure surmise of I know not what, *matter.*

Phil. But are you not sensible, Hylas, that two things must concur to take away all scruple, and work a plenary assent in the mind? Let a visible object be set in never so clear a light, yet if there is any imperfection in the sight, or if the eye is not directed towards it, it will not be distinctly seen. And though a demonstration be never so well grounded and fairly proposed, yet if there is withal a stain of prejudice, or a wrong bias on the understanding, can it be expected on a sudden to perceive clearly and adhere firmly to the truth? No, there is need of time and pains; the attention must be awakened and detained by a frequent repetition of the same thing placed oft in the same, oft in different lights. I have said it already, and I find I must still repeat and inculcate, that it is an unaccountable license you take in pretending to maintain you know not what, for you know not what reason, to you know not what purpose. Can this be paralleled in any art or science, any sect or profession of men? Or is there any thing so barefacedly groundless and unreasonable to be met with even in the lowest of common conversation? But perhaps you will still say, matter may exist, though at the same time you neither know what is meant by *matter*, nor by its *existence*. This indeed is surprising, and the more so because it is altogether voluntary, you not being led to it by any one reason; for I challenge you to show me that thing in nature which needs matter to explain or account for it.

Hyl. The reality of things cannot be maintained without supposing the existence of matter. And is not this, think you, a good reason why I should be earnest in its defence?

Phil. The reality of things! What things, sensible or intelligible?

Hyl. Sensible things.

Phil. My glove, for example?

Hyl. That or any other thing perceived by the senses.

Phil. But to fix on some particular thing; is it not a sufficient evidence to me of the existence of this *glove*, that I see it, and feel it, and wear it? Or if this will not do, how is it possible I should be assured of the reality of this thing, which I actually see in this place, by supposing that some unknown thing, which I never did or can see, exists after an unknown manner, in an unknown place, or in no place at all? How can the supposed reality of that which is intangible, be a proof that any thing tangible really exists? Or of that which is invisible, that any visible thing, or in general of any thing which is imperceptible, that a perceptible exists? Do but explain this, and I shall think nothing too hard for you.

Hyl. Upon the whole, I am content to own the existence of matter is highly improbable; but the direct and absolute impossibility of it does not appear to me.

Phil. But granting matter to be possible, yet upon that account merely it can have no more claim to existence, than a golden mountain or a centaur.

Hyl. I acknowledge it; but still you do not deny it is possible; and that which is possible, for aught you know, may actually exist.

Phil. I deny it to be possible; and have, if I mistake not, evidently proved from your own concessions that it is not. In the common sense of the word *matter*, is there any more implied than an extended, solid, figured, moveable substance, existing without the mind? And have not you acknowledged over and over, that you have seen evident reason for denying the possibility of such a substance.

Hyl. True, but that is only one sense of the term *matter*.

Phil. But is it not the only proper genuine received sense? and if matter in such a sense be proved impossible, may it not be thought with good grounds absolutely impossible? Else how could any thing be proved impossible? Or indeed how could there be any proof at all one way or other, to a man who takes the liberty to unsettle and change the common signification of words?

Hyl. I thought philosophers might be allowed to speak

more accurately than the vulgar, and were not always confined to the common acceptation of a term.

Phil. But this now mentioned is the common received sense among philosophers themselves. But not to insist on that, have you not been allowed to take matter in what sense you pleased? And have you not used this privilege in the utmost extent, sometimes entirely changing, at others leaving out or putting into the definition of it whatever for the present best served your design, contrary to all the known rules of reason and logic? And hath not this shifting, unfair method of yours spun out our dispute to an unnecessary length; matter having been particularly examined, and by your own confession refuted in each of those senses? And can any more be required to prove the absolute impossibility of a thing, than the proving it impossible in every particular sense, that either you or any one else understands it in?

Hyl. But I am not so thoroughly satisfied that you have proved the impossibility of matter in the last most obscure, abstracted and indefinite sense.

Phil. When is a thing shown to be impossible?

Hyl. When a repugnancy is demonstrated between the ideas comprehended in its definition.

Phil. But where there are no ideas, there no repugnancy can be demonstrated between ideas.

Hyl. I agree with you.

Phil. Now in that which you call the obscure, indefinite sense of the word *matter*, it is plain, by your own confession, there was included no idea at all, no sense except an unknown sense, which is the same thing as none. You are not therefore to expect I should prove a repugnancy between ideas where there are no ideas, or the impossibility of matter taken in an *unknown* sense, that is no sense at all. My business was only to show, you meant *nothing*: and this you were brought to own. So that in all your various senses, you have been shown either to mean nothing at all, or if any thing, an absurdity. And if this be not sufficient to prove the impossibility of a thing, I desire you will let me know what is.

Hyl. I acknowledge you have proved that matter is impossible; nor do I see what more can be said in defence of it. But at the same time that I give up this, I suspect all my other notions. For surely none could be more seemingly evident than this once was: and yet it now seems as false and absurd as ever it did true before. But I think we have discussed the point sufficiently for the present. The remaining part of the day I would willingly spend, in running over in my thoughts the several heads of this morning's conversation, and to-morrow shall be glad to meet you here again about the same time.

Phil. I will not fail to attend you.

THE THIRD DIALOGUE

Philonous. Tell me, Hylas, what are the fruits of yesterday's meditation? Hath it confirmed you in the same mind you were in at parting? or have you since seen cause to change your opinion?

Hylas. Truly my opinion is, that all our opinions are alike vain and uncertain. What we approve to-day, we condemn to-morrow. We keep a stir about knowledge, and spend our lives in the pursuit of it, when, alas! we know nothing all the while : nor do I think it possible for us ever to know any thing in this life. Our faculties are too narrow and too few. Nature certainly never intended us for speculation.

Phil. What! say you we can know nothing, Hylas?

Hyl. There is not that single thing in the world, whereof we can know the real nature, or what it is in itself.

Phil. Will you tell me I do not really know what fire or water is?

Hyl. You may indeed know that fire appears hot, and water fluid : but this is no more than knowing what sensations are produced in your own mind, upon the application of fire and water to your organs of sense. Their internal constitution, their true and real nature, you are utterly in the dark as to that.

Phil. Do I not know this to be a real stone that I stand on, and that which I see before my eyes to be a real tree?

Hyl. Know? No, it is impossible you or any man alive should know it. All you know is, that you have such a certain idea or appearance in your own mind. But what is this to the real tree or stone? I tell you, that colour, figure, and hardness, which you perceive, are not the real natures of those things, or in the least like them. The same may be said of all other real things or corporeal substances which compose the world. They have none of them any thing in themselves, like those sensible qualities by us perceived. We should not therefore pretend to affirm or know any thing of them, as they are in their own nature.

Phil. But surely, Hylas, I can distinguish gold, for example, from iron : and how could this be, if I knew not what either truly was?

Hyl. Believe me, Philonous, you can only distinguish between your own ideas. That yellowness, that weight, and other sensible qualities, think you they are really in the gold? They are only relative to the senses, and have no absolute existence in nature. And in pretending to distinguish the species of real things, by the appearances in your mind, you may perhaps act as wisely as he that should conclude two men were of a different species, because their clothes were not of the same colour.

Phil. It seems then we are altogether put off with the appearances of things, and those false ones too. The very meat I eat, and the cloth I wear, have nothing in them like what I see and feel.

Hyl. Even so.

Phil. But is it not strange the whole world should be thus imposed on and so foolish as to believe their senses? And yet I know not how it is, but men eat, and drink, and sleep, and perform all the offices of life as comfortably and conveniently, as if they really knew the things they are conversant about.

Hyl. They do so : but you know ordinary practice does not require a nicety of speculative knowledge. Hence the vulgar retain their mistakes, and for all that, make a shift to bustle through the affairs of life. But philosophers know better things.

Phil. You mean, they know that they *know nothing.*

Hyl. That is the very top and perfection of human knowledge.

Phil. But are you all this while in earnest, Hylas; and

are you seriously persuaded that you know nothing real in the world? Suppose you are going to write, would you not call for pen, ink, and paper, like another man; and do you not know what it is you call for?

Hyl. How often must I tell you, that I know not the real nature of any one thing in the universe? I may, indeed, upon occasion, make use of pen, ink, and paper. But what any one of them is in its own true nature, I declare positively I know not. And the same is true with regard to every other corporeal thing. And, what is more, we are not only ignorant of the true and real nature of things, but even of their existence. It cannot be denied that we perceive such certain appearances or ideas; but it cannot be concluded from thence that bodies really exist. Nay, now I think on it, I must, agreeably to my former concessions, further declare, that it is impossible any real corporeal thing should exist in nature.

Phil. You amaze me. Was ever any thing more wild and extravagant than the notions you now maintain : and is it not evident you are led into all these extravagancies by the belief of *material substance*? This makes you dream of those unknown natures in every thing. It is this occasions your distinguishing between the reality and sensible appearances of things. It is to this you are indebted for being ignorant of what every body else knows perfectly well. Nor is this all : you are not only ignorant of the true nature of every thing, but you know not whether any thing really exists, or whether there are any true natures at all; forasmuch as you attribute to your material beings an absolute or external existence, wherein you suppose their reality consists. And as you are forced in the end to acknowledge such an existence means either a direct repugnancy, or nothing at all, it follows that you are obliged to pull down your own hypothesis of material substance, and positively to deny the real existence of any part of the universe. And so you are plunged into the deepest and most deplorable *scepticism* that ever man was. Tell me, Hylas, is it not as I say?

Hyl. I agree with you. *Material substance* was no more than an hypothesis, and a false and groundless one too. I will no longer spend my breath in defence of it. But whatever hypothesis you advance, or whatsoever scheme of things you introduce in its stead, I doubt not it will appear every whit as false : let me but be allowed to question you upon it. That is, suffer me to serve you in your own kind, and I warrant it shall conduct you through as many perplexities and contradictions, to the very same state of scepticism that I myself am in at present.

Phil. I assure you, Hylas, I do not pretend to frame any hypothesis at all. I am of a vulgar cast, simple enough to believe my senses, and leave things as I find them. To be plain, it is my opinion, that the real things are those very things I see and feel, and perceive by my senses. These I know, and finding they answer all the necessities and purposes of life, have no reason to be solicitous about any other unknown beings. A piece of sensible bread, for instance, would stay my stomach better than ten thousand times as much of that insensible, unintelligible, real bread you speak of. It is likewise my opinion, that colours and other sensible qualities are on the objects. I cannot for my life help thinking that snow is white, and fire hot. You indeed, who by *snow* and *fire* mean certain external, unperceived, unperceiving substances, are in the right to deny whiteness or heat to be affections inherent in them. But I, who understand by those words the things I see and feel, am obliged to think like other folks. And as I am no sceptic with regard to the nature of things, so neither am I as to their existence. That a thing should be really perceived by my senses, and at the same time not really exist, is to me a plain contradiction; since I cannot prescind or abstract, even in thought, the existence of a sensible thing from its being perceived. Wood, stones, fire,

water, flesh, iron, and the like things, which I name and
discourse of, are things that I know. And I should not
have known them, but that I perceived them by my senses;
and things perceived by the senses are immediately perceived; and things immediately perceived are ideas; and
ideas cannot exist without the mind; their existence therefore consists in being perceived; when therefore they are
actually perceived, there can be no doubt of their existence.
Away then with all that scepticism, all those ridiculous
philosophical doubts. What a jest is it for a philosopher to
question the existence of sensible things, till he hath it
proved to him from the veracity of God : or to pretend our
knowledge in this point falls short of intuition or demonstration ! I might as well doubt of my own being, as of
the being of those things I actually see and feel.

Hyl. Not so fast, Philonous : you say you cannot conceive how sensible things should exist without the mind.
Do you not?

Phil. I do.

Hyl. Supposing you were annihilated, cannot you conceive it possible that things perceivable by sense may still
exist?

Phil. I can; but then it must be in another mind. When
I deny sensible things in existence out of the mind, I do
not mean my mind in particular, but all minds. Now it is
plain they have an existence exterior to my mind, since I
find them by experience to be independent of it. There is
therefore some other mind wherein they exist, during the
intervals between the times of my perceiving them : as likewise they did before my birth, and would do after my
supposed annihilation. And as the same is true with
regard to all other finite created spirits, it necessarily
follows, there is an *omnipresent, eternal Mind,* which
knows and comprehends all things, and exhibits them to
our view in such a manner, and according to such rules
as he himself hath ordained, and are by us termed the
laws of nature.

Hyl. Answer me, Philonous. Are all our ideas perfectly inert beings? Or have they any agency included in them?

Phil. They are altogether passive and inert.

Hyl. And is not God an agent, a being purely active?

Phil. I acknowledge it.

Hyl. No idea therefore can be like unto, or represent the nature of God.

Phil. It cannot.

Hyl. Since therefore you have no idea of the mind of God, how can you conceive it possible, that things should exist in his mind? Or, if you can conceive the mind of God without having an idea of it, why may not I be allowed to conceive the existence of matter, notwithstanding that I have no idea of it?

Phil. As to your first question : I own I have properly no idea, either of God or any other spirit; for these being active, cannot be represented by things perfectly inert, as our ideas are. I do nevertheless know, that I, who am a spirit or thinking substance, exist as certainly as I know my ideas exist. Further, I know what I mean by the terms *I* and *myself*; and I know this immediately, or intuitively, though I do not perceive it as I perceive a triangle, a colour, or a sound. The mind, spirit, or soul, is that indivisible, unextended thing, which thinks, acts, and perceives. I say *indivisible*, because unextended; and *unextended*, because extended, figured, moveable things, are ideas; and that which perceives ideas, which thinks and wills, is plainly itself no idea, nor like an idea. Ideas are things inactive, and perceived : and spirits a sort of beings altogether different from them. I do not therefore say my soul is an idea, or like an idea. However, taking the word *idea* in a large sense, my soul may be said to furnish me with an idea, that is, an image, or likeness of God, though indeed extremely inadequate. For all the notion I have of God is obtained by reflecting on my own soul, heightening its powers, and removing its imperfections. I have therefore, though not an inactive idea, yet in myself some sort of an active thinking image of the Deity. And though I perceive him not by sense, yet I have a notion of him, or know him by reflection and reasoning. My own mind and my own ideas I have an immediate knowledge of; and by the help of these, do mediately apprehend the possibility of the existence of other spirits and ideas. Further, from my own being, and from the dependency I find in myself and my ideas, I do by an act of reason necessarily infer the existence of a God, and of all created things in the mind of God. So much for your first question. For the second: I suppose by this time you can answer it yourself. For you neither perceive matter objectively, as you do an inactive being or idea, nor know it, as you do yourself, by a reflex act: neither do you mediately apprehend it by similitude of the one or the other: nor yet collect it by reasoning from that which you know immediately. All which makes the case of *matter* widely different from that of the *Deity*.

Hyl. You say your own soul supplies you with some sort of an idea or image of God. But at the same time you acknowledge you have, properly speaking, no idea of your own soul. You even affirm that spirits are a sort of beings altogether different from ideas. Consequently that no idea can be like a spirit. We have therefore no idea of any spirit. You admit nevertheless that there is spiritual substance, although you have no idea of it; while you deny there can be such a thing as material substance, because you have no notion or idea of it. Is this fair dealing? To act consistently, you must either admit matter or reject spirit. What say you to this?

Phil. I say in the first place, that I do not deny the existence of material substance merely because I have no notion of it, but because the notion of it is inconsistent, or in other words, because it is repugnant that there should be a notion of it. Many things, for aught I know, may exist, whereof neither I nor any other man hath or can have any idea or notion whatsoever. But then those things must be possible, that is, nothing inconsistent must be included in their definition. I say secondly, that although we believe things to exist which we do not perceive; yet we may not believe that any particular thing exists, without some reason for such belief: but I have no reason for believing the existence of matter. I have no immediate intuition thereof: neither can I mediately from my sensations, ideas, notions, actions, or passions, infer an unthinking, unperceiving, inactive substance, either by probable deduction, or necessary consequence. Whereas the being of myself, that is, my own soul, mind, or thinking principle, I evidently know by reflection. You will forgive me if I repeat the same things in answer to the same objections. In the very notion or definition of material substance, there is included a manifest repugnance and inconsistency. But this cannot be said of the notion of spirit. That ideas should exist in what doth not perceive, or be produced by what doth not act, is repugnant. But it is no repugnancy to say, that a perceiving thing should be the subject of ideas, or an active thing the cause of them. It is granted we have neither an immediate evidence nor a demonstrative knowledge of the existence of other finite spirits; but it will not thence follow that such spirits are on a foot with material substances: if to suppose the one be inconsistent, and it be not inconsistent to suppose the other; if the one can be inferred by no argument, and there is a probability for the other; if we see signs and effects indicating distinct finite agents like ourselves, and see no sign or symptom whatever that leads to a rational belief of matter. I say lastly, that I have a notion of spirit, though I have not, strictly speaking, an idea of it. I do not perceive it as an idea or by means of an idea, but know it by reflection.

Hyl. Notwithstanding all you have said, to me it seems, that according to your own way of thinking, and in consequence of your own principles, it should follow that you are only a system of floating ideas, without any substance to support them. Words are not to be used without a meaning. And as there is no more meaning in spiritual substance than in material substance, the one is to be exploded as well as the other.

Phil. How often must I repeat, that I know or am conscious of my own being; and that I myself am not my ideas, but somewhat else, a thinking, active principle that perceives, knows, wills, and operates about ideas? I know that I, one and the same self, perceive both colours and sounds : that a colour cannot perceive a sound, nor a sound a colour : that I am therefore one individual principle, distinct from colour and sound; and, for the same reason, from all other sensible things and inert ideas. But I am not in like manner conscious either of the existence or essence of matter. On the contrary, I know that nothing inconsistent can exist, and that the existence of matter implies an inconsistency. Further, I know what I mean, when I affirm that there is a spiritual substance or support of ideas, that is, that a spirit knows and perceives ideas. But I do not know what is meant, when it is said, that an unperceiving substance hath inherent in it and supports either ideas or the archetypes of ideas. There is therefore upon the whole no parity of case between spirit and matter.

Hyl. I own myself satisfied in this point. But do you in earnest think, the real existence of sensible things consists in their being actually perceived? If so, how comes it that all mankind distinguish between them? Ask the first man you meet, and he shall tell you, *to be perceived* is one thing, and *to exist* is another.

Phil. I am content, Hylas, to appeal to the common sense of the world for the truth of my notion. Ask the gardener, why he thinks yonder cherry-tree exists in the garden, and he shall tell you, because he sees and feels it; in a word, because he perceives it by his senses. Ask him, why he thinks an orange-tree not to be there, and he shall tell you, because he does not perceive it. What he perceives by sense, that he terms a real being, and saith it *is*, or *exists*; but that which is not perceivable, the same, he saith, hath no being.

Hyl. Yes, Philonous, I grant the existence of a sensible thing consists in being perceivable, but not in being actually perceived.

Phil. And what is perceivable but an idea? And can an idea exist without being actually perceived? These are points long since agreed between us.

Hyl. But be your opinion never so true, yet surely you will not deny it is shocking, and contrary to the common sense of men. Ask the fellow, whether yonder tree hath an existence out of his mind : what answer, think you, he would make?

Phil. The same that I should myself, to wit, that it doth exist out of his mind. But then to a Christian it cannot surely be shocking to say, the real tree existing without his mind is truly known and comprehended by (that is, *exists in*) the infinite mind of God. Probably he may not at first glance be aware of the direct and immediate proof there is of this, inasmuch as the very being of a tree, or any other sensible thing, implies a mind wherein it is. But the point itself he cannot deny. The question between the materialists and me is not, whether things have a real existence out of the mind of this or that person, but whether they have an absolute existence, distinct from being perceived by God, and exterior to all minds. This indeed some heathens and philosophers have affirmed, but whoever entertains notions of the Deity suitable to holy scriptures, will be of another opinion.

Hyl. But according to your notions, what difference is there between real things, and chimeras formed by the imagination, or the visions of a dream, since they are all equally in the mind?

Phil. The ideas formed by the imagination are faint and indistinct; they have besides an entire dependence on the will. But the ideas perceived by sense, that is, real things,

are more vivid and clear, and being imprinted on the min
by a spirit distinct from us, have not a like dependence o
our will. There is therefore no danger of confoundin
these with the foregoing : and there is as little of confoun
ing them with the visions of a dream, which are dim
irregular, and confused. And though they should happe
to be never so lively and natural, yet by their not bein
connected, and of a piece with the preceding and subse
quent transactions of our lives, they might easily be di
tinguished from realities. In short, by whatever metho
you distinguish *things* from *chimeras* on your own schem
the same, it is evident, will hold also upon mine. For
must be, I presume, by some perceived difference, and
am not for depriving you of any one thing that you per
ceive.

Hyl. But still, Philonous, you hold, there is nothing i
the world but spirits and ideas. And this, you must nee
acknowledge, sounds very oddly.

Phil. I own the word *idea,* not being commonly use
for *thing,* sounds something out of the way. My reason fo
using it was, because a necessary relation to the mind
understood to be implied by that term; and it is no
commonly used by philosophers, to denote the immediat
objects of the understanding. But however oddly the pro
position may sound in words, yet it includes nothing s
very strange or shocking in its sense, which in effec
amounts to no more than this, to wit, that there are onl
things perceiving, and things perceived; or that ever
unthinking being is necessarily, and from the very natur
of its existence, perceived by some mind; if not by an
finite created mind, yet certainly by the infinite mind c
God, in whom " we live, and move, and have our being.
Is this as strange as to say, the sensible qualities are not o
the objects : or, that we cannot be sure of the existence c
things, or know any thing of their real natures, though w
both see and feel them, and perceive them by all ou
senses?

Hyl. And in consequence of this, must we not think there are no such things as physical or corporeal causes; but that a spirit is the immediate cause of all the phenomena in nature? Can there be any thing more extravagant than this?

Phil. Yes, it is infinitely more extravagant to say, a thing which is inert, operates on the mind, and which is unperceiving, is the cause of our perceptions. Besides, that which to you, I know not for what reason, seems so extravagant, is no more than the holy scriptures assert in a hundred places. In them God is represented as the sole and immediate author of all those effects, which some heathens and philosophers are wont to ascribe to nature, matter, fate, or the like unthinking principle. This is so much the constant language of scripture, that it were needless to confirm it by citations.

Hyl. You are not aware, Philonous, that in making God the immediate author of all the motions in nature, you make him the author of murder, sacrilege, adultery, and the like heinous sins.

Phil. In answer to that, I observe first, that the imputation of guilt is the same, whether a person commits an action with or without an instrument. In case therefore you suppose God to act by the mediation of an instrument, or occasion, called *matter*, you as truly make him the author of sin as I, who think him the immediate agent in all those operations vulgarly ascribed to nature. I further observe, that sin or moral turpitude doth not consist in the outward physical action or motion, but in the internal deviation of the will from the laws of reason and religion. This is plain, in that the killing an enemy in a battle, or putting a criminal legally to death, is not thought sinful, though the outward act be the very same with that in the case of murder. Since therefore sin doth not consist in the physical action, the making God an immediate cause of all such actions, is not making him the author of sin. Lastly, I have no where said that God is the only agent who

produces all the motions in bodies. It is true, I hav
denied there are any other agents beside spirits : but thi
is very consistent with allowing to thinking, rational beings
in the production of motions, the use of limited powers
ultimately indeed derived from God, but immediatel
under the direction of their own wills, which is sufficien
to entitle them to all the guilt of their actions.

Hyl. But the denying matter, Philonous, or corporea
substance; there is the point. You can never persuade m
that this is not repugnant to the universal sense of man
kind. Were our dispute to be determined by most voices
I am confident you would give up the point, withou
gathering the votes.

Phil. I wish both our opinions were fairly stated and
submitted to the judgment of men who had plain commor
sense, without the prejudices of a learned education. Le
me be represented as one who trusts his senses, who
thinks he knows the things he sees and feels, and enter
tains no doubts of their existence; and you fairly set fortl
with all your doubts, your paradoxes, and your scepticism
about you, and I shall willingly acquiesce in the determina
tion of any indifferent person. That there is no substance
wherein ideas can exist beside spirit, is to me evident. And
that the objects immediately perceived are ideas, is or
all hands agreed. And that sensible qualities are object
immediately perceived, no one can deny. It is therefore
evident there can be no *substratum* of those qualities bur
spirit, in which they exist, not by way of mode or property, but as a thing perceived in that which perceives it.
I deny therefore that there is any unthinking *substratum*
of the objects of sense, and in that acceptation that there
is any material substance. But if by *material substance* is
meant only sensible body, that which is seen and felt (and
the unphilosophical part of the world, I dare say, mean
no more), then I am more certain of matter's existence
than you, or any other philosopher, pretend to be. If there
be any thing which makes the generality of mankind

averse from the notions I espouse, it is a misapprehension
that I deny the reality of sensible things : but as it is you
who are guilty of that and not I, it follows that in truth
their aversion is against your notions, and not mine. I do
therefore assert that I am as certain as of my own being,
that there are bodies or corporeal substances (meaning the
things I perceive by my senses); and that granting this,
the bulk of mankind will take no thought about, nor think
themselves at all concerned in the fate of those unknown
natures, and philosophical quiddities, which some men are
so fond of.

Hyl. What say you to this? Since, according to you,
men judge of the reality of things by their senses, how
can a man be mistaken in thinking the moon a plain lucid
surface, about a foot in diameter; or a square tower, seen
at a distance, round; or an oar, with one end in the water,
crooked?

Phil. He is not mistaken with regard to the ideas he
actually perceives; but in the inferences he makes from
his present perceptions. Thus in the case of the oar, what
he immediately perceives by sight is certainly crooked;
and so far he is in the right. But if he thence conclude,
that upon taking the oar out of the water he shall perceive the same crookedness, or that it would affect his
touch as crooked things are wont to do, in that he is mistaken. In like manner, if he should conclude from what
he perceives in one station, that in case he advances to-
ward the moon or tower, he should still be affected with
the like ideas, he is mistaken. But his mistake lies not in
what he perceives immediately and at present (it being a
manifest contradiction to suppose he should err in respect
of that), but in the wrong judgment he makes concerning
the ideas he apprehends to be connected with those immediately perceived : or concerning the ideas that, from
what he perceives at present, he imagines would be perceived in other circumstances. The case is the same with
regard to the Copernican system. We do not here per-

ceive any motion of the earth : but it were erroneous
thence to conclude, that in case we were placed at as great
a distance from that, as we are now from the other
planets, we should not then perceive its motion.

Hyl. I understand you; and must needs own you say
things plausible enough : but give me leave to put you in
mind of one thing. Pray, Philonous, were you not formerly as positive that matter existed, as you are now that
it does not?

Phil. I was. But here lies the difference. Before, my
positiveness was founded without examination, upon prejudice; but now, after inquiry, upon evidence.

Hyl. After all, it seems our dispute is rather about words
than things. We agree in the thing, but differ in the
name. That we are affected with ideas from without is
evident; and it is no less evident, that there must be (I
will not say archetypes, but) powers without the mind,
corresponding to those ideas. And as these powers cannot
subsist by themselves, there is some subject of them necessarily to be admitted, which I call *matter,* and you call
spirit. This is all the difference.

Phil. Pray, Hylas, is that powerful being, or subject of
powers, extended?

Hyl. It hath not extension; but it hath the power to
raise in you the idea of extension.

Phil. It is therefore itself unextended.

Hyl. I grant it.

Phil. Is it not also active?

Hyl. Without doubt : otherwise, how could we attribute powers to it?

Phil. Now let me ask you two questions : first, whether
it be agreeable to the usage either of philosophers or
others, to give the name *matter* to an unextended active
being? And secondly, whether it be not ridiculously
absurd to misapply names contrary to the common use of
language?

Hyl. Well then, let it not be called matter, since you

will have it so, but some *third nature* distinct from matter and spirit. For, what reason is there why you should call it spirit? Does not the notion of spirit imply, that it is thinking as well as active and unextended?

Phil. My reason is this : because I have a mind to have some notion or meaning in what I say; but I have no notion of any action distinct from volition, neither can I conceive volition to be any where but in a spirit : therefore when I speak of an active being, I am obliged to mean a spirit. Beside, what can be plainer than that a thing which hath no ideas in itself, cannot impart them to me; and if it hath ideas, surely it must be a spirit. To make you comprehend the point still more clearly, if it be possible : I assert as well as you, that since we are affected from without, we must allow powers to be without in a being distinct from ourselves. So far we are agreed. But then we differ as to the kind of this powerful being. I will have it to be spirit, you matter, or I know not what (I may add too, you know not what) third nature. Thus I prove it to be spirit. From the effects I see produced, I conclude there are actions; and because actions, volitions; and because there are volitions, there must be a will. Again, the things I perceive must have an existence, they or their archetypes, out of my mind : but being ideas, neither they nor their archetypes can exist otherwise than in an understanding : there is therefore an understanding. But will and understanding constitute in the strictest sense a mind or spirit. The powerful cause therefore of my ideas, is in strict propriety of speech a *spirit*.

Hyl. And now I warrant you think you have made the point very clear, little suspecting that what you advance leads directly to a contradiction. Is it not an absurdity to imagine any imperfection in God?

Phil. Without doubt.

Hyl. To suffer pain is an imperfection.

Phil. It is.

Hyl. Are we not sometimes affected with pain and uneasiness by some other being?

Phil. We are.

Hyl. And have you not said that being is a spirit, and is not that spirit God?

Phil. I grant it.

Hyl. But you have asserted, that whatever ideas we perceive from without, are in the mind which affects us. The ideas therefore of pain and uneasiness are in God; or in other words, God suffers pain : that is to say, there is an imperfection in the divine nature, which you acknowledged was absurd. So you are caught in a plain contradiction.

Phil. That God knows or understands all things, and that he knows among other things what pain is, even every sort of painful sensation, and what it is for his creatures to suffer pain, I make no question. But that God, though he knows and sometimes causes painful sensations in us, can himself suffer pain, I positively deny. We who are limited and dependent spirits, are liable to impressions of sense, the effects of an external agent, which being produced against our wills, are sometimes painful and uneasy. But God, whom no external being can affect, who perceives nothing by sense as we do, whose will is absolute and independent, causing all things, and liable to be thwarted or resisted by nothing; it is evident, such a being as this can suffer nothing, nor be affected with any painful sensation, or indeed any sensation at all. We are chained to a body, that is to say, our perceptions are connected with corporeal motions. By the law of our nature we are affected upon every alteration in the nervous parts of our sensible body : which sensible body rightly considered, is nothing but a complexion of such qualities or ideas, as have no existence distinct from being perceived by a mind; so that this connexion of sensations with corporeal motions, means no more than a correspondence in the order of nature between two sets of ideas, or things immediately erceivable. But God is a pure spirit, disengaged from ll such sympathy or natural ties. No corporeal motions re attended with the sensations of pain or pleasure in his ind. To know every thing knowable is certainly a perfection; but to endure, or suffer, or feel any thing by sense, an imperfection. The former, I say, agrees to God, but ot the latter. God knows or hath ideas : but his ideas are ot conveyed to him by sense, as ours are. Your not distinguishing where there is so manifest a difference, makes ou fancy you see an absurdity where there is none.

Hyl. But all this while you have not considered, that he quantity of matter hath been demonstrated to be proportioned to the gravity of bodies. And what can withstand demonstration?

Phil. Let me see how you demonstrate that point?

Hyl. I lay it down for a principle, that the moments or quantities of motion in bodies, are in a direct compounded eason of the velocities and quantities of matter contained n them. Hence, where the velocities are equal, it follows, he moments are directly as the quantity of matter in each. But it is found by experience, that all bodies (bating the mall inequalities arising from the resistance of the air) lescend with an equal velocity; the motion therefore of lescending bodies, and consequently their gravity, which s the cause or principle of that motion, is proportional to he quantity of matter : which was to be demonstrated.

Phil. You lay it down as a self-evident principle, that he quantity of motion in any body is proportional to the velocity and *matter* taken together : and this is made use of to prove a proposition, from whence the existence of *matter* is inferred. Pray is not this arguing in a circle?

Hyl. In the premise I only mean, that the motion is proportional to the velocity, jointly with the extension and solidity.

Phil. But allowing this to be true, yet it will not thence follow, that gravity is proportional to *matter,* in your philosophic sense of the word; except you take it for

granted, that unknown *substratum*, or whatever else yo
call it, is proportional to those sensible qualities; which
suppose is plainly begging the question. That there
magnitude, and solidity, or resistance, perceived by sens
I readily grant; as likewise that gravity may be propo
tional to those qualities, I will not dispute. But that eithe
these qualities as perceived by us, or the powers produc
ing them, do exist in a *material substratum*; this is what
deny, and you indeed affirm, but notwithstanding you
demonstration, have not yet proved.

Hyl. I shall insist no longer on that point. Do yo
think, however, you shall persuade me that natural phil
sophers have been dreaming all this while? pray wha
becomes of all their hypotheses and explications of th
phenomena, which suppose the existence of matter?

Phil. What mean you, Hylas, by the phenomena?

Hyl. I mean the appearances which I perceive by m
senses.

Phil. And the appearances perceived by sense, are the
not ideas?

Hyl. I have told you so a hundred times.

Phil. Therefore, to explain the phenomena, is to sho
how we come to be affected with ideas, in that manner an
order wherein they are imprinted on our senses. Is it not

Hyl. It is.

Phil. Now if you can prove, that any philosopher hath
explained the production of any one idea in our minds b
the help of *matter*, I shall for ever acquiesce, and look o
all that hath been said against it as nothing: but if yo
cannot, it is in vain to urge the explication of phenomena
That a being endowed with knowledge and will, shoul
produce or exhibit ideas, is easily understood. But that a
being which is utterly destitute of these faculties shoul
be able to produce ideas, or in any sort to affect an intel
ligence, this I can never understand. This I say, though
we had some positive conception of matter, though w
knew its qualities, and could comprehend its existence

would yet be so far from explaining things, that it is itself the most inexplicable thing in the world. And yet for all this, it will not follow, that philosophers have been doing nothing; for by observing and reasoning upon the connexion of ideas, they discover the laws and methods of nature, which is a part of knowledge both useful and entertaining.

Hyl. After all, can it be supposed God would deceive all mankind? Do you imagine, he would have induced the whole world to believe the being of matter, if there was no such thing?

Phil. That every epidemical opinion arising from prejudice, or passion, or thoughtlessness, may be imputed to God, as the author of it, I believe you will not affirm. Whatsoever opinion we father on him, it must be either because he has discovered it to us by supernatural revelation, or because it is so evident to our natural faculties, which were framed and given us by God, that it is impossible we should withhold our assent from it. But where is the revelation, or where is the evidence that extorts the belief of matter? Nay, how does it appear that matter, taken for something distinct from what we perceive by our senses, is thought to exist by all mankind, or indeed by any except a few philosophers, who do not know what they would be at? Your question supposes these points are clear; and when you have cleared them, I shall think myself obliged to give you another answer. In the mean time let it suffice that I tell you, I do not suppose God has deceived mankind at all.

Hyl. But the novelty, Philonous, the novelty! There lies the danger. New notions should always be discountenanced; they unsettle men's minds, and nobody knows where they will end.

Phil. Why the rejecting a notion that hath no foundation either in sense, or in reason, or in divine authority, should be thought to unsettle the belief of such opinions as are grounded on all or any of these, I cannot imagine.

That innovations in government and religion are dangerous, and ought to be discountenanced, I freely own. But is there the like reason why they should be discouraged in philosophy? The making any thing known which was unknown before, is an innovation in knowledge: and if all such innovations had been forbidden, men would have made a notable progress in the arts and sciences. But it is none of my business to plead for novelties and paradoxes. That the qualities we perceive are not on the objects: that we must not believe our senses: that we know nothing of the real nature of things, and can never be assured even of their existence: that real colours and sounds are nothing but certain unknown figures and motions: that motions are in themselves neither swift nor slow: that there are in bodies absolute extensions, without any particular magnitude or figure: that a thing stupid, thoughtless, and inactive, operates on a spirit: that the least particle of a body contains innumerable extended parts. These are the novelties, these are the strange notions which shock the genuine uncorrupted judgment of all mankind; and being once admitted, embarrass the mind with endless doubts and difficulties. And it is against these and the like innovations, I endeavour to vindicate common sense. It is true, in doing this, I may perhaps be obliged to use some *ambages,* and ways of speech not common. But if my notions are once thoroughly understood, that which is most singular in them will in effect be found to amount to no more than this: that it is absolutely impossible, and a plain contradiction to suppose, any unthinking being should exist without being perceived by a mind. And if this notion be singular, it is a shame it should be so at this time of day, and in a Christian country.

Hyl. As for the difficulties other opinions may be liable to, those are out of the question. It is your business to defend your own opinion. Can any thing be plainer, than that you are for changing all things into ideas? You, I ly, who are not ashamed to charge me with *scepticism*. This is so plain, there is no denying it.

Phil. You mistake me. I am not for changing things into ideas, but rather ideas into things; since those immediate objects of perception, which, according to you, are only appearances of things, I take to be the real things themselves.

Hyl. Things! you may pretend what you please; but it is certain, you leave us nothing but the empty forms of things, the outside only which strikes the senses.

Phil. What you call the empty forms and outside of things, seems to me the very things themselves. Nor are they empty or incomplete otherwise, than upon your supposition, that matter is an essential part of all corporeal things. We both therefore agree in this, that we perceive only sensible forms: but herein we differ, you will have them to be empty appearances, I real beings. In short you do not trust your senses, I do.

Hyl. You say you believe your senses; and seem to applaud yourself that in this you agree with the vulgar. According to you therefore, the true nature of a thing is discovered by the senses. If so, whence comes that disagreement? Why is not the same figure, and other sensible qualities, perceived all manner of ways? and why should we use a microscope, the better to discover the true nature of a body, if it were discoverable to the naked eye?

Phil. Strictly speaking, Hylas, we do not see the same object that we feel; neither is the same object perceived by the microscope, which was by the naked eye. But in case every variation was thought sufficient to constitute a new kind or individual, the endless number or confusion of names would render language impracticable. Therefore to avoid this as well as other inconveniences which are obvious upon a little thought, men combine together several ideas, apprehended by divers senses, or by the same sense at different times, or in different circumstances, but

observed however to have some connexion in nature, either
with respect to co-existence or succession; all which they
refer to one name, and consider as one thing. Hence it
follows that when I examine by my other senses a thing I
have seen, it is not in order to understand better the
same object which I had perceived by sight, the object of
one sense not being perceived by the other senses. And
when I look through a microscope, it is not that I may perceive more clearly what I perceived already with my bare
eyes, the object perceived by the glass being quite different from the former. But in both cases my aim is only to
know what ideas are connected together; and the more a
man knows of the connexion of ideas, the more he is said
to know of the nature of things. What therefore if our
ideas are variable? What if our senses are not in all
circumstances affected with the same appearances? It
will not thence follow, they are not to be trusted, or that
they are inconsistent either with themselves or any thing
else, except it be with your preconceived notion of (I know
not what) one single, unchanged, unperceivable, real
nature, marked by each name : which prejudice seems to
have taken its rise from not rightly understanding the
common language of men speaking of several distinct
ideas, as united into one thing by the mind. And indeed
there is cause to suspect several erroneous conceits of the
philosophers are owing to the same original : while they
began to build their schemes, not so much on notions as
words, which were framed by the vulgar, merely for conveniency and despatch in the common actions of life,
without any regard to speculation.

Hyl. Methinks I apprehend your meaning.

Phil. It is your opinion, the ideas we perceive by our
senses are not real things, but images, or copies of them.
Our knowledge therefore is no further real, than as our
ideas are the true representations of those originals. But
as these supposed originals are in themselves unknown, it
is impossible to know how far our ideas resemble them; or

whether they resemble them at all. We cannot therefore be sure we have any real knowledge. Further, as our ideas are perpetually varied, without any change in the supposed real things, it necessarily follows they cannot all be true copies of them; or if some are, and others are not, it is impossible to distinguish the former from the latter. And this plunges us yet deeper in uncertainty. Again, when we consider the point, we cannot conceive how any idea, or any thing like an idea, should have an absolute existence out of a mind; nor consequently, according to you, how there should be any real thing in nature. The result of all which is, that we are thrown into the most hopeless and abandoned *scepticism*. Now give me leave to ask you, first, whether your referring ideas to certain absolutely existing unperceived substances, as their originals, be not the source of all this *scepticism*? Secondly, whether you are informed, either by sense or reason, of the existence of those unknown originals? And in case you are not, whether it be not absurd to suppose them? Thirdly, whether upon inquiry, you find there is any thing distinctly conceived or meant by the *absolute or external existence of unperceiving substances*? Lastly, whether, the premises considered, it be not the wisest way to follow nature, trust your senses, and laying aside all anxious thought about unknown natures or substances, admit with the vulgar those for real things, which are perceived by the senses?

Hyl. For the present, I have no inclination to the answering part. I would much rather see how you can get over what follows. Pray are not the objects perceived by the senses of one, likewise perceivable to others present? If there were a hundred more here, they would all see the garden, the trees, and flowers as I see them. But they are not in the same manner affected with the ideas I frame in my imagination. Does not this make a difference between the former sort of objects and the latter?

Phil. I grant it does. Nor have I ever denied a difference between the objects of sense and those of imagina-

tion. But what would you infer from thence? You canno
say that sensible objects exist unperceived, because the
are perceived by many.

Hyl. I own, I can make nothing of that objection, bu
it hath led me into another. Is it not your opinion that by
our senses we perceive only the ideas existing in our
minds?

Phil. It is.

Hyl. But the same idea which is in my mind, cannot be
in yours, or in any other mind. Doth it not therefore
follow from your principles, that no two can see the same
thing? And is not this highly absurd?

Phil. If the term *same* be taken in the vulgar acceptation, it is certain (and not at all repugnant to the principles I maintain) that different persons may perceive the
same thing; or the same thing or idea exist in different
minds. Words are of arbitrary imposition; and since men
are used to apply the word *same* where no distinction or
variety is perceived, and I do not pretend to alter their
perceptions, it follows, that as men have said before,
several saw the same thing, so they may upon like occasions still continue to use the same phrase, without any
deviation either from propriety of language, or the truth
of things. But if the term *same* be used in the acceptation
of philosophers, who pretend to an abstracted notion of
identity, then, according to their sundry definitions of this
notion (for it is not yet agreed wherein that philosophic
identity consists), it may or may not be possible for divers
persons to perceive the same thing. But whether philosophers shall think fit to call a thing the *same* or no, is, I
conceive, of small importance. Let us suppose several
men together, all endued with the same faculties, and
consequently affected in like sort by their senses, and
who had yet never known the use of language; they would
without question agree in their perceptions. Though perhaps, when they came to the use of speech, some regarding

the uniformness of what was perceived, might call it the *same* thing: others especially regarding the diversity of persons who perceived, might choose the denomination of different things. But who sees not that all the dispute is about a word; to wit, whether what is perceived by different persons, may yet have the term *same* applied to it? Or suppose a house, whose walls or outward shell remaining unaltered, the chambers are all pulled down, and new ones built in their place; and that you should call this the *same,* and I should say it was not the *same* house: would we not for all this perfectly agree in our thoughts of the house, considered in itself? And would not all the difference consist in a sound? If you should say, we differ in our notions; for that you superadded to your idea of the house the simple abstracted idea of identity, whereas I did not; I would tell you I know not what you mean by that *abstracted idea of identity*; and should desire you to look into your own thoughts, and be sure you understood yourself.——Why so silent, Hylas? Are you not yet satisfied, men may dispute about identity and diversity, without any real difference in their thoughts and opinions, abstracted from names? Take this further reflection with you: that whether matter be allowed to exist or no, the case is exactly the same as to the point in hand. For the materialists themselves acknowledge what we immediately perceive by our senses to be our own ideas. Your difficulty therefore, that no two see the same thing, makes equally against the materialists and me.

Hyl. But they suppose an external archetype, to which referring their several ideas, they may truly be said to perceive the same thing.

Phil. And (not to mention your having discovered those archetypes) so may you suppose an external archetype on my principles: *external,* I mean, to your own mind; though indeed it must be supposed to exist in that mind which comprehends all things; but then this serves all the ends of identity, as well as if it existed out of a mind. And I am sure you yourself will not say, it is less intelligible.

Hyl. You have indeed clearly satisfied me, either that there is no difficulty at bottom in this point; or if there be, that it makes equally against both opinions.

Phil. But that which makes equally against two contradictory opinions, can be a proof against neither.

Hyl. I acknowledge it. But after all, Philonous, when I consider the substance of what you advance against scepticism, it amounts to no more than this. We are sure that we really see, hear, feel; in a word, that we are affected with sensible impressions.

Phil. And how are we concerned any further? I see this *cherry*, I feel it, I taste it: and I am sure *nothing* cannot be seen, or felt, or tasted: it is therefore *real*. Take away the sensations of softness, moisture, redness, tartness, and you take away the *cherry*. Since it is not a being distinct from sensations; a *cherry*, I say, is nothing but a congeries of sensible impressions, or ideas perceived by various senses; which ideas are united into one thing (or have one name given them) by the mind; because they are observed to attend each other. Thus when the palate is affected with such a particular taste, the sight is affected with a red colour, the touch with roundness, softness, &c. Hence, when I see, and feel, and taste, in sundry certain manners, I am sure the *cherry* exists, or is real; its reality being in my opinion nothing abstracted from those sensations. But if by the word *cherry* you mean an unknown nature distinct from all those sensible qualities, and by its existence something distinct from its being perceived; then indeed I own, neither you, nor I, nor any one else can be sure it exists.

Hyl. But what would you say, Philonous, if I should bring the very same reasons against the existence of sensible things in a mind, which you have offered against their existing in a material *substratum*?

Phil. When I see your reasons, you shall hear what I have to say to them.

Hyl. Is the mind extended or unextended?

Phil. Unextended, without doubt.

Hyl. Do you say the things you perceive are in your mind?

Phil. They are.

Hyl. Again, have I not heard you speak of sensible impressions?

Phil. I believe you may.

Hyl. Explain to me now, O Philonous! how it is possible there should be room for all those trees and houses to exist in your mind. Can extended things be contained in that which is unextended? or are we to imagine impressions made on a thing void of all solidity? You cannot say objects are in your mind, as books in your study: or that things are imprinted on it, as the figure of a seal upon wax. In what sense therefore are we to understand those expressions? Explain me this if you can: and I shall then be able to answer all those queries you formerly put to me about my substratum.

Phil. Look you, Hylas, when I speak of objects as existing in the mind or imprinted on the senses, I would not be understood in the gross literal sense, as when bodies are said to exist in a place, or a seal to make an impression upon wax. My meaning is only that the mind comprehends or perceives them; and that it is affected from without, or by some being distinct from itself. This is my explication of your difficulty; and how it can serve to make your tenet of an unperceiving material substratum intelligible, I would fain know.

Hyl. Nay, if that be all, I confess I do not see what use can be made of it. But are you not guilty of some abuse of language in this?

Phil. None at all : it is no more than common custom, which you know is the rule of language, hath authorized : nothing being more usual, than for philosophers to speak

of the immediate objects of the understanding as thing
existing in the mind. Nor is there any thing in this, but
what is conformable to the general analogy of language
most part of the mental operations being signified by word
borrowed from sensible things; as is plain in the term
comprehend, reflect, discourse, &c., which being applied
to the mind, must not be taken in their gross original
sense.

Hyl. You have, I own, satisfied me in this point; but
there still remains one great difficulty, which I know not
how you will get over. And, indeed, it is of such importance, that if you could solve all others, without being
able to find a solution for this, you must never expect to
make me a proselyte to your principles.

Phil. Let me know this mighty difficulty.

Hyl. The scripture account of the creation is what
appears to me utterly irreconcilable with your notions.
Moses tells us of a creation : a creation of what? of ideas?
No, certainly, but of things, of real things, solid corporeal
substances. Bring your principles to agree with this, and
I shall perhaps agree with you.

Phil. Moses mentions the sun, moon, and stars, earth
and sea, plants and animals : that all these do really exist,
and were in the beginning created by God, I make no
question. If by *ideas* you mean fictions and fancies of the
mind, then these are no ideas. If by *ideas* you mean
immediate objects of the understanding, or sensible things
which cannot exist unperceived, or out of a mind, then
these things are ideas. But whether you do or do not call
them *ideas,* it matters little. The difference is only about
a name. And whether that name be retained or rejected,
the sense, the truth, and reality of things continues the
same. In common talk, the objects of our senses are not
termed *ideas,* but *things.* Call them so still; provided
you do not attribute to them any absolute external existence, and I shall never quarrel with you for a word. The
creation, therefore, I allow to have been a creation of

things, of *real* things. Neither is this in the least inconsistent with my principles, as is evident from what I have now said; and would have been evident to you without this, if you had not forgotten what had been so often said before. But as for solid corporeal substances, I desire you to show where Moses makes any mention of them; and if they should be mentioned by him, or any other inspired writer, it would still be incumbent on you to show those words were not taken in the vulgar acceptation, for things falling under our senses, but in the philosophic acceptation, for matter, or an unknown quiddity, with an absolute existence. When you have proved these points, then (and not till then) may you bring the authority of Moses into our dispute.

Hyl. It is in vain to dispute about a point so clear. I am content to refer it to your own conscience. Are you not satisfied there is some peculiar repugnancy between the Mosaic account of the creation and your notions?

Phil. If all possible sense, which can be put on the first chapter of Genesis, may be conceived as consistently with my principles as any other, then it has no peculiar repugnancy with them. But there is no sense you may not as well conceive, believing as I do. Since, beside spirits, all you conceive are ideas, and the existence of these I do not deny. Neither do you pretend they exist without the mind.

Hyl. Pray let me see any sense you can understand it in.

Phil. Why I imagine that if I had been present at the creation, I should have seen things produced into being; that is, become perceptible, in the order described by the sacred historian. I ever before believed the Mosaic account of the creation, and now find no alteration in my manner of believing it. When things are said to begin or end their existence, we do not mean this with regard to God, but his creatures. All objects are eternally known by God, or, which is the same thing, have an eternal existence in his mind: but when things before imperceptible to creatures, are by a decree of God, made perceptible to them; then are they said to begin a relative existence with respect to created minds. Upon reading therefore the Mosaic account of the creation, I understand that the several parts of the world became gradually perceivable to finite spirits, endowed with proper faculties; so that, whoever such were present, they were in truth perceived by them. This is the literal, obvious sense suggested to me by the words of the holy scripture : in which is included no mention or no thought, either of substratum, instrument, occasion, or absolute existence. And upon inquiry, I doubt not it will be found, that most plain, honest men, who believe the creation, never think of those things any more than I. What metaphysical sense you may understand it in, you only can tell.

Hyl. But, Philonous, you do not seem to be aware, that you allow created things in the beginning only a relative, and, consequently, hypothetical being; that is to say, upon supposition there were men to perceive them, without which they have no actuality of absolute existence, wherein creation might terminate. Is it not, therefore, according to you plainly impossible, the creation of any inanimate creatures should precede that of man? And is not this directly contrary to the Mosaic account?

Phil. In answer to that I say, first, created beings might begin to exist in the mind of other created intelligences, beside men. You will not therefore be able to prove any contradiction between Moses and my notions, unless you first show, there was no other order of finite created spirits in being before man. I say further, in case we conceive the creation, as we should at this time a parcel of plants or vegetables of all sorts, produced by an invisible power, in a desert where nobody was present : that this way of explaining or conceiving it, is consistent with my principles, since they deprive you of nothing, either sensible or imaginable : that it exactly suits with the common, natural, undebauched notions of mankind : that it manifests the dependence of all things on God; and consequently hath all the good effect or influence, which it is possible that important article of our faith should have in making men humble, thankful, and resigned to their Creator. I say moreover, that in this naked conception of things, divested of words, there will not be found any notion of what you call the *actuality of absolute existence.* You may indeed raise a dust with those terms, and so lengthen our dispute to no purpose. But I entreat you calmly to look into your own thoughts, and then tell me if they are not a useless and unintelligible jargon.

Hyl. I own I have no very clear notion annexed to them. But what say you to this? Do you not make the existence of sensible things consist in their being in a mind? and were not all things eternally in the mind of God? Did they not therefore exist from all eternity, according to you? And how could that which was eternal be created in time? Can any thing be clearer or better connected than this?

Phil. And are not you too of opinion, that God knew all things from eternity?

Hyl. I am.

Phil. Consequently they always had a being in the divine intellect.

Hyl. This I acknowledge.

Phil. By your own confession therefore, nothing is new, or begins to be, in respect of the mind of God. So we are agreed in that point.

Hyl. What shall we make then of the creation?

Phil. May we not understand it to have been entirely in respect of finite spirits; so that things, with regard to us, may properly be said to begin their existence, or be created, when God decreed they should become perceptible to intelligent creatures, in that order and manner which he then established, and we now call the laws of nature? You may call this a *relative,* or *hypothetical existence* if you please. But so long as it supplies us with the most natural, obvious, and literal sense of the Mosaic history of the creation; so long as it answers all the religious ends of that great article; in a word, so long as you can assign no other sense or meaning in its stead; why should we reject this? Is it to comply with a ridiculous sceptical humour of making every thing nonsense and unintelligible? I am sure you cannot say it is for the glory of God. For allowing it to be a thing possible and conceivable, that the corporeal world should have an absolute subsistence extrinsical to the mind of God, as well as to the minds of all created spirits : yet how could this set forth either the immensity or omniscience of the Deity, or the necessary and immediate dependence of all things on him? Nay, would it not rather seem to derogate from those attributes?

Hyl. Well, but as to this decree of God's, for making things perceptible : what say you, Philonous, is it not plain, God did either execute that decree from all eternity, or at some certain time began to will what he had not actually willed before, but only designed to will? If the former, then there could be no creation or beginning of existence in finite things. If the latter, then we must acknowledge something new to befall the Deity; which implies a sort of change; and all change argues imperfection.

Phil. Pray consider what you are doing. Is it not evident, this objection concludes equally against a creation in any sense; nay, against every other act of the Deity, discoverable by the light of nature? None of which can we conceive, otherwise than as performed in time, and having a beginning. God is a being of transcendent and unlimited perfections : his nature therefore is incomprehensible to finite spirits. It is not therefore to be expected, that any man, whether *materialist* or *immaterialist,* should have exactly just notions of the Deity, his attributes, and ways of operation. If then you would infer any thing against me, your difficulty must not be drawn from the inadequateness of our conceptions of the divine nature, which is unavoidable on any scheme : but from the denial of matter, of which there is not one word, directly or indirectly, in what you have now objected.

Hyl. I must acknowledge the difficulties you are concerned to clear, are such only as arise from the non-existence of matter, and are peculiar to that notion. So far you are in the right. But I cannot by any means bring myself to think there is no such peculiar repugnancy between the creation and your opinion; though indeed where to fix it, I do not distinctly know.

Phil. What would you have? Do I not acknowledge a twofold state of things, the one ectypal or natural, the other archetypal and eternal? The former was created in time; the latter existed from everlasting in the mind of God. Is not this agreeable to the common notions of divines? or is any more than this necessary in order to conceive the creation? But you suspect some peculiar repugnancy, though you know not where it lies. To take away all possibility of scruple in the case, do but consider this one point. Either you are not able to conceive the creation on any hypothesis whatsoever; and if so, there is no ground for dislike or complaint against my particular opinion on that score : or you are able to conceive it; and if so, why not on my principles, since thereby nothing conceivable is taken away? You have all along been allowed the full scope of sense, imagination, and reason. Whatever therefore you could before apprehend, either immediately or mediately by your senses, or by ratiocination from your senses; whatever you could perceive, imagine, or understand, remains still with you. If therefore the notion you have of the creation by other principles be intelligible, you have it still upon mine; if it be not intelligible, I conceive it to be no notion at all; and so there is no loss of it. And indeed it seems to me very plain, that the supposition of matter, that is, a thing perfectly unknown and inconceivable, cannot serve to make us conceive any thing. And I hope, it need not be proved to you, that if the existence of matter doth not make the creation conceivable, the creation's being without it inconceivable, can be no objection against its non-existence.

Hyl. I confess, Philonous, you have almost satisfied me in this point of the creation.

Phil. I would fain know why you are not quite satisfied. You tell me indeed of a repugnancy between the Mosaic history and immaterialism : but you know not where it lies. Is this reasonable, Hylas? Can you expect I should solve a difficulty without knowing what it is? But to pass by all that, would not a man think you were assured there is no repugnancy between the received notions of materialists and the inspired writings?

Hyl. And so I am.

Phil. Ought the historical part of scripture to be understood in a plain, obvious sense, or in a sense which is metaphysical and out of the way?

Hyl. In the plain sense, doubtless.

Phil. When Moses speaks of herbs, earth, water, &c. as having been created by God; think you not the sensible things, commonly signified by those words, are suggested to every unphilosophical reader?

Hyl. I cannot help thinking so.

Phil. And are not all ideas, or things perceived by sense, to be denied a real existence by the doctrine of the materialists?

Hyl. This I have already acknowledged.

Phil. The creation therefore, according to them, was not the creation of things sensible, which have only a relative being, but of certain unknown natures, which have an absolute being, wherein creation might terminate.

Hyl. True.

Phil. Is it not therefore evident, the asserters of matter destroy the plain obvious sense of Moses, with which their notions are utterly inconsistent; and instead of it obtrude on us I know not what, something equally unintelligible to themselves and me.

Hyl. I cannot contradict you.

Phil. Moses tells us of a creation. A creation of what? unknown quiddities, of occasions, or substratums? No, ertainly; but of things obvious to the senses. You must st reconcile this with your notions, if you expect I should e reconciled to them.

Hyl. I see you can assault me with my own weapons.

Phil. Then as to *absolute existence*; was there ever nown a more jejune notion than that? Something it is, abstracted and unintelligible, that you have frankly wned you could not conceive it, much less explain any ing by it. But allowing matter to exist, and the notion f absolute existence to be as clear as light, yet was this ver known to make the creation more credible? Nay, ath it not furnished the atheists and infidels of all ages ith the most plausible argument against a creation? hat a corporeal substance, which hath an absolute existnce without the minds of spirits, should be produced out f nothing by the mere will of a spirit, hath been looked pon as a thing so contrary to all reason, so impossible and bsurd, that not only the most celebrated among the ncients, but even divers modern and Christian philoophers, have thought matter co-eternal with the Deity. ay these things together, and then judge you whether naterialism disposes men to believe the creation of things.

Hyl. I own, Philonous, I think it does not. This of the *reation* is the last objection I can think of; and I must eeds own it hath been sufficiently answered as well as he rest. Nothing now remains to be overcome, but a sort f unaccountable backwardness that I find in myself oward your notions.

Phil. When a man is swayed, he knows not why, to one ide of a question, can this, think you, be any thing else ut the effect of prejudice, which never fails to attend old and rooted notions? And indeed in this respect I cannot deny the belief of matter to have very much the advan-

tage over the contrary opinion, with men of a learne
education.

Hyl. I confess it seems to be as you say.

Phil. As a balance therefore to this weight of pr
judice, let us throw into the scale the great advantage
that arise from the belief of immaterialism, both in regar
to religion and human learning. The being of a God, an
incorruptibility of the soul, those great articles of religion
are they not proved with the clearest and most immediat
evidence? When I say the being of a *God,* I do not mea
an obscure, general cause of things, whereof we have n
conception, but *God,* in the strict and proper sense of th
word. A being whose spirituality, omnipresence, pro
vidence, omniscience, infinite power, and goodness, are a
conspicuous as the existence of sensible things, of whicl
(notwithstanding the fallacious pretences and affecte
scruples of sceptics) there is no more reason to doubt thar
of our own being. Then with relation to human sciences
in natural philosophy, what intricacies, what obscurities
what contradictions, hath the belief of matter led mer
into! To say nothing of the numberless disputes about it
extent, continuity, homogeneity, gravity, divisibility, &c.
do they not pretend to explain all things by bodies operat
ing on bodies, according to the laws of motion? and yet
are they able to comprehend how any one body shoulc
move another? Nay, admitting there was no difficulty ir
reconciling the notion of an inert being with a cause; or ir
conceiving how an accident might pass from one body tt
another; yet by all their strained thoughts and extravagant
suppositions, have they been able to reach the mechanical
production of any one animal or vegetable body? Can
they account by the laws of motion, for sounds, tastes,
smells, or colours, or for the regular course of things?
Have they accounted by physical principles for the aptitude and contrivance, even of the most inconsiderable
parts of the universe? By laying aside matter and corporeal causes, and admitting only the efficiency of an all-

perfect mind, are not all the effects of nature easy and intelligible? If the phenomena are nothing else but *ideas*; God is a *spirit*, but matter an unintelligent, unperceiving being. If they demonstrate an unlimited power in their cause; God is active and omnipotent, but matter an inert mass. If the order, regularity, and usefulness of them can never be sufficiently admired; God is infinitely wise and provident, but matter destitute of all contrivance and design. These surely are great advantages in *physics*. Not to mention that the apprehension of a distant Deity naturally disposes men to a negligence in their *moral* actions, which they would be more cautious of in case they thought him immediately present, and acting on their minds without the interposition of matter, or unthinking second causes. Then in *metaphysics*; what difficulties concerning entity in abstract, substantial forms, hylarchic principles, plastic natures, substance and accident, principle of individuation, possibility of matter's thinking, origin of ideas, the manner how two independent substances, so widely different as *spirit* and *matter*, should mutually operate on each other! what difficulties, I say, and endless disquisitions concerning these and innumerable other the like points, do we escape by supposing only spirits and ideas? Even the *mathematics* themselves, if we take away the absolute existence of extended things, become much more clear and easy; the most shocking paradoxes and intricate speculations in those sciences, depending on the finite divisibility of finite extension, which depends on that supposition. But what need is there to insist on the particular sciences? Is not that opposition to all science whatsoever, that frenzy of the ancient and modern sceptics, built on the same foundation? Or can you produce so much as one argument against the reality of corporeal things, or in behalf of that avowed utter ignorance of their natures, which doth not suppose their reality to consist in an external absolute existence. Upon this supposition indeed, the objections from the change of colours in a pigeon's neck, or the appearances of a broken oar in the water, must be allowed to have weight. But those and the like objections vanish, if we do not maintain the being of absolute external originals, but place the reality of things in ideas, fleeting indeed, and changeable; however not changed at random, but according to the fixed order of nature. For herein consists that constancy and truth of things, which secures all the concerns of life, and distinguishes that which is *real* from the irregular visions of the fancy.

Hyl. I agree to all you have now said, and must own that nothing can incline me to embrace your opinion, more than the advantages I see it is attended with. I am by nature lazy, and this would be a mighty abridgment in knowledge. What doubts, what hypotheses, what labyrinths of amusement, what fields of disputation, what an ocean of false learning, may be avoided by that single notion of *immaterialism*!

Phil. After all, is there any thing further remaining to be done? You may remember you promised to embrace that opinion which upon examination should appear most agreeable to common sense, and remote from scepticism. This, by your own confession, is that which denies matter, or the absolute existence of corporeal things. Nor is this all; the same notion has been proved several ways, viewed in different lights, pursued in its consequences, and all objections against it cleared. Can there be a greater evidence of its truth? or is it possible it should have all the marks of a true opinion, and yet be false?

Hyl. I own myself entirely satisfied for the present in all respects. But what security can I have that I shall still continue the same full assent to your opinion, and that no unthought-of objection or difficulty will occur hereafter?

Phil. Pray, Hylas, do you in other cases, when a point is once evidently proved, withhold your assent on account of objections or difficulties it may be liable to? Are the difficulties that attend the doctrine of incommensurable quantities, of the angle of contact, of the asymptotes to curves, or the like, sufficient to make you hold out against mathematical demonstration? Or will you disbelieve the providence of God, because there may be some particular things which you know not how to reconcile with it? If there are difficulties attending immaterialism, there are at the same time direct and evident proofs for it. But for the existence of matter there is not one proof, and far more numerous and insurmountable objections lie against it. But where are those mighty difficulties you insist on? Alas! you know not where or what they are; something which may possibly occur hereafter. If this be a sufficient pretence for withholding your full assent, you should never yield it to any proposition, how free soever from exceptions, how clearly and solidly soever demonstrated.

Hyl. You have satisfied me, Philonous.

Phil. But to arm you against all future objections, do but consider, that which bears equally hard on two contradictory opinions, can be a proof against neither. Whenever therefore any difficulty occurs, try if you can find a solution for it on the hypothesis of the *materialists*. Be not deceived by words; but sound your own thoughts. And in case you cannot conceive it easier by the help of *materialism*, it is plain it can be no objection against *immaterialism*. Had you proceeded all along by this rule, you would probably have spared yourself abundance of trouble in objecting; since of all your difficulties I challenge you to show one that is explained by matter; nay, which is not more unintelligible with, than without that supposition, and consequently makes rather *against* than *for* it. You should consider in each particular, whether the difficulty arises from the *non-existence of matter*. If it doth not, you might as well argue from the infinite divisibility of extension against the divine prescience, as from such a difficulty against *immaterialism*. And yet upon recollection I believe you will find this to have been often, if not always the case. You should likewise take heed not to argue on a *petitio principii*. One is apt to say, the unknown substances ought to be esteemed real things, rather than the ideas in our minds: and who can tell but the unthinking external substance may concur as a cause or instrument in the production of our ideas? But is not this proceeding on a supposition that there are such external substances? And to suppose this, is it not begging the question? But above all things you should beware of imposing on yourself by that vulgar sophism, which is called *ignoratio elenchi*. You talked often as if you thought I maintained the non-existence of sensible things: whereas in truth no one can be more thoroughly assured of their existence than I am, and it is you who doubt; I should have said, positively deny it. Every thing that is seen, felt, heard, or any way perceived by the senses, is, on the principles I embrace, a real being, but not on yours. Remember the matter you contend for is an unknown somewhat (if indeed it may be termed *somewhat*), which is quite stripped of all sensible qualities, and can neither be perceived by sense, nor apprehended by the mind. Remember, I say, that it is not any object which is hard or soft, hot or cold, blue or white, round or square, &c. For all these things I affirm do exist. Though indeed I deny they have any existence distinct from being perceived; or that they exist out of all minds whatsoever. Think on these points; let them be attentively considered and still kept in view. Otherwise you will not comprehend the state of the question; without which your objections will always be wide of the mark, and instead of mine, may possibly be directed (as more than once they have been) against your own notions.

Hyl. I must needs own, Philonous, nothing seems to have kept me from agreeing with you more than this same *mistaking the question*. In denying matter, at first glimpse I am tempted to imagine you deny the things we see and feel; but upon reflection find there is no ground for it. What think you therefore of retaining the name *matter,*

ıd applying it to sensible things? This may be done
ithout any change in your sentiments : and believe me it
ould be a means of reconciling them to some persons,
ho may be more shocked at an innovation in words than
opinion.

Phil. With all my heart : retain the word *matter*, and
ɔply it to the objects of sense, if you please, provided you
ɔ not attribute to them any subsistence distinct from their
eing perceived. I shall never quarrel with you for an
xpression. *Matter, or material substance,* are terms intro-
uced by philosophers; and as used by them, imply a sort
f independency, or a subsistence distinct from being per-
eived by a mind : but are never used by common people;
r if ever, it is to signify the immediate objects of sense.
ɔne would think therefore, so long as the names of all
articular things, with the terms *sensible, substance, body,*
uff, and the like, are retained, the word *matter* should be
ever missed in common talk. And in philosophical dis-
ourses it seems the best way to leave it quite out; since
ıere is not perhaps any one thing that hath more fav-
ured and strengthened the depraved bent of the mind
ɔward *atheism,* than the use of that general confused
erm.

Hyl. Well but, Philonous, since I am content to give up
ıe notion of an unthinking substance exterior to the mind,
think you ought not to deny me the privilege of using
ıe word *matter* as I please, and annexing it to a collec-
ion of sensible qualities subsisting only in the mind. I
reely own there is no other substance in a strict sense, than
pirit. But I have been so long accustomed to the term
natter, that I know not how to part with it. To say,
ıere is no *matter* in the world, is still shocking to me.
Whereas to say, there is no *matter,* if by that term be
ıeant an unthinking substance existing without the mind;
ut if by matter is meant some sensible thing, whose existnce consists in being perceived, then there is *matter* :
ıis distinction gives it quite another turn : and men will

come into your notions with small difficulty, when the
are proposed in that manner. For after all, the contr
versy about matter, in the strict acceptation of it, li
altogether between you and the philosophers, whose pri
ciples, I acknowledge, are not near so natural, or so agre
able to the common sense of mankind, and holy scriptur
as yours. There is nothing we either desire or shun, bu
as it makes, or is apprehended to make some part of ou
happiness or misery. But what hath happiness or misery
joy or grief, pleasure or pain, to do with absolute existenc
or with unknown entities, abstracted from all relation t
us? It is evident, things regard us only as they are plea
ing or displeasing: and they can please or displease onl
so far forth as they are perceived. Further therefore w
are not concerned; and thus far you leave things as yo
found them. Yet still there is something new in thi
doctrine. It is plain, I do not now think with the philo
sophers, nor yet altogether with the vulgar. I would kno
how the case stands in that respect: precisely what yo
have added to, or altered in my former notions.

Phil. I do not pretend to be a setter-up of *new notions*
My endeavours tend only to unite and place in a cleare
light that truth, which was before shared between th
vulgar and the philosophers: the former being of opinion
that *those things they immediately perceive are the rea
things*: and the latter, that *the things immediately per
ceived are ideas which exist only in the mind*. Whic
two notions put together, do in effect constitute the sub
stance of what I advance.

Hyl. I have been a long time distrusting my senses
methought I saw things by a dim light, and through false
glasses. Now the glasses are removed, and a new ligh
breaks in upon my understanding. I am clearly convinced
that I see things in their native forms; and am no longe
in pain about their unknown natures or absolute existence
This is the state I find myself in at present: though in
deed the course that brought me to it I do not yet tho-

oughly comprehend. You set out upon the same principles that Academics, Cartesians, and the like sects, usually do; and for a long time it looked as if you were advancing their philosophical scepticism; but in the end your conclusions are directly opposite to theirs.

Phil. You see, Hylas, the water of yonder fountain, how it is forced upwards, in a round column, to a certain height; at which it breaks and falls back into the basin from whence it rose : its ascent, as well as descent, proceeding from the same uniform law or principle of *gravitation*. Just so, the same principles which at first view lead to scepticism, pursued to a certain point, bring men back to common sense.

APPENDIX
BIBLIOGRAPHY
CHRONOLOGICAL TABLE
INDEX

APPENDIX

It may be of interest to append here a specimen of Berkeley's rather meagre philosophical correspondence. What follows is the first of two letters to Berkeley from Samuel Johnson, with his reply. This Samuel Johnson is not the celebrated English lexicographer—whose opinion of Berkeley's philosophy was, so Boswell reports, pretty low— but a distinguished American divine and man of learning. Born in 1696, he was educated at Yale, and for a short time held an academic appointment there. Having taken orders in the Church of England in 1722, he was made a Doctor of Divinity by Oxford in 1743; and in 1754, the year after Berkeley's death, he became the first President of King's College, New York—now Columbia University. His *Elementa Philosophica,* published in 1752 by Benjamin Franklin in Philadelphia, was dedicated to Berkeley.

Their correspondence took place during Berkeley's period of residence at Newport, Rhode Island, at which time Johnson was living at Stratford, Connecticut. It is clear that the two men met on several occasions, and Johnson elsewhere refers to "many letters" exchanged between them. Besides the two here printed, however, only two others are known that deal with philosophical matters. Berkeley's reply to Johnson's very natural doubts and queries is perhaps rather perfunctory, but states his position on the points raised with much clearness and brevity.

Stratford, Sept. 10, 1729

Rev'd Sir:

The kind invitation you gave me to lay before you any difficulties that should occur to me in reading those excellent books which you was pleased to order into my hands, is all the apology I shall offer for the trouble I now presume to give you. But nothing could encourage me to expose to your view my low and mean way of thinking and writing, but my hopes of an interest in that candor and tenderness which are so conspicuous both in your writings and conversation.

These books (for which I stand humbly obliged to you) contain speculations the most surprisingly ingenious I have ever met with, and I must confess that the reading of them has almost convinced me that matter as it has been commonly defined for an unknown Quiddity is but a mere non-entity. That it is a strong presumption against the existence of it, that there never could be conceived any manner of connection between it and our ideas. That the *esse* of things is only their *percipi*; and that the rescuing us from the absurdities of abstract ideas and the gross notion of matter that have so much obtained, deserves well of the learned world, in that it clears away very many difficulties and perplexities in the sciences.

And I am of opinion that this way of thinking can't fail of prevailing in the world, because it is likely to prevail very much among us in these parts, several ingenious men having entirely come in to it. But there are many others on the other hand that cannot be reconciled to it; though of these there are some who have a very good opinion of it and plainly see many happy consequences attending it, on account of which they are well inclined to embrace it, but think they find some difficulties in their way which they can't get over, and some objections not

fficiently answered to their satisfaction. And since you
ave condescended to give me leave to do so, I will make
old to lay before you sundry things, which yet remain in
he dark either to myself or to others, and which I can't
account for either to my own, or at least to their satis-
action.

1. The great prejudice that lies against it with some is
s repugnancy to and subversion of Sir I. Newton's philo-
phy in sundry points; to which they have been so much
ttached that they can't suffer themselves in the least to
all it in question in any instance, but indeed it does not
ppear to me so inconsistent therewith as at first blush it
id, for the laws of nature which he so happily explains
re the same whether matter be supposed or not. How-
ver, let Sir Isaac Newton, or any other man, be heard
nly so far as his opinion is supported by reason :—but
fter all I confess I have so great a regard for the philo-
ophy of that great man, that I would gladly see as much
f it as may be, to obtain in this ideal scheme.

2. The objection, that it takes away all subordinate
atural causes, and accounts for all appearances merely
y the immediate will of the supreme spirit, does not seem
o many to be answered to their satisfaction. It is readily
ranted that our ideas are inert, and can't cause one
nother, and are truly only signs one of another. For
nstance my idea of fire is not the cause of my idea of
urning and of ashes. But inasmuch as these ideas are so
onnected as that they seem necessarily to point out to us
he relations of cause and effect, we can't help thinking
hat our ideas are pictures of things without our minds
t least, tho' not without the Great Mind, and which are
heir archetypes, between which these relations do obtain.
 kindle a fire and leave it, no created mind beholds it; I
eturn again and find a great alteration in the fuel; has
here not been in my absence all the while that gradual
alteration making in the archetype of my idea of wood
which I should have had the idea of if I had been pre-

sent? And is there not some archetype of my idea of th
fire, which under the agency of the Divine Will ha
gradually caused this alteration? And so in all oth
instances, our ideas are so connected, that they seer
necessarily to refer our minds to some originals which a
properly (tho' subordinate) causes and effects one of an
other; insomuch that unless they be so, we can't hel
thinking ourselves under a perpetual delusion.

3. That all the phenomena of nature, must ultimatel
be referred to the will of the Infinite Spirit, is what mu
be allowed; but to suppose his immediate energy in th
production of every effect, does not seem to impress s
lively and great a sense of his power and wisdom upo
our minds, as to suppose a subordination of causes an
effects among the archetypes of our ideas, as he tha
should make a watch or clock of ever so beautiful a
appearance and that should measure the time ever s
exactly yet if he should be obliged to stand by it an
influence and direct all its motions, he would seem bu
very deficient in both his ability and skill in compariso
with him who should be able to make one that woul
regularly keep on its motion and measure the time for
considerable while without the intervention of any imme
diate force of its author or any one else impressed upon i

4. And as this tenet seems thus to abate our sense o
the wisdom and power of God, so there are some tha
cannot be persuaded that it is sufficiently cleared from
bearing hard on his holiness; those who suppose that th
corrupt affections of our souls and evil practices conse
quent to them, are occasioned by certain irregular mech
anical motions of our bodies, and that these motions com
to have an habitual irregular bias and tendency by mean
of our own voluntary indulgence to them, which we migh
have governed to better purpose, do in this way of think
ing, sufficiently bring the guilt of those ill habits and
actions upon ourselves; but if in an habitual sinner, every

bject and motion be but an idea, and every wicked
appetite the effect of such a set of ideas, and these ideas,
he immediate effect of the Almighty upon his mind; it
seems to follow, that the immediate cause of such ideas
must be the cause of those immoral appetites and actions;
because he is borne down before them seemingly, even in
spite of himself. At first indeed they were only occasions,
which might be withstood, and so, proper means of trial,
but now they become causes of his immoralities. When
therefore a person is under the power of a vicious habit,
and it can't but be foreseen that the suggestion of such
and such ideas will unavoidably produce those immorali-
ies, how can it consist with the holiness of God to suggest
hem?

5. It is, after all that has been said on that head, still
something shocking to many to think that there should be
nothing but a mere show in all the art and contrivance
appearing in the structure (for instance) of a human body,
particularly of the organs of sense. The curious structure
of the eye, what can it be more than merely a fine show,
if there be no connection more than you admit of, between
that and vision? It seems from the make of it to be
designed for an instrument or means of conveying the
images of external things to the perceptive faculty within;
and if it be not so, if it be really of no use in conveying
visible objects to our minds, and if our visible ideas are
immediately created in them by the will of the Almighty,
why should it be made to seem to be an instrument or
medium as much as if indeed it really were so? It is
evident, from the conveying of images into a dark room
thro' a lens, that the eye is a lens, and that the images
of things are painted on the bottom of it. But to what
purpose is all this, if there be no connection between this
fine apparatus and the act of vision; can it be thought a
sufficient argument that there is no connection between
them because we can't discover it, or conceive how it
should be?

6. There are some who say, that if our sensations don'
depend on any bodily organs—they don't see how deati
can be supposed to make any alteration in the manner o
our perception, or indeed how there should be (properl
speaking) any separate state of the soul at all. For if ou
bodies are nothing but ideas, and if our having ideas i
this present state does not depend on what are thought t
be the organs of sense, and lastly, if we are supposed (a
doubtless we must) to have ideas in that state; it shoulc
seem that immediately upon our remove from our presen
situation, we should still be attended with the same idea:
of bodies as we have now, and consequently with the
same bodies or at least with bodies however different, anc
if so, what room is there left for any resurrection, properly
so-called? So that while this tenet delivers us from the
embarrassments that attend the doctrine of a material resurrection, it seems to have no place for any resurrection
at all, at least in the sense that word seems to bear in St.
John 5; 28, 29.

7. Some of us are at a loss to understand your meaning
when you speak of archetypes. You say the being of
things consists in their being perceived. And that things
are nothing but ideas, that our ideas have no unperceived
archetypes, but yet you allow archetypes to our ideas
when things are not perceived by our minds; they exist in,
i.e. are perceived by, some other mind. Now I understand
you, that there is a two-fold existence of things or ideas,
one in the divine mind, and the other in created minds;
the one archetypal, and the other ectypal; that, therefore,
the real original and permanent existence of things is
archetypal, being ideas in *mente Divinâ,* and that our ideas
are copies of them, and so far forth real things as they
are correspondent to their archetypes and exhibited to us,
or begotten in us by the will of the Almighty, in such
measure and degrees and by such stated laws and rules as
He is pleased to observe; that, therefore, there is no unper-

eived substance intervening between the divine ideas and ours as a medium, occasion or instrument by which He begets our ideas in us, but that which was thought to be the material existence of things is in truth only ideal in the divine mind. Do I understand you right? Is it not therefore your meaning, that the existence of our ideas (*i.e.* the ectypal things) depends upon our perceiving them, yet there are external to any created mind, in the all-comprehending Spirit, real and permanent archetypes (as stable and permanent as ever matter was thought to be), to which these ideas of ours are correspondent, and so that ('tho' our visible and tangible ideas are *toto coelo* different and distinct things, yet) there may be said to be external to my mind, in the divine mind, an archetype (for instance of the candle that is before me) in which the originals of both my visible and tangible ideas, light, heat, whiteness, softness, etc., under such a particularly cylindrical figure, are united, so that it may be properly said to be the same thing that I both see and feel?

8. If this, or something like it might be understood to be your meaning, it would seem less shocking to say that we don't see and feel the same thing, because we can't dispossess our minds of the notion of an external world, and would be allowed to conceive that, 'tho' there were no intelligent creature before Adam to be a spectator of it, yet the world was really six days in *archetypo,* gradually proceeding from an informal chaotic state into that beautiful show wherein it first appeared to his mind, and that the comet that appeared in 1680 (for instance) has now, 'tho' no created mind beholds it, a real existence in the all-comprehending spirit, and is making its prodigious tour through the vast fields of ether, and lastly that the whole vast congeries of heaven and earth, the mighty systems of worlds with all their furniture, have a real being in the eternal mind antecedent to and independent on the perception of created spirit, and that when we see and feel,

etc., that that almighty wind, by his immediate *fiat*, begets
in our minds (*pro nostro modulo*) ideas correspondent to
them, and which may be imagined in some degree resemblances of them.

9. But if there be archetypes to our ideas, will it not
follow that there is external space, extension, figure and
motion, as being archetypes of our ideas, to which we give
these names. And indeed for my part I cannot disengage
my mind from the persuasion that there is external space,
when I have been trying ever so much to conceive of space
as being nothing but an idea in my mind, it will return
upon me even in spite of my utmost efforts, certainly
there must be, there can't but be, external space. The
length, breadth, and thickness of any idea, it's true, are
but ideas; the distance between two trees in my mind is
but an idea, but if there are archetypes to the ideas of the
trees, there must be an archetype to the idea of the distance between them. Nor can I see how it follows that
there is no external absolute height, bigness, or distance
of things, because they appear greater or less to us
according as we are nearer or remote from them, or see
them with our naked eyes, or with glasses; any more than
it follows that a man, for instance, is not really absolutely
six foot high measured by a two foot rule applied to his
body, because divers pictures of him may be drawn some
six, some four, some two foot long according to the same
measure. Nobody ever imagined that the idea of distance
is without the mind, but does it therefore follow that there
is no external distance to which the idea is correspondent,
for instance, between Rhode Island and Stratford? Truly
I wish it were not so great, that I might be so happy as to
have a more easy access to you, and more nearly enjoy
the advantages of your instructions.

10. You allow spirits to have a real existence external
to one another. Methinks, if so, there must be distance
between them, and space wherein they exist, or else they
must all exist in one individual spot or point, and as it

vere coincide one with another. I can't see how external space and duration are any more abstract ideas than spirits. As we have (properly speaking) no ideas of spirits, so, indeed, neither have we of external space and duration. But it seems to me that the existence of these must unavoidably follow from the existence of those, insomuch that I can no more conceive of their not being, than I can conceive of the non-existence of the infinite and eternal mind. They seem as necessarily existent independent of any created mind as the Deity Himself. Or must we say there is nothing in Dr. Clarke's argument *a priori,* in his demonstration of the being and attributes of God, or in what Sir Isaac Newton says about the infinity and eternity of God in his *Scholium Generale* to his *Principia*? I should be glad to know your sense of what those two authors say upon this subject.

11. You will forgive the confusedness of my thoughts and not wonder at my writing like a man something bewildered, since I am, as it were, got into a new world amazed at everything about me. These ideas of ours, what are they? Is the substance of the mind the *substratum* to its ideas? Is it proper to call them modifications of our minds? Or impressions upon them? Or what? Truly I can't tell what to make of them, any more than of matter itself. What is the *esse* of spirits?—you seem to think it impossible to abstract their existence from their thinking. *Princip.* p. 143 sec. 98. Is then the *esse* of minds nothing else but *percipere,* as the *esse* of ideas is *percipi*? Certainly, methinks there must be an unknown somewhat that thinks and acts, as difficult to be conceived of as matter, and the creation of which, as much beyond us as the creation of matter. Can actions be the *esse* of anything? Can they exist or be exerted without some being who is the agent? And may not that being be easily imagined to exist without acting, *e.g.* without thinking? And consequently (for you are there speaking of duration) may he not be said *durare, etsi non cogitet,* to persist in

being, tho' thinking were intermitted for a while? And i
not this sometimes fact? The duration of the eterna
mind, must certainly imply some thing besides an eterna
succession of ideas. May I not then conceive that, tho'
get my idea of duration by observing the succession o
ideas in my mind, yet there is a *perseverare in existendo,*
duration of my being, and of the being of other spirit
distinct from, and independent of, this succession of ideas

But, Sir, I doubt I have more than tried your patienc
with so many (and I fear you will think them impertinent
questions; for tho' they are difficulties with me, or at leas
with some in my neighbourhood for whose sake, in part
I write, yet I don't imagine they can appear such to you
who have so perfectly digested your thoughts upon thi
subject. And perhaps they may vanish before me upon a
more mature consideration of it. However, I should be
very thankful for your assistance, if it were not a pity you
should waste your time (which would be employed to
much better purposes) in writing to a person so obscure
and so unworthy of such a favor as I am. But I shall
live with some impatience till I see the second part of
your design accomplished, wherein I hope to see these (if
they can be thought such) or any other objections, that
may have occurred to you since your writing the first
part, obviated; and the usefulness of this doctrine more
particularly displayed in the further application of it to
the arts and sciences. May we not hope to see logic,
mathematics, and natural philosophy, pneumatology, theo-
logy and morality, all in their order, appearing with a new
lustre under the advantages they may receive from it?
You have at least given us to hope for a geometry cleared
of many perplexities that render that sort of study trouble-
some, which I shall be very glad of, who have found that
science more irksome to me than any other, tho', indeed,
I am but very little versed in any of them. But I will
not trespass any further upon your patience. My very

humble service to Mr. James and Mr. Dalton, and I am
with the greatest veneration,
Rev'd Sir,
   your most obliged
      and most obedient
         humble servant
            Samuel Johnson

II. BERKELEY TO JOHNSON
Nov. 25, 1729

Reverend Sir,

   The ingenious letter you favoured me with found me
very much indisposed with a gathering or imposthumation
in my head, which confined me several weeks, and is now,
I thank God, relieved. The objections of a candid thinking man to what I have written will always be welcome,
and I shall not fail to give all the satisfaction I am able,
not without hopes of convincing or being convinced. It is
a common fault for men to hate opposition, and be too
much wedded to their own opinions. I am so sensible of
this in others that I could not pardon it to myself if I
considered mine any further than they seem to me to be
true; which I shall the better be able to judge of when
they have passed the scrutiny of persons so well qualified
to examine as you and your friends appear to be, to whom
my illness must be an apology for not sending this answer
sooner.

   1. The true use and end of Natural Philosophy is to
explain the phenomena of nature; which is done by discovering the laws of nature, and reducing particular appearances to them. This is Sir Isaac Newton's method;
and such method or design is not in the least inconsistent
with the principles I lay down. This mechanical philosophy doth not assign or suppose any one natural efficient
cause in the strict and proper sense; nor is it, as to its use,
concerned about matter; nor is matter connected there-

with; nor doth it infer the being of matter. It must be owned, indeed, that the mechanical philosophers do suppose (though unnecessarily) the being of matter. They do even pretend to demonstrate that matter is proportional to gravity, which, if they could, this indeed would furnish an unanswerable objection. But let us examine their demonstration. It is laid down in the first place, that the momentum of any body is the product of its quantity by its velocity, *moles in celeritatem ducta*. If, therefore, the velocity is given, the momentum will be as its quantity. But it is observed that bodies of all kinds descend in vacuo with the same velocity; therefore the momentum of descending bodies is as the quantity of moles, *i.e.* gravity is as matter. But this argument concludes nothing, and is a mere circle. For, I ask, when it is premised that the momentum is equal to the *moles in celeritatem ducta*, how the moles or quantity of matter is estimated? If you say, by extent, the proposition is not true; if by weight, then you suppose that the quantity of matter is proportional to matter; *i.e.* the conclusion is taken for granted in one of the premises. As for absolute space and motion, which are also supposed without any necessity or use, I refer you to what I have already published; particularly in a Latin treatise, *De Motu,* which I shall take care to send to you.

2. Cause is taken in different senses. A proper active efficient cause I can conceive none but Spirit; nor any action, strictly speaking, but where there is Will. But this doth not hinder the allowing occasional causes (which are in truth but signs); and more is not requisite in the best physics, *i.e.* the mechanical philosophy. Neither doth it hinder the admitting other causes besides God; such a spirits of different orders, which may be termed active causes, as acting indeed, though by limited and derivative powers. But as for an unthinking agent, no point of physics is explained by it, nor is it conceivable.

3. Those who have all along contended for a material

orld have yet acknowledged that *natura naturans* (to use
ue language of the Schoolmen) is God; and that the
vine conservation of things is equipollent to, and in fact
ue same thing with, a continued repeated creation : in a
ord, that conservation and creation differ only in the
rminus a quo. These are the common opinions of the
choolmen; and Durandus, who held the world to be a
aachine like a clock, made and put in motion by God,
ut afterwards continuing to go of itself, was therein
articular, and had few followers. The very poets teach
doctrine not unlike the schools—*Mens agitat molem*
Virg. *Aeneid* VI). The Stoics and Platonists are every-
here full of the same notion. I am not therefore singular
a this point itself, so much as in my way of proving it.
urther, it seems to me that the power and wisdom of
od are as worthily set forth by supposing Him to act
nmediately as an omnipresent infinitely active Spirit, as
y supposing Him to act by the mediation of subordinate
auses, in preserving and governing the natural world. A
lock may indeed go independent of its maker or artificer,
aasmuch as the gravitation of its pendulum proceeds
rom another cause, and that the artificer is not the ade-
uate cause of the clock; so that the analogy would not
e just to suppose a clock is in respect of its artist what
he world is in respect of its Creator. For aught I can
ee, it is no disparagement to the perfections of God to
ay that all things necessarily depend on Him as their
Conservator as well as Creator, and that all nature would
hrink to nothing, if not upheld and preserved in being by
he same force that first created it. This I am sure is
greeable to Holy Scripture, as well as to the writings of
he most esteemed philosophers; and if it is to be con-
dered that men make use of tools and machines to supply
efect of power in themselves, we shall think it no honour
o the Divinity to attribute such things to Him.

4. As to guilt, it is the same thing whether I kill a man
ith my hands or an instrument; whether I do it myself

or make use of a ruffian. The imputation therefore upo
the sanctity of God is equal, whether we suppose ou
sensations to be produced immediately by God, or by th
mediation of instruments and subordinate causes, all whic
are His creatures, and moved by His laws. This thec
logical consideration, therefore, may be waived, as leadin
beside the question; for such I hold all points to be whic
bear equally hard on both sides of it. Difficulties abou
the principle of moral actions will cease, if we conside
that all guilt is in the will, and that our ideas, from wha
ever cause they are produced, are alike inert.

5. As to the art and contrivance in the parts of animal
&c., I have considered that matter in the *Principles o
Human Knowledge,* and, if I mistake not, sufficientl
shewn the wisdom and use thereof, considered as sign
and means of information. I do not indeed wonder tha
on first reading what I have written, men are not tho
roughly convinced. On the contrary, I should very muc
wonder if prejudices, which have been many years takin
root, should be extirpated in a few hours' reading. I ha
no inclination to trouble the world with large volumes
What I have done was rather with a view of giving hint
to thinking men, who have leisure and curiosity to go t
the bottom of things, and pursue them in their own mind
Two or three times reading these small tracts, and makin
what is read the occasion of thinking, would, I believe
render the whole familiar and easy to the mind, and tak
off that shocking appearance which hath often been ob
served to attend speculative truths.

6. I see no difficulty in conceiving a change of state
such as is vulgarly called Death, as well without as wit
material substance. It is sufficient for that purpose tha
we allow sensible bodies, *i.e.* such as are immediatel
perceived by sight and touch; the existence of which I a
so far from questioning (as philosophers are used to do
that I establish it, I think, upon evident principles. Now
it seems very easy to conceive the soul to exist in a separ

ate state (*i.e.* divested from those limits and laws of
motion and perception with which she is embarrassed
here), and to exercise herself on new ideas, without the
intervention of these tangible things we call bodies. It is
even very possible to apprehend how the soul may have
ideas of colour without an eye, or of sounds without an
ear.

And now, Sir, I submit these hints (which I have hastily
thrown together as soon as my illness gave me leave) to
your own maturer thoughts, which after all you will find
the best instructors. What you have seen of mine was
published when I was very young, and without doubt
hath many defects. For though the notions should be true
(as I verily think they are), yet it is difficult to express
them clearly and consistently, language being framed to
common use and received prejudices. I do not therefore
pretend that my books can teach truth. All I hope for is,
that they may be an occasion to inquisitive men of discovering truth, by consulting their own minds, and
looking into their own thoughts. As to the Second Part
of my treatise concerning the *Principles of Human Knowledge*, the fact is that I had made a considerable progress
in it; but the manuscript was lost about fourteen years
ago, during my travels in Italy, and I never had leisure
since to do so disagreeable a thing as writing twice on the
same subject.

Objections passing through your hands have their full
force and clearness. I like them the better. This intercourse with a man of parts and philosophic genius is very
agreeable. I sincerely wish we were nearer neighbours.
In the meantime, whenever either you or your friends
favour me with their thoughts, you may be sure of a
punctual correspondence on my part. Before I have done
I will venture to recommend these points: (1) To consider well the answers I have already given in my books
to several objections. (2) To consider whether any new
objection that shall occur doth not suppose the doctrine of

abstract general ideas. (3) Whether the difficulties proposed in objection to my scheme can be solved by the
contrary; for if they cannot, it is plain they can be no
objections to mine.

I know not whether you have got my treatise concerning the *Principles of Human Knowledge*. I intend to send
it to you with my tract *De Motu*. My humble service to
your friends, to whom I understand I am indebted for
some part of your letter.

I am your faithful humble servant,
 George Berkeley

BIBLIOGRAPHY

A BERKELEY'S WRITINGS

1. The following are the chief works of Berkeley as published during his own life-time:

An Essay towards a New Theory of Vision, Dublin, 1709:
appended to *Alciphron* (see below), London &
Dublin, 1732.

*A Treatise concerning the Principles of Human Knowl-
edge,* Dublin, 1710: with *Three Dialogues* (see
below), London, 1734.

Three Dialogues between Hylas and Philonous, London,
1713.

De Motu, London, 1721.

Alciphron; or, The Minute Philosopher, London &
Dublin, 1732: 3rd edition, 1752.

Theory of Vision Vindicated, London, 1733.

*The Analyst; or, A Discourse addressed to an Infidel
Mathematician,* London & Dublin, 1734.

*Siris: a Chain of Philisophical Reflexions and Inquiries
concerning the Virtues of Tar-water, and divers other
Subjects,* London, 1744.

2. The earliest collected edition of Berkeley's writings
was published in London and Dublin in 1784, probably
edited by Joseph Stock. Another was published in London
in 1843, edited by G. N. Wright.

The first really complete edition was A. C. Fraser's, published by the Clarendon Press in Oxford in 1871. This
edition was re-issued, with extensive revisions, in 1901.

But what must now be regarded as the definitive edition
is *The Works of George Berkeley,* edited in nine volumes
by A. A. Luce and T. E. Jessop, published by Nelson in

London between 1949 and 1957. This is as complete as
could be, and most exhaustively annotated.

Many texts of the *Essay*, *Principles*, and *Dialogues* are
readily available; we may mention that in Everyman's
Library, edited with an introduction by A. D. Lindsay.
First issued in 1910, this text was re-issued in 1957.

B WORKS ON BERKELEY

The Development of Berkeley's Philosophy, by G. A.
Johnston, London, 1923. A careful, if rather old-fashioned,
survey of Berkeley's thought, tracing the "underlying
unity" in his diverse interests.

Locke, Berkeley, Hume, by C. R. Morris, Oxford, 1931.
A brief and somewhat unimaginative study of Berkeley
in the context of so-called "British Empiricism."

Berkeley, by G. Dawes Hicks, London, 1932. A com-
petent general survey, somewhat lacking in vivacity.

Berkeley's Immaterialism, by A. A. Luce, London,
1945. A commentary on and exposition of Berkeley's
Principles. The author is the unchallenged authority on
all aspects of Berkeley's life and character, but his account of the philosophy is apt to be uncritically partisan.
In particular Luce is very much concerned to play down,
and indeed scarcely admits at all, the extreme *oddness* of
Berkeley's ontological convictions.

Berkeley, by the present editor, London, 1953, gives a
critical survey of Berkeley's thought with (as I now
think) too much emphasis on his defence of "common
sense", and too little on his religious and metaphysical
views.

The Unconscious Origin of Berkeley's Philosophy, by
J. O. Wisdom, London, 1953. This book is a rather interesting oddity. The author stresses, and indeed consider-
ably exaggerates, the strangeness of Berkeley's doctrine of
"immaterialism", and dwells also on his surprising en-

usiasm for tar-water. He submits that these call for xplanation in psycho-analytical terms, and devizes a ghly conjectural "interpretation" to account for them. his throws no light on Berkeley's philosophy.

Berkeley's Theory of Vision, by D. M. Armstrong, Ielbourne, 1960. A brief but detailed critical examinaon of the theory of vision expounded in Berkeley's ssay.

The authoritative *Life* of Berkeley is by A. A. Luce, ublished by Nelson in London in 1949, uniformly with eir new edition of Berkeley's *Works*. This book is a odel of scholarship and pertinacity, and most agreeably ritten.

CHRONOLOGICAL TABLE

1685 Birth of George Berkeley.

1687 Publication of Newton's *Principia*.

1688 Deposition of James II, accession of William and Mary.

1690 Battle of the Boyne—effectively the end of Stuart resistance to the new English monarchy.

1690 Publication of Locke's *Essay concerning Human Understanding*.

1700 Berkeley entered Trinity College, Dublin.

1702 Accession of Queen Anne.

1704 Graduated B.A. Death of Locke.

1707 Berkeley elected to a Fellowship.

1709 *Essay towards a New Theory of Vision*.

1710 *Principles of Human Knowledge*.

1713 Berkeley's first visit to England.
Three Dialogues between Hylas and Philonous.

1714 Accession of George I.

1716 Travel in France and Italy as tutor to the son of the Bishop of Clogher.

1720 The "South Sea bubble"—a financial disaster which moved Berkeley to many reflections on morals and economics.

1721 *De Motu*, composed while in France.
Return to Ireland.

1724 Appointed Dean of Derry, and resigned his Fellowship of Trinity College. Publicly launched his scheme for a College in Bermuda.

1727 Accession of George II.

1728 Berkeley married Anne, eldest daughter of Sir John Forster, and set sail for America. For nearly three years he lived at Newport, Rhode Island.

731 Return to London, abandoning the Bermuda project.

732 *Alciphron.*

734 *The Analyst.* Berkeley appointed Bishop of Cloyne.

739 Publication of Hume's *Treatise of Human Nature.*

744 *Siris.*

752 Berkeley in Oxford, supervising his son's entry to Christ Church.

753 Death of Berkeley.

INDEX

Abstract ideas, 26-30, 38, 47-63, 71, 105, 113-15, 125, 127, 129-30, 138, 175, 200, 264, 278; and existence, 67; and identity, 241

Abstraction, 130

Academics, 259

Accidents, 72, 181, 182

Action (activity) of the mind, in perception, 178-80; in volition, 204, 231

Agency, agent (i.e. efficient cause), 76, 78, 96, 115, 118, 139, 221

America, Berkeley in, 8-9, 263, 282-3

Animal, abstract idea of, 49, 56

Animals, mental processes of, 51

Archetypes of ideas, 201, 211, 241, 268-70

Aristotle, 60, 70

Arithmetic, 125-8

Astronomy, 94

Atheism, Berkeley's answer to, 22, 81, 111, 112, 134, 144, 145, 198-9, 251, 257

Attraction (gravitational and magnetic), 116, 118

Austin, J. L., 38n.

"Author of Nature" (see also God), 79, 80, 119, 143, 196

Ayer, A. J., 37

Beauty, 193, 195, 197

Being, 72

Berkeley, G.: life, 7-9, 263, 282-3; publications, 8, 277; philosophical position, 10-34; notebooks, 7-8, 20, 33; relations with later philosophy, 35-9; correspondence, 263-78; studies of, 280-1;
Works, 279-80; *Essay to wards a New Theory of Vision*, 8, 33, 84-5, 124, *Principles of Human Knowl edge*, 8, 23, 26, 33-4, 65n, 276, 277, 278; *Three Dia logues betwen Hylas an Philonous*, 8, 23, 34; *D Motu*, 24, 34, 274, 278 other works, 34-5

Body (see also matter), 173, 19

Bodies, human, 80, 85, 14 267; animal and vegetable 196, 252

Brain, the, 194

Cartesians, 259

Causal theory of perceptio 36, 38, 39, cf. 173

Causation, 19, 79-80, 90, 97-8 115, 117, 118, 227, 265-6 273-5; of our ideas, 18, 2 77, 202-3, 211

Cause, God as supreme, 202, 20

Centaur, possibility of, 213

Change, whether possible i God, 248

Children, 54-5

Chimeras, 225-6

Christianity, 112, cf. 129, 142 *and see* Scripture, religion

Clarke, Dr., 271

Colour, 48, 68, 114, 163-9 177-8, 179, 180, 216, 252, 25

Columbia University, 263

Comet of 1680, the, 269

Common sense, 10-11, 30, 31 34, 150, 236, 258

Conception, 183-4

Copernican system, 89, 229-3

Creation, 15-16, 119, 197 Mosaic account of, 244-6

284

250-1, 269; philosophical critique of, 246-50

Death, 16, 268, 276
Definition, 58
Demonstration, 55
Distance, perception of, 84, 185
Dreams, 73, 184-5, 225-6
Durandus, 275
Duration, 271, 272

Emotive use of language, 59-60
Entity, 209, 210
Epicureans, 112
Esse and *percipi*, relation of, 30, 66-8, 109, 133, 154, 219-20, 264, 271 and *percipere*, 30, 271
Essence, 115
Eternity, 247
Existence, 37, 105; of sensible objects, 66, 109, 154, 197, 217, 219-20, 245-7; of matter, alleged (*see also* matter, substance), 210; "absolute existence," 251, 253, 258
Extension, 48, 52, 69-70, 72, 88, 114, 128, 169-72, 173, 174-5, 176, 177-8, 233, 270
"External world," in Locke, 13, 18, 31; Berkeley's treatment of, 21, 31; in Malebranche, 200
Evil, God and, 227; *see also* sin

Fatalism, 112
Figure (i.e. shape), 169-72, 177-8, 216, 270
Fire, 216
Force (in Newtonian physics), 121
Franklin, Benjamin, 263
Freedom (of will), 93, 111, 144

General ideas, 52

General names, 60
Geometry, 128-33, 272
Geulinx, 90n.
God, current ideas about, 10, 15-16, 46, 74, 101, 102-3, 124, 152-3, 176, 199, 271; Berkeley's doctrine of, as universal perceiving mind, 21-2, 37, 103, 225, 226, 245; as spiritual substance, 29; existence of, 43, 140, 141, 145-6, 198-202, 252; as universal efficient cause, 90, 101, 142, 203, 205, 207, 221, 227, 247, 275; relation to laws of nature, 96, 118, 119, 143; providence of, 102, 255; perfection of, 206, 231-3, 235, 266-7; *see also* mind, divine; Author of Nature; Spirit, supreme
Goodness, 114
Gravitation, *see* attraction
Gravity, 173, 233, 234

Happiness, 114
Heat and cold, 71, 154-9, 171, 174, 216
Hobbes, T., 199; Hobbists, 112
Hume, D., 35
Hypotheses, in natural science, 234

Ideas: in Locke's theory, 12-13, 16, 31-2; Berkeley's treatment of, 20-21, 30, 31-2, 37, 47-134 passim; contrasted with "notions," 24, 109-10; general (not abstract), 52, 58; relation to language, 58-9, 61, 62; immediacy of, 61, 186-7, 200-1, 226; origin of, in perception, 65, 103, 110; relation to external world, 68, 107, 109, 110, 187-91, 238, 253;

causation of, 77, 193-5, 234; in mind of God, 100, 103, 221; relation to spirit, 134-6, 199-200; connection of, 235, 238; Berkeley's use of the word, 83, 136, 216, 244; its larger sense, 221

Identity, 240-1

Idolatry, 112

Illusions, in perception, 229, 254

Image, in thought, 221

Imagination, contrasted with abstraction, 49-50; with sense, 78, 80, 201, 225-6, 239-40

Immaterialism, 252, 254, 255

Immortality of the soul, 136-7

Inference from sense-perceptions, 229

Infinite divisibility, 128-30

Infinitesimals, 131-2

Innovations, danger of, 236

Instrument, matter as, 205-6, 211, 269

Insubstantiality of Berkeley's world, 31

Intellect, pure, 176

Intelligences, created, other than man, 246

Jargon, 211

Jaundice, 166

Johnson, Samuel (the Lexicographer), 263

Johnson, Samuel (of New York), 263-73

Knowledge, Locke on, 13-14; Berkeley on, 107

Language, 47, 51, 57-9, 89-90, 106, 238, 243-4

Light, 167, 179, 180

Locke, J., 7, 10, 11-20, 21, 22, 23, 25, 26, 27, 28, 29, 31, 33, 34, 35-6, 38, 39; *Essa, concerning Human Under standing,* 7, 50-51, 52, 53 4, 58, 68n., 115n.

Logic, 272

Magnitude, 234

Malebranche, 90n., 200

Man, abstract idea of, 49, 56 perception of, 141

Mathematics, 35, 93, 115, 124 33, 175, 253, 272

Matter: Locke's theory of, 12 69; Berkeley's denial of, 20 30, 264; alleged existence of disputed, 71, 72-6, 81, 86-7 91, 98, 106, 111-12, 133-4 150-1, 180-1, 208-15, 230 256; puzzles about, 106 112-13, 182, 251, 253; al leged cause of ideas, 202 230-1, 256; role in physica sciences, 233-4, 274; Berke ley's use of the word, 257-8

Meaning, propositions without 86, 91, 104, 211, 214

Mechanism, 19-20, 22, cf. 116 119

Memory, 188

Metaphysics, 138, 253; revol from, 150

Microscopes, 165

Mind, as perceiving agent, 88 102, 114, 184, 201, 220, 242-3; as efficient cause (*see also* spirit), 118, 201

Mind, divine, 79, 80, 81, 112, 196, 197, 198, 220

Minds, human, 29, 30, 65-6, 74, 76, 81, 220

Miracle, 92, 96, 106

Mode, 181

Moore, G. E., 38

Morality, 20, 114, 138, 253, 272, 276

Motion, 48, 53, 68, 69-70, 71,

113, 114, 115, 119, 172-3, 176, 270, 274; absolute and relative, 120-3, 174-5; as alleged material cause of sensation, 203-4, 252

Natura naturans, 275
Natural philosophy (natural science), 88-9, 115-24, 252, 272, 273
Nature, laws of, 79, 117, 119, 206, 235; works of, 139, 142-3; order of, 186, 254; as source of truth, 193; beauties of, 195-7
Newton, Sir I., 7, 9, 14, 23, 265, 271, 273; his *Principia*, 119, 122, 271; Newtonian idea of universe, 15, 265
Notions, 29, 109-10, 136, 138, 152, 210, 211, 222
Number, 70, 125-8

Objects, 16-18, 31-2, 33, 36, 66, 72, 92, 177, 178, 187-9
Occasion, 99-100; matter as, 206-8, 211, 251, 269
Occasionalists, 90n.
Odours, 160-1; *see also* smells
Ontology, Berkeley's, 34, 37, 38
'Outness or distance," 185
Oxford University, 7, 9, 263

Pain, 83-4, 97, 99, 139, 144, 155, 173, 180, 231-2
Paradoxes 128, 149, 163, 197
Passivity of mind in perception, 179-80; of ideas, 204
Perceivability, relation to existence, 225
Perception, Locke's theory of, 12-13; Berkeley's treatment of, 30-2; mediate and immediate, 188-9; *see also under* sensation, etc., *and* ideas
Phenomenalism, 36-39

Physical sciences, Berkeley and, 23-5, 252. *See also* natural philosophy
Place, 113, 120
Platonists, 275. *See also* Academics
Pleasure, 114, 139, 156-7, 173
Power (i.e. causative power), 76, 90
Primary qualities, 13, 14, 17, 68-9, 71-2, 77, 101, 169, 174, 176
Providence, 95, 111, 255

Quantity, 124

Reality, 80, 81-2, 106, 107-8, 109, 110, 114, 115, 197, 212, 242, 254; " real things," 189-90, 201, 216, 225, 245
Reason, 73, 109, 134, 176, 188, 211, 222
Reflection, 109, 189, 222
Regularity of nature (*see also* uniformity), 139
Relations, notion of, 110, 138
Religion, 16, 20, 22, 33, 35, 134, 137; arguments from, 105-7; consequences for, 199, 252
Resistance, 234
Resurrection, of Christ, 112; general, 268
Revelation, 211, 235

Same, meaning of, 240
Scepticism, 16-7, 30, 33, 43, 45, 108-9, 111, 134, 135, 149, 151-2, 191, 195, 197, 216-17, 237, 239, 242, 252, 254, 259
Schoolmen, 57, 60, 86, 275
Sciences, the (*see also* physical sciences, natural philosophy), 152, 252
Scripture, Holy, 105-7, 142, 200, 225, 227, 244-6, 258, 275
Secondary qualities, 13, 17, 68,

69, 71, 86, 101, 169, 174, 176, 183

Seeing, see sight

Self, the, 65, 136, 221, 223

Sensation, 18-19, 66, 114, 135, 177, 180, 201

Sense-data, 36, 37, cf. 66, 68, 177

Sense-perception, 73, 78, 153, 237

Sensible things, 152-4, 160, 212, 242, 252, 256

Sight, 84-5, 179, 185

Sin, God not author of, 227, 266-7, 276

Smells (see also odours), 160-1, 179, 252

Socinians, 112

Solidity, 173, 233, 234

Soul, the, 16, 43, 65, 77, 89, 111, 114, 135, 136, 138, 199, 221; immortality of, 136-7

Sounds, 161, 252

Space, 119-20, 123, 270-1, 274

Spinoza, 199

Spirit (i.e. thinking substance), 21, 29, 30, 37, 65, 74, 77, 80, 81, 95, 101, 109, 110, 114, 133, 134-9, 172, 184, 197, 253; definition of, 231; the only substance, 68, 134-5, 257; the only efficient cause, 115, 117, 118, 201, 204, 227, 274; human knowledge of, 134-6, 195

Spirit, the supreme (eternal, governing, etc., i.e. God, q.v.), 68, 85, 92, 94, 100, 105, 110, 118, 139-40, 143, 201, 203, 265, 266

Spirits, created, 67, 246, 270-1; our knowledge of other spirits, 139, 140-1, 221, cf. 246

" Spirits," physiological), 194

Stoics, 275

Substance, 14-15, 88; alleged

corporeal (see also matter), 69, 71, 73, 82, 86, 10₁, 111, 150, 163-4, 182, 216, 17, 222, 257; immateria (incorporeal, active, spiritual etc.), 16, 21, 68, 77, 134-5, 136, 222-4, 257; popula understanding of, 82, 228

" Substratum, material," 180, 228, 234, 251; mental, 27

" Suppositions " (in physica sciences), 24

Taste, sensations of, 71, 159, 60, 252

Thing, meaning of, 65, 82-3, 109, 237-8, 242, 244, 269

Time, 28, 113-14, 119-20. Se also duration

Touch, 84-5

Triangle, abstract idea of a 27, 53-4, 55

Trinity College, Dublin, 7.

Truth, 193

Understanding, 77

Uniformity of nature, 79, 92 96, 119

Unity, 70-1, 125-6

Universal ideas, 130; notions, 5

Vanini, 199 and n.

Velocity (and momentum etc.) 233

Virtue, 137, 145, 152-3, 176

Vision, Berkeley on, 33. Se also Berkeley, works

Volition (see also will), 179 204, 231

Will, 77, 117, 234, 274 human, 19, 138-9, 178-9 201, 204, 228; non-human i.e. divine, 21, 201

Wittgenstein, L., 38

Words, influence of in philo sophy, 238